AF226142

One Gospel

One Gospel

Paul's Use of the Abraham Story in Romans 4:1–25

NATHAN N. HOFF

Foreword by Elliott Johnson

WIPF & STOCK · Eugene, Oregon

ONE GOSPEL
Paul's Use of the Abraham Story in Romans 4:1–25

Wipf & Stock
An Imprint of Wipf and Stock Publishers
199 W. 8th Ave., Suite 3
Eugene, OR 97401

www.wipfandstock.com

PAPERBACK ISBN: 978-1-6667-7938-7
HARDCOVER ISBN: 978-1-6667-7939-4
EBOOK ISBN: 978-1-6667-7940-0

12/13/23

Contents

Foreword

Elliott Johnson

Few dissertations address several central issues with greater clarity than Nathan Hoff. His dissertation, *One Gospel: Paul's Use of the Abraham Story in Rom. 4:1–25* addresses four. First, One Gospel with a common content of faith but a change in wording from the Old Testament to the New Testament. Second, Dispensational Theology has been challenged concerning one gospel. Some say that there is little continuity while Hoff contends for continuity. The continuity is between the position (promised heir) and the person (Jesus). Third, hermeneutics which seeks textual understanding. Paul's understanding in Romans 4:3 represents an understanding of Genesis 15:6: "what does the Scripture say, Abraham believed God and it (the faith resting in Jesus the heir) was accounted for righteousness." Forth, literary genre which follows the narrative plot from stated promise to believed promise (12:3c): "in you all families of the earth shall be blessed," which is ambiguous;

what does "in you" mean? in you as an example?

in you as Savior?

or in you in your descendant?

12:7 the ambiguity is clarified: "to your descendant I will give this land" and 13:18, 14:20–22 (he believed God) "a burnt offering to the Lord"

(but he hadn't believed in the heir).

15:2 "Lord what will you give me seeing I go childless and

my heir of my house is Eliezer of Damascus"

15:4 "This one shall not be your heir,

but one who comes from your own body"

15:6 "And he believed in the Lord" (for an heir from his body)

Author's Preface

Dispensationalism has been criticized for what opponents see as a lack of clarity with respect to God's plan of salvation. While dispensationalists have affirmed that this plan has a common *basis* (Christ's death), a common *requirement* (faith), and a common *object* (God), they have not agreed on what continuity is found in the *content* of faith. The purpose of this study is to show that Paul's use of the Abraham story in Rom 4:1–25 demonstrates that faith in the promised seed, Messiah, is a *sine qua non* of God's plan of salvation. To accomplish this purpose, this study shows that Abraham's faith in Genesis was in God's promised Seed of blessing, Abraham's Heir. In Rom 4:1–25, Paul announces that the heir whose identity was unknown in Abraham's day was revealed to be Jesus Christ. The change, then, between Abraham's faith and the faith of New Testament believers is found in what could be known of this seed/heir.

This study has three parts. Part one provides a history of the interpretation of Rom 4:1–25 in the dispensational tradition. Through this history, it is shown that dispensationalists have been divided when it comes to the content of saving faith. There have been those who argue that little continuity is to be found in the content of faith and those who, from the beginning, have believed that Messiah is a continuous element of faith's content, past and present. The difference between these two factions hinges on what each believed was revealed in the Genesis account of Abraham's faith.

Part two examines the faith of Abraham in Genesis 15:6 and demonstrates that Abraham's faith was in God's promise of an heir through whom the nations of the earth would be blessed (12:3). This content formed part of Abraham's faith and led to his justification.

Part three examines Paul's use of the Abraham story in Rom 4:1–25 and shows that Abraham's faith was in God's promise of an heir. Although the identity of this heir was unknown to Abraham, Paul revealed that this heir was Jesus in whom New Testament believers place their faith.

Abbreviations

PRIMARY LITERATURE

1QS	*Rule of the Congregation*
4QMMT	*4Q Halakhic Letter*
Jub.	*Jubilees*
LXX	Septuagint

SECONDARY LITERATURE

ESV	English Standard Version
KJV	King James Version
NASB	New America Standard Bible
NKJV	New King James Version
WCF	Westminster Confession of Faith

1

Introduction

STATEMENT OF THE PROBLEM

During the last half century, biblical scholarship has gained a growing interest in the way the apostle Paul utilized the Old Testament Scriptures.[1] Beginning with the writings of Krister Stendahl in 1963, whose ideas would give birth to the New Perspective on Paul, and continuing through the works of notable scholars such as E. P. Sanders, N. T. Wright, and James D. G. Dunn, academics and pastors alike have had to reevaluate their understanding of some of most foundational elements in the Christian faith such as the Pauline views of sin, justification, and the nature of the gospel message itself.[2]

Attempting to slice through the complexities introduced by these writers, D. A. Carson notes that despite the Second Temple Judaic *Umwelt* in which Paul wrote, one must account for the fact that something changed in Paul's own reading of the Old Testament after his conversion experience on the Damascus road. In other words, Paul the apostle finds Christian themes

---

1. Carson, "Mystery and Fulfillment," 410.

2. Stendahl, "Apostle Paul and the Introspective Conscience of the West," 199–215; Sanders, *Paul and Palestinian Judaism*; Sanders, *Paul, the Law, and the Jewish People*; Sanders, *Paul*; Wright, *Justification*; Dunn, "New Perspective on Paul," 95–122; Dunn, "Justice of God," 1–22; Dunn, *Theology of Paul the Apostle*; Dunn, *New Perspective on Paul*; Dunn, "New Perspective on the New Perspective on Paul," 157–82. For a good overview of the major theses presented by each of these scholars, see Allman, "Gaining Perspective on the New Perspective on Paul," 51–68.

permeating the Old Testament in a way that he could not see prior to his conversion because Christ had taken away the "veil" which prohibited his Jewish brethren from understanding the Scriptures as he did (2 Cor 3:14–15).[3]

Therefore, while some have suggested that Paul is simply using hermeneutical techniques such as *midrash* or *pesher*, common among the rabbis in his day, in an attempt to make the Old Testament fit his newfound Christian faith,[4] Carson notes that a careful reading of Paul reveals that he is doing and claiming something far more significant than what a *midrash* interpretation would allow. Paul believes that what he finds in the Old Testament has always been there.[5] "Judging by his passionate handling of Scripture in Galatians, and in his slightly less passionate but scarcely less intense handling of Scripture in Romans, Paul is concerned to show that the gospel he preaches has in fact actually been announced by what we now refer to as the Old Testament . . . How does he himself seek to warrant his Christian reading *in the Scriptures themselves*, and thereby convince his readers."[6]

As one looks at Paul's understanding of the Old Testament's proclamation of the gospel, it becomes clear that Paul himself sees both a continuity and discontinuity between the Old Testament's proclamation and its fulfillment in the person and work of Jesus of Nazareth. In Rom 3:21, Paul claims that the righteous of God (δικαιοσύνη θεοῦ) received through faith in Jesus Christ was something to which the Law and the prophet bore witness.[7] However, in the doxology at the end of his letter to the Romans

3. Carson, "Mystery and Fulfillment," 411. In his analysis of the New Perspective, Mark A. Seifrid also acknowledges the important role that Paul's conversion to Christianity had on his theology. See Seifrid, "Paulus und seine neue Perspektive," 268–83.

4. Advocating for this view, Ellis summarizes what he believes the apostle Paul is doing as he uses the Old Testament Scripture. "In selecting a particular version or in creating an *ad hoc* rendering Paul views his citation as thereby more accurately expressing the true meaning of Scripture. For Paul, as for the rabbis, the 'letter' was sacred; but unlike some rabbis, Paul valued the 'letter' not for itself alone but for the meaning which it conveyed. His idea of a quotation was not a worshipping of the letter or 'parroting' of the text; neither was it an eisegesis which arbitrarily imposed a foreign meaning upon the text. It was rather, in his eyes, a quotation-exposition, a *midrash pesher*, which drew from the text the meaning originally planted there by the Holy Spirit and expressed that meaning in the most appropriate words and phrases known to him." Ellis, *Prophecy and Hermeneutic in Early Christianity*, 179–8).

5. Carson, "Mystery and Fulfillment," 410.

6. Carson, "Mystery and Fulfillment," 411. Emphasis his.

7. This is not the first occasion in the book of Romans where Paul claims that the Old Testament bore witness to the gospel he preached. In fact, Paul begins the epistle with this announcement (Rom 1:1–2). This claim is also reflected in Paul's letter to the Galatians (Gal 3:8) where he argues that the gospel, specifically gentile justification by faith, was anticipated in Gen 12:3.

(Rom 16:25–27), Paul claims that elements of God's plan were a mystery (μυστήριον) kept secret in the past but made manifest to gentiles in the present age (cf. 11:16–25).[8] Recognizing both continuity and discontinuity in Pauline thought, Carson identifies two polarities that help the reader shape his understanding of Pauline theology with respect to the gospel message. Since Paul argues that the gospel he preaches is something to which the Old Testament Scriptures bore witness, the first Pauline polarity should be thought of as *promise* and *fulfillment*. However, since Paul also acknowledges that the gospel he preaches contains elements of mystery previously unrevealed, the second polarity should be construed as *hiddenness* and *revelation*.[9] In light of these polarities, Carson raises a fundamental problem present in Pauline thought. "How can the very things that are said, on the one hand, to be predicted in the past and now fulfilled, be said, on the other, to be hidden in the past and only now, in the fullness of time, revealed?"[10]

However one understands the development of the gospel throughout the Old Testament and the New, one must wrestle with the continuity and discontinuity found in Pauline theology and, therefore, the theology taught in the New Testament Scriptures. The soteriology promoted and taught by different theological traditions centers on the different ways they attempt resolve the tension created by this continuity and discontinuity. Traditionally, covenant theology has placed a greater emphasis on continuity in its development of the gospel message throughout the Bible while dispensationalism

---

8. The term μυστήριον finds distinct uses in Pauline writings. It can refer to something which was previously revealed but not understood (1 Cor 2:7). It can refer to something that was previously hidden and only hinted at (Eph 5:31–32). It can refer to something that was completely unrevealed because it was not the topic of previous written revelation (Eph 3:3–10). In Rom 11:25, Paul specifically addresses the gentiles in his audience and reveals something which had previously not been discussed in Scripture. Although the Old Testament was clear that Israel would reject Messiah, the means by which Israel's ministry would be carried out after this rejection had not been revealed. Here Paul fills that void by explaining that gentiles have been given equal status with Jews in the Church during the delay of the kingdom until God's dealings with Israel resume. See Johnson, *Dispensational Biblical Theology*, 392–94. For a good discussion of the term μυστήριον see Bornkamm, "μυστήριον," 802–28.

The authenticity of this final doxology in the book of Romans has been questioned. For a thorough discussion and defense of the passage as a genuine part of Paul's original letter, see Marshall, "Romans 16:25–27—An Apt Conclusion," 170–84. In Romans, the term μυστήριον is used only one other time by Paul (16:25) to refer to the grafting in of gentile believers in the present age and is likely the content of the mystery to which he refers in the doxology. For a good discussion regarding the Greek syntax of Romans 16:25, see Cranfield, *Romans*, 383; Dunn, *Romans 9–16*, 914–15; Moo, *Epistle to the Romans*, 938–39; Schreiner, *Romans*, 811–12.

9. Carson, "Mystery and Fulfillment," 397.

10. Carson, "Mystery and Fulfillment," 397–98.

has attempted to eliminate anachronistic readings from the New Testament into the Old Testament context. As a result, it has traditionally worked to emphasize the need for a healthy discontinuity with respect to the gospel's development in a biblical theology.[11]

Covenant Theology and Continuity

Although the elements of what today is called covenant theology can be traced throughout church history, as a systematized theological system, covenant theology is of recent origin.[12] Without wholly discounting discontinuity, the covenant tradition has sought to emphasize continuity between the testaments, especially as it pertains to God's one method of salvation. The Westminster Confession of Faith, a foundational creed in the covenant tradition, states the continuity in the following way (WCF 7.5–6).

> This covenant [the covenant of grace] was differently administered under the time of the law, and in the time of the gospel; under the law it was administered by promises, prophecies, sacrifices, circumcision, the paschal lamb, and other types and ordinances delivered to the people of the Jews, and all foresignifying Christ to come, which were for that time sufficient and efficacious, through the operation of the Spirit, to instruct and build up the elect in faith in the promised Messiah, by whom they had full remission of sins and eternal salvation; and is called the Old Testament. Under the gospel when Christ the substance was exhibited, the ordinances in which this covenant

11. It is important to note that both covenant and dispensational theologies hold to aspects of continuity and discontinuity in their systems. The difference is one of emphasis. In a show of good faith, dispensationalist Kenneth L. Barker authored an article for the Evangelical Theological Society in which he acknowledged false dichotomies (i.e., discontinuities) between the testaments. See Barker, "False Dichotomies between the Testaments," *Journal of the Evangelical Theological Society* 25 (1982): 3–16. In response to this work, covenant theologian Mark W. Karlberg penned an article in which he acknowledged that legitimate discontinuities existed between the testaments as well. See Karlberg, "Legitimate Discontinuities between the Testaments," 9–20.

12. In 1955, Cornelius Van Till wrote, "The idea of covenant theology has only in modern times been thus broadly conceived" (Van Til, "Covenant Theology," 306). Charles C. Ryrie notes the recent systematization of covenant theology in response to a similar critique of dispensationalism. "Systematized covenant theology is recent. It was not the expressed doctrine of the early church. It was never taught by church leaders in the Middle Ages. It was not even mentioned by the primary leaders of the Reformation. Indeed, covenant theology as a system is only a little older than dispensationalism" (Ryrie, *Dispensationalism*, 215). For a thorough history of covenant theology, see Woolsey, *Unity and Continuity in Covenantal Thought*.

> is dispensed are the preaching of the word, and the administration of the sacraments of baptism and the Lord's Supper. . .[13]

According to this creed, then, the so-called covenant of grace grants both Old and New Testament believers salvation. Yet the creed clarifies the elements of continuity and discontinuity in God's method of salvation according to a covenant formulation. Continuity is found in one's faith in Messiah, while the elements of discontinuity pertain to the various ordinances and revelation through which one's faith in Messiah was expressed.

In his attempt to put forth a systematized covenant theology, Charles Hodge articulates a similar view.

> As the same promise was made to those who lived before the advent which is now made to us in the gospel, as the same Redeemer was revealed to them who is presented as the object of faith to us, it of necessity follows that the condition, or terms of salvation, was the same then as now. It was not mere faith or trust in God, or simply piety, which was required, but faith in the promised Redeemer, or faith in the promise of redemption through Messiah.[14]

While dispensationalists such as Charles Ryrie and John Feinberg believe that the covenant position achieves this continuity through an a theological reading that forces the clarity of New Testament revelation onto the Old,[15] Hodge's writings reveal that he himself saw a level of discontinuity in what could be known of Messiah and his work in the Old Testament under the covenant of grace.[16] He distinguishes this progress in the revelation of

13. Macpherson, *Westminster Confession of Faith*, 69. WCF 8.7 again emphasizes Christ as the mediator of salvation in both the Old Testament and the New.

14. Hodge, *Systematic Theology*, 371–72.

15. Ryrie aggressively makes this argument in his 1965 work, *Dispensationalism Today* (Ryrie, *Dispensationalism Today*, 122–23). See also Ryrie, *Dispensationalism*, 94–95; Feinberg, "Salvation in the Old Testament," 51. A recent theological movement known as New Covenant Theology has shared this criticism of covenant theology with dispensationalism. While the movement has not yet been systematized in any serious fashion, Douglas J. Moo writes the following in his foreword to a work helping to identify the trajectories of the movement. "While expressing deep appreciation for the heritage of Reformed theology, Wells and Zaspel nevertheless argue that the emphasis on the continuity of revelation in much of that tradition has been overdone" (Moo, "Foreword," xiii).

16. More recently, covenant theologian Fred H. Klooster has admitted that while faith in Messiah is to be considered a point of continuity in the gospel message across the testaments, one must be careful not to read later revelation into earlier expressions of the gospel. In his interaction with dispensationalist John S. Feinberg, Klooster writes, "[Feinberg] has made a worthy contribution to the discussion which helps to avoid

Messiah and the administration of forgiveness of sins by faith in Messiah through four dispensations: Adam to Abraham, Abraham to Moses, Moses to Christ, and the gospel age.[17] Therefore, while one may question whether all that covenant theology claims was revealed from the beginning, it is clear that the covenant tradition attempts to deal seriously with both continuities and discontinuities in God's method of salvation.

Dispensational Theology and Discontinuity

While covenant theology attempts to emphasize the continuity in God's one method of salvation, dispensationalists have typically sought to argue for a healthy discontinuity in an attempt to acknowledge the progressive unfolding of God's plan in history.[18] For dispensationalists, the concern is to understand what could be known of God's plan in each era in history so as to not read the clarity of New Testament soteriology onto the Old. This emphasis on discontinuity has caused many non-dispensationalists to criticize the tradition for what they perceive to be a lack of clarity and, at times, an advocacy for multiple ways of salvation. In his critique of dispensational soteriology, John H. Gerstner writes,

> We must sadly accuse dispensationalists (of all varieties) of teaching, always implicitly and sometimes explicitly, that there

---

misunderstanding by sharply distinguishing what has been revealed and what could be known in each specific period of redemptive revelation" (Klooster, "Biblical Method of Salvation," 143–44). Klooster notes that the Heidelberg Catechism (19Q), written in 1563 to articulate a covenant soteriology, evidences such progress, and therefore a discontinuity, in what could be known of the gospel as developed in Scripture (Klooster, "Biblical Method of Salvation," 144). For the text of the Heidelberg Catechism (19Q), see Christian Reformed Church, *Psalter Hymnal*, 866. Vern S. Poythress notes the increasing focus of covenant theology on the role that the progress of revelation plays in a biblical theology. "Covenant theologians have not simply stood still with the Westminster Confession. Geerhardus Vos began a program of examining the progressive character of God's revelation and the progressive character of God's redemptive action in history. Vos's reflection has issued in a whole movement of "biblical theology," emphasizing much more the discontinuities and advances not only between the Old Testament and the New Testament, but between successive epochs within the Old Testament" (Poythress, *Understanding Dispensationalists*, 40).

17. Hodge, *Systematic Theology*, 373–77.

18. Charles F. Baker describes this concern of dispensationalism in his systematic theology (Baker, *Dispensational Theology*, 324–25). See also Nevin, "Some Major Problems in Dispensational Interpretation," 130–31. Article V of the doctrinal statement of Dallas Theological Seminary acknowledges the role that progressive revelation necessarily plays in a dispensational view of God's method of salvation. See Dallas Theological Seminary, "DTS Doctrinal Statement."

is more than one way of salvation and, in the process of developing that theology, excluding the one and only way even from this dispensation of grace.[19]

Although dispensationalists have adamantly denied these accusations, this critique continues to be advanced despite repeated rebuttals.[20] Writing as recently as 2012, Walter C. Kaiser claims that a dispensational development of the gospel message throughout each age emphasizes discontinuity to the point that it inevitably leads to a general theistic soteriology in the Old Testament that lacks any distinctively Christian qualities.[21] In light of this continued line of attack, one is left to wonder whether covenant theologians simply misunderstand dispensational soteriology,[22] or is it possible that,

19. Gertner, *Wrongly Dividing the Word of Truth*, 168. Writing in 1936, Oswald T. Allis published two articles in which he criticized dispensationalism for compartmentalizing the Bible through its literal hermeneutic and thereby creating a soteriological crisis (multiple ways of salvation) in the resulting distinction between law and grace (Allis, "Modern Dispensationalism and the Doctrine of Unity of Scripture," 22–35); Allis, "Modern Dispensationalism and the Law of God," 272–89). This criticism was developed by Daniel P. Fuller who, having sorted through the works of various dispensationalists in his time, concluded that dispensationalism continued to promote a dubious soteriology despite claims to the contrary (Fuller, "The Hermeneutics of Dispensationalism," 139–89). See also *Gospel and Law: Contrast or Continuum?* 18–46. Writing a response to Wayne G. Strickland's dispensational view of the gospel, Greg L. Bahnsen finds fault with the dispensational view relating the gospel and law. See Bahnsen, "Response to Wayne G. Strickland," 291.

20. See Chafer, "Dispensational Distinctions Denounced," 258–59; Chafer, "Inventing Heretics through Misunderstanding," 1; Feinberg, "Salvation in the Old Testament," 53; Ross, "The Biblical Method of Salvation: A Case for Discontinuity," 166–67; Kreider, "What is Dispensationalism?," 17.

21. Kaiser Jr., "Is It the Case that Christ is the Same Object of Faith in the Old Testament? (Genesis 15:1–6)," 292.

22. In his doctoral dissertation written at Dallas Theological Seminary in 1956, dispensationalist H. Chester Woodring argued that the tradition has not done a good job explaining how salvation by grace through faith operates under the traditional dispensational distinction between grace and law (Woodring, "Grace under the Mosaic Covenant," 208). Woodring's criticism is understandable since some dispensational writers, such as C. I. Scofield, were not careful in explaining the distinction. In the 1909 version of his reference Bible, Scofield writes, "The point of testing is no longer legal obedience as the condition of salvation [as under the law], but acceptance or rejection of Christ, with good works as a fruit of salvation . . ." (Scofield, *Scofield Reference Bible*, 1115, note 2). A. C. Gaebelein similarly writes, "[Israel] had received grace, they needed grace. With the vow they had made, they had put themselves under the law" (Gaebelein, *Annotated Bible*, 152). Despite these phraseologies, dispensationalist William L. Pettingill provided a more nuanced statement when he wrote, "The dispensational tests [including law] served to show man's utter helplessness, in order to bring him to faith, that he might be saved by grace through faith plus nothing" (Pettingill, *Bible Questions Answered*, 470).

despite its best efforts, dispensationalists have not adequately addressed the unity of the gospel message between the Old Testament and the New?

Charles Ryrie, who during his life was widely recognized as a leading spokesman for the dispensational movement, attempted to defend the tradition against the charge of differing methods of salvation in his work, *Dispensationalism*, which was written to clarify and explain the essential elements in the dispensational system.

> The dispensationalist's answer to the question of the relation of grace and law is this: The basis of salvation in every age is the death of Christ; the *requirement* for salvation in every age is faith; the *object* of faith in every age is God; the *content* of faith changes in the various dispensations. It is the last point, of course, that distinguishes dispensationalism from covenant theology, but it is not a point to which the charge of teaching two ways of salvation can be attached.[23]

At first glance, it may appear that Ryrie's statement should, once and for all, lay to rest any doubts that dispensationalism promotes multiple ways of salvation. However, his clarification of this general statement introduces a dilemma that leaves the door open to continued criticism of dispensational soteriology.

> In examining salvation under the Mosaic Law, the principal question is simply, How much of what God was going to do in the future did the Old Testament believer comprehend? According to both Old and New Testament revelation, it is impossible to say that he saw the same promise, the same Savior as we do today . . . If by "ways of salvation is meant different content of faith, then dispensationalism does teach various "ways" because the Scriptures reveal differing contents for faith in the progressive nature of God's revelation to mankind. But if by "ways" is meant more than one basis or means of salvation, then dispensationalism most emphatically does not teach more than one way, for salvation has been, is, and always will be based on the substitutionary death of Jesus Christ.[24]

It is clear that, for Ryrie, the continuity in God's method of salvation between the testaments is found in a common *object* of faith, God, and a common *basis* for salvation, the substitutionary death of Christ, rather than in an essential *content* to be believed. As such, he feels comfortable saying

23. Ryrie, *Dispensationalism*, 134. Emphasis his.

24. Ryrie, *Dispensationalism*, 140.

that continuity found in both the promise of the gospel and the savior of the gospel are not necessary elements of saving faith in every dispensation. The changing content of faith in each dispensation is, therefore, not to be seen as the clarification of a set of essential components to be believed—such as knowledge regarding the person and work of Christ—but could, foreseeably, refer to an array of disparate promises which God made at various points through the progress of revelation.[25]

Before Ryrie, Lewis Sperry Chafer articulated the same basic viewpoint in his defense against the charge of multiple methods of salvation.

> Are there two ways by which one may be saved? In reply to this question it may be stated that salvation of whatever specific character is always the work of God in behalf of man and never a work of man in behalf of God. This is to assert that God never saved any one person or group of persons on any other ground than that righteous freedom to do so which the Cross of Christ secured. . . .The far lesser question as to the precise human terms upon which men may be saved is quite a different issue.[26]

Recognizing the unifying nature of Christ's death as the basis of salvation, Chafer uses Gen 15:2–6 and Rom 4:23–24 as an example of the different contents of faith required for salvation. "From this [Romans 4:23–24] it will be seen that, though the specific object of faith—Isaac in the case of Abraham and Jesus Christ in the case of those becoming Christians—varies, both have a promise of God on which to rest and both believe in God."[27]

---

25. Feinberg and Ross share Ryrie's view that the continuous element throughout the dispensations is found in a common basis rather than in a common content to be believed. See Feinberg, "Salvation in the Old Testament," 54–56; Ross, "Biblical Method of Salvation," 171–72.

26. Chafer, "Inventing Heretics through Misunderstanding," 1. While he wrote this statement in 1945, Chafer was not always clear on what he held to be the basis upon which men were saved. In 1946, he wrote, "A distinction must be observed between just men of the Old Testament and the justified according to the New Testament. According to the Old Testament, men were just because they were true and faithful in keeping the Mosaic law . . . Men were therefore just because of their own works for God, whereas New Testament justification is God's work for man in answer to faith (Rom. 5:1)" (Chafer, "Editorials: Justification," 130). In his systematic theology, Chafer adds to the confusion when he writes, "When the Law was proposed, the children of Israel deliberately forsook their position under the grace of God which had been their relationship to God until that day, and placed themselves under the Law" (Chafer, Systematic Theology, 162). However in that same volume, he also writes, "The law was never given as a means of salvation or justification . . . The law was effective only as it drove the transgressor to Christ" (Chafer, Systematic Theology: Ecclesiology, 162).

27. Chafer, "Inventing Heretics through Misunderstanding," 2–3.

Like Ryrie, Chafer agrees that continuity in the promise and savior are not essential components of a saving faith in every dispensation.

However, not all dispensationalists agree with Chafer and Ryrie. Some dispensationalists argue that additional continuity is to be found in faith's *content* which has always included belief in God's revelation of Messiah in each dispensation. William L. Pettingill, a contemporary of Scofield and Chafer, believed that both Old and New Testament believers were saved by their faith in Messiah. The difference, in Pettingill's mind, was dispensational in nature. "Old Testament believers were saved by faith in the coming One, as we are saved by faith in the One who has already come."[28] More recently, Elliott E. Johnson continues to give life to this alternative dispensational perspective when he claims that a continuity in the content of faith in every dispensation can be found in Messiah who, in the Old Testament, was progressively revealed as the "seed of the woman," the "seed of Abraham," and the "Son of David," and is revealed to be Jesus of Nazareth once the "promised one" has come.[29]

The Debate within Dispensational Theology

While it seems fair to claim that the dispensational tradition, on the whole, has acknowledged that continuity is to be found in faith as common *requirement* of salvation, God as the common *object* of salvation, and the substitutionary death of Christ as the common *basis* for salvation, there is disagreement as to the nature of discontinuity involved in the *content* of saving faith. Some dispensationalists, like Chafer and Ryrie, believe that there is no essential and common content to be believed in God's plan of salvation. As one places his faith in God, God justifies the believer on the basis of Christ's substitutionary death, whether before or after the resurrection. This view does not dismiss the importance of faith's content but simply holds that the essence of this content has changed in the progress of revelation. Other dispensationalists, like Pettingill and Johnson, argue that while discontinuity exists, continuity in the content of saving faith exists and is to be found in the promised seed, Messiah.[30] For them, the element of discontinuity pertains to what could be known of Messiah in a given dispensation. In the Old Testament, then, believers were saved as they placed their faith

28. Pettingill, *Bible Questions Answered*, 380.

29. Johnson, *Dispensational Biblical Theology*, 8–9.

30. Although the term "Messiah" is first applied to this coming one in Ps 2:2, the title has been chosen as a comprehensive and unifying term to identify this important individual and what God has revealed about him throughout redemptive history.

(requirement) in God (object) who justified them on the basis of Christ's death (basis) as they believed what God had revealed about Messiah in their time (content). In the New Testament, believers are saved in the same way. However, because of the progress of revelation, these believers know Messiah to be Jesus of Nazareth.

To date, no serious work has been written to address this crucial conversation within the dispensational tradition and, specifically, to advocate for the view that Messiah is an essential component of saving faith. However, the continued criticism by non-dispensationalists as well as the disagreement that exists within the dispensational tradition require that a serious work be written to answer some fundamental questions. Is faith in Messiah a point of continuity in God's method of salvation in the Old Testament and in the New?

PURPOSE OF THE STUDY

When considering God's one method of salvation in dispensational theology, Rom 4:1–25 becomes a sort of *crux interpretum* for it is here that Paul uses the Abraham story in the book of Genesis to speak to the role that faith plays in God's singular program for salvation both past and present. The purpose of this study is to show that Paul's use of the Abraham story in Rom 4:1–25 demonstrates that faith in the promised seed, Messiah, is a *sine qua non* of God's one method of salvation as he interprets the Genesis account of Abraham's faith and its progress in history.[31] In order to accomplish this purpose, it will be shown that Abraham's faith in Genesis, by which he was justified, was in God's promised seed of blessing, Abraham's heir. Although Isaac was an immediate seed and heir, he was not the seed or heir which God had promised or ultimately the heir in which Abraham believed. In Rom 4:1–25, Paul announced that the heir whose full identity was unknown in Abraham's day was revealed to be Jesus Christ. The change, then, between Abraham's faith and the faith of New Testament believers is found in what could be known of this seed/heir and his work. When understood in conjunction with preceding literary unit, Rom 3:21—4:25 exists as a thought unity that describes God's one method of salvation as having a common *basis* (Christ's death), a common *requirement* (faith), a common *object* (God), and a common *content* (faith in God's promised seed, Messiah). The purpose of this study is merely to demonstrate that the content of saving faith includes belief in Messiah. It is not meant to determine what must be

---

31. This is the thesis statement of this study.

believed about Messiah in each dispensation, although such a study would be a welcomed companion to this present study.

LIMITATIONS OF THE STUDY

This study will be limited by four factors. First, it will be written exclusively within the dispensational tradition. Other Christian traditions will not be a primary focus of discussion in this work. Second, this investigation will examine the biblical texts through a consistent literal method of interpretation which denies the legitimacy of anachronistic readings in the Old Testament texts by New Testament authors. Third, this study will limit itself to Abraham's expression of saving faith as developed by Paul in Rom 4:1–25. While further work must be done to account for other instances of saving faith in the Old Testament, such a discussion will not be part of the current work.[32] Fourth, the broad nature of this study means that the emphasis of this study will be on synthesis as opposed to depth. While dissertations have and certainly will be written on many of the topics addressed, the current investigation by necessity must assume the legitimacy of certain textual readings and positions in order to make a case for the larger argument. To show the legitimacy of certain readings, where such proofs go beyond the scope of the discussion, footnotes will be used to direct the reader to more thorough discussions of the issues in which the legitimacy of certain positions has been demonstrated.

Because of the synthetic nature of this study, the purpose of the work is not to prove that the proposed argument is the only way to read or synthesize the text. Such a claim would be far beyond the scope of what is possible to achieve in a work of this nature. Rather, the goal is simply to demonstrate that the proposed argument for the thesis is a legitimate way to both read and synthesize the text.

DEFINITIONS PRELIMINARY TO THE STUDY

At the outset of this study, it seems prudent to provide a brief description of the interpretive approach that will be used in this work. As Ryrie noted, an essential element of dispensationalism has been its commitment to the "consistent" use of a literal, or historical-grammatical, hermeneutic as a means to establish the meaning intended by both the divine and human

---

32. See Kaiser for other examples of saving faith in the Old Testament. Kaiser, "Is It the Case That Christ Is the Same Object of Faith in the Old Testament?," 296–98.

author(s) of Scripture.[33] The heart behind the literal method of interpretation is a desire to find meanings that are textually based rather than imported from extra-textual sources, whatever they might be.[34] However, as John H. Sailhamer notes, the historical-grammatical method of interpretation has suffered from ambiguity throughout its history.[35] Because of this, it seems sensible to provide a brief explanation of philosophical basis behind the dispensational hermeneutic which this study will employ.

Literary Genre

Perhaps one of the most welcome developments in biblical studies generally, and in the field of biblical hermeneutics specifically, is a growing appreciation for the role that the literary genre of a work plays not only in describing the work but in interpreting the component parts of the work.[36] In his early writing, *Validity in Interpretation*, E. D. Hirsch Jr. gave recognition to the role that genre plays in the interpretive process when he observed that the genre of a work sets up a set of "expectations" that influences what the reader understands.[37] Identifying a work as narrative history actualizes a set of expectations on the part of the reader that he will use to make sense of the work as a whole. These "expectations" or rules would be different if the genre of the text were parable, poetry, or any other type of literature. The literary genre of the whole provides the broad framework within which the exegesis of particular subunits occurs as the interpreter attempts to discern what an author meant by what he wrote. These expectations actualized by the genre

33. Ryrie, *Dispensationalism*, 91–93. Dispensationalist Nathan D. Holsteen also gives recognition to the emphasis on literal interpretation in the dispensational tradition. "The same traditional attraction to the principle of authorial intent gave rise to another distinct hermeneutic. While the seeds of this hermeneutic may be traced, at least in snippets, to earlier stages in Christian history, its developed form—again like the covenant hermeneutic—appeared after the Reformation. This approach to the reading of Scripture we might call the dispensational hermeneutic" (Holsteen, "Hermeneutic of Dispensationalism," 109).

34. Johnson, *Expository Hermeneutics*, 31.

35. Sailhamer, "Johann August Ernesti," 194–97.

36. See Long, *Reign and Rejection of King Saul*, 14.

37. Hirsch Jr., *Validity in Interpretation*, 71–72. Tremper Longman III recognizes the relationship between genre and expectations when he writes, "Readers approach texts with certain expectations that arise as soon as they begin reading it and that are grounded in their previous reading. When they start to read a text, they make a conscious or unconscious genre identification, which involves further expectations concerning what is to come. Texts may trigger generic expectations in different ways" (Longman III, *Literary Approaches to Biblical Interpretation*, 77).

are an important part of the process of communication because they align expectations of the reader with the literary design, i.e., the expectations, intended by the author, making it more likely that communication will take place.[38] Recognizing the interpretive power of a work's literary genre, Kevin Vanhoozer writes,

> Recent literary studies show that literary forms serve more than classificatory purposes. The genre provides the literary context for a given sentence and, therefore, partly determines what the sentence means and how it should be taken . . . But genre as constitutive of meaning conditions our expectations as readers and permits understanding to take place.[39]

There is a difference, however, between talking about literary genre in general (e.g., narrative history, allegory, poetry, etc.) and interpreting a particular work of literature. The former emphasizes basic similarity and, therefore, interpretive expectations on a generic level. The latter includes these basic expectations but narrows the focus to the specific and perhaps more detailed expectations that an author placed in the literary design of a particular text, what some might call an "intrinsic genre."[40] This more detailed conception of genre includes both the generic expectations actualized by the basic literary genre of the work as well as the "conception of the whole," determined by an author in a particular literary work. Hirsch states,

> In what sense is verbal meaning genre-bound? First of all, it is obvious that not only understanding but also speaking must be governed and constituted by a sense of the whole utterance. How does a speaker manage to put one word after another unless his choices and usages are governed by a controlling conception? There must be some kind of overarching notion which controls the temporal sequence of speech, and this controlling

---

38. "Genre as a whole comes into play at the focal point between the author and the text and then again between the text and the reader. As such it brings together all three components of the interpretation process: writer, text, reader. The key is for the reader to align himself/herself with the originally intended genre, and as argued above this is both a possible and a necessary enterprise" (Vanhoozer, "Semantics of Biblical Literature," 26). Robert D. Bergen argues that human communication takes place at the paragraph and genre level rather than at the sentence level. "Within the past three decades, however, an ever-increasing amount of attention has been given to the study of the larger units of human communication, from paragraphs to entire genres. It is now recognized that human communication as it is normally practiced actually occurs only above the sentence level" (Bergen, "Text as a Guide to Authorial Intention," 327). See also Long, *Art of Biblical History*, 43.

39. Vanhoozer, "Semantics of Biblical Literature," 80.

40. Hirsch, *Validity in Interpretation*, 78.

notion of the speaker, like that of the interpreter, must embrace a set of expectations.[41]

If a literal, or historical-grammatical, hermeneutic attempts to find only those meanings which are textually based, then the hermeneutic in the broadest sense must first deal with the generic genre and concept of the whole so that the interpretive expectations of the reader are keenly aligned with "intrinsic genre" established by the author through the text he wrote.[42]

Verbal Meaning as a "Willed-Type"

In his attempt to define "literal" or "grammatical-historical" interpretation in the dispensational tradition, Ryrie proposed that the literal meaning of a word is "the same meaning it would have in normal usage, whether employed in writing, speaking, or thinking."[43] However, this understanding of literal interpretation fails to account for the difference that exists between the public use of a word during a particular time period and an author's meaning of a word in a particular context. To facilitate communication, an author must necessarily intend a meaning that accounts for the public usage

41. Hirsch, *Validity in Interpretation*, 78. Because of the controlling nature of the "sense of the whole" on the interpretation of textual subunits, Elliott E. Johnson argues that literary should be added to historical-grammatical. "The premise of textual design (literary) affirms that the textually based sense of any subsection is determined within the limits of the textual design of the composition as a whole. This premise is important because verbal communication requires our knowing more than the grammar and the historical realm of a text. The textually based sense of any part of a written work is determined in part by the textual design of the composition considered as a whole. Textual design contributes to the way something is said, which in turn contributes to what is said" (Johnson, *Expository Hermeneutics*, 43).

42. While he does not deal with "concept of the whole," J. R. Porter argues that Hebrew narrative must be allowed its distinctive elements when attempting to find similarities with its ancient Near Eastern counterparts. "[I]t is perhaps just when we consider the character of these ancient Near Eastern materials and the use made of similar types in the Old Testament, that we may find a clue to the distinctive character of Hebrew historiography, and this along two lines. In the first place, in the cultures surrounding Israel, these literary forms are found almost entirely as separate units . . . By contrast, in the Old Testament, all these elements, as far as the Pentateuch and the Former Prophets are concerned, are embedded in a chronologically added narrative. It is this that provides their setting, it is only in this framework that they have eventually been preserved, and it is the narrative which is intended to determine their significance. Nowhere else in the ancient Near East is there to be found anything strictly comparable to this collecting and arranging of traditions and documents as successive elements in larger corpora and, ultimately into a single corpus" (Porter, "Old Testament Historiography," 130–31).

43. Ryrie, *Dispensationalism*, 91.

of a word or his meaning may not be understood by his intended audience. Nevertheless, an author is the determiner of meaning, and he may, at times, intend a meaning that goes beyond what the public use of a term would normally entail. Therefore, the task to determine the public meaning of a word during a particular historical period is not precisely the same task as to determine an author's use of the word in a particular context. The author's or user's authority to determine what he/she means by a word is simply one of the features of language that enable the semantic domains of words to develop over time.[44] Upon closer examination, the reader may find that the author intended a sense of a word firmly within the public use of the word during a particular historical period, or he may discover a nuance that a study of the public use of the word would not have surfaced. A satisfactory theory of verbal meaning must be able to distinguish between the public use and an author's use of a word, if such a distinction exists.

Although he would later revise his theory of verbal meaning, E. D. Hirsch had originally sought to provide a theory of meaning that accounted for the facts of communications and enabled the reader to recognize what perhaps might be an author's determinate usage in a given context.[45] In his study of language in general, Hirsch observed that a single unifying feature of all language was to be found in its "shareability."[46] Regardless of the particular mechanics of a given language, all languages function as vehicles of communication. For Hirsch, this normative principle of language held significant implications with respect to the nature of meaning. If meanings constructed through language were capable of being shared, i.e., communicated, then these meanings must be "determinate," for indeterminate meanings cannot be shared since they cannot be recognized or reproduced as anything in particular by the reader. Furthermore, this "determinate"

44. G. B. Caird recognizes the important distinction between the public use of a word and a user's use when he writes, "When we turn from language and what words are capable of meaning to what they actually do mean in any given item of speech, then, as we have already seen, the user is in control. Within the latitude of correctness marked out by public usage, or even slightly beyond it, he determines the sense of the words he uses . . ." (Caird, *Language and Imagery of the Bible*, 49).

45. Although in his original work, *Validity in Interpretation*, Hirsch limited meaning to what an author meant to convey by what he wrote, in his subsequent work, *The Aims of Interpretation*, he began to expand his conception of meaning to include any meaning that a reader construed from a text. Although he still acknowledged that an author's meaning was accessible through the text he wrote, meaning need only refer to "meaning-for-an-interpreter," whether it be the author's meaning or not. See E. D. Hirsch Jr., *Aims of Interpretation*, 79. The final evolution of Hirsch can be seen in his defense of allegorical interpretation late in his career. See Hirsch Jr., "Transhistorical Intentions and the Persistence of Allegory: Part 1," 549–67.

46. Hirsch, *Validity in Interpretation*, 31.

meaning must be a stable meaning since a meaning intended by an author could not be shared with a reader if the author's meaning were somehow capable of being transformed or altered.[47]

For Hirsch, the concept of shareability also implied something important with respect to the relationship between the author and his words. For communication to transpire, it was the meaning intended by the author that must be shared through the words of the text. In Hirsch's model of verbal meaning, the connection between the author and text was crucial and indispensable. With these considerations in mind, Hirsch described verbal meaning as a "willed-type."[48] It was "willed" in the sense that an author meant something particular to be shared through the words of the text. As a "type," the meaning contained recognizable boundaries (i.e., was pattern bound) enabling the reader to apprehend the author's meaning through the medium of the text. Because of the boundaries defined by the type, the reader is able to recognize the author's meaning as "this type of meaning" as opposed to "that type of meaning." Verbal meaning, then, is an abstract object of consciousness that can be represented by multiple instances. This reproducibility is the very thing that enables communication to happen. In written communication, the author intends a particular type of meaning through the medium of the text. As the reader encounters the text, he attempts to reproduce the author's type of meaning as he interprets what he reads. When the type of meaning intended by the author is apprehended (i.e., reproduced) by the reader, communication takes place.[49]

Hirsch's model of verbal meaning provides the biblical interpreter with a way to relate the divine and human authors of Scripture.[50] Through the medium of the inspired text, the divine and human author share the same type of meaning. That meaning is what is capable of being shared through

47. Hirsch, *Validity in Interpretation*, 49–50. See also Hirsch, *Aims of Interpretation*, 3. L. Jonathan Cohen recognized the importance of stability and determinacy to a theory of verbal meaning when he wrote, "When a speech is over nothing can change what is meant. What has been said cannot be unsaid, though later remarks may contradict it. Even the ambiguities in this evening's speech must remain such forever, though tomorrow's press conference may clarify the speaker's intentions. Though the speech may be differently translated in different countries or at different periods, no one could judge the correctness of each new translation unless he assumed the meaning of the original speech to remain the same." See Cohen, *Diversity of Meaning*, 3.

48. Hirsch, *Validity in Interpretation*, 49. This same idea of verbal meaning undergirds Nicholas Wolterstorff's view of "authorial discourse interpretation," which is a type of reading that seeks to understand what an author sought to communicate through what he wrote (Wolterstorff, *Divine Discourse*, 134–35).

49. Hirsch, *Validity in Interpretation*, 50.

50. It also provides a model to relate the meaning shared by God and his chosen stewards in instances of divine discourse, such as that found in covenant promises.

the language of the text to a reader. Although the divine and human author share the same type of meaning, the divine author's knowledge transcends that of the human author enabling him to know more details regarding the meaning he shared through the human author in an original context. The divine author is aware of the details that will be revealed in history, but details that at the time of the original revelation have not yet been disclosed. The divine author's more detailed knowledge of the type of meaning is not a different meaning but, rather, a more detailed version of the same meaning. This model for relating the divine and human authors of Scripture seems to be consistent with the testimony of Scripture itself. In 1 Peter 1:10–11, the apostle explains that the prophets who testified concerning the coming salvation through Messiah studied the inspired revelation given to them to discern the historical referents intended by God but unspecified in Scripture. They understood what it was God had promised, i.e., they shared the same meaning, yet they understood that God's knowledge transcended their own knowledge and included details related to that shared meaning which the original words given to them did not disclose.[51] Peter, in his day, recognized that the meaning shared by the divine and human authors in the Old Testament had been fulfilled in Jesus Christ. In recognizing the fulfillment, Peter necessarily shared the same type of meaning as the prophets before him or he would have had no basis upon which to recognize or claim fulfillment. However, in recognizing Jesus as the fulfillment, Peter now shared details which God, the divine author, had always known but details which the human authors of the Old Testament Scripture were not necessarily aware.[52]

Viewing meaning as a "willed-type" is a model that works well within the dispensational tradition, specifically as it relates to literal interpretation. It is a model that attempts to discern the meaning of an author through the medium of the text so that the reader can share this meaning through an act of communication. As a "willed-type," meaning is textually based since the reader examines the text with the goal of discerning the author's "willed" meaning. Yet, because it is precisely the "will" of the author that the reader seeks, the primary goal of interpretation is not the public use of words, although that is a good starting point, but rather the particular meaning an author intended by what he wrote. Considering this theory, then, literal interpretation can be summarized quite simply as the endeavor that seeks to discover what an author meant by what he wrote.

51. See Johnson, *Expository Hermeneutics*, 51–52. For an alternative model, see Kaiser Jr., "The Single Intent of Scripture," 125–26.

52. There are also examples of details revealed in the Old Testament which were always there but not recognized at the time (cf. 1 Cor 2:7). Here, though, the discussion relates to generic descriptions that are fleshed out in the progress of revelation.

Verbal Meaning as a Speech-Act

In his description of verbal meaning as an act of the "will," Hirsch opened the door to understanding and classifying meaning in terms of its corresponding speech-action. In 1955, J. L. Austin delivered a series of lectures at Harvard University in which he examined the ways in which language is used to accomplish things. While Austin focused his attention primarily on verbal speech, his theory has been applied more broadly to include written and literary forms of communication.[53] For Austin, it was not sufficient to see language simply in an informative fashion, although he would not discount this function of language. Focusing on what he called "performatives,"[54] Austin demonstrated that those who use language frequently do something, that is to say, perform an action by the saying of something in the hope of affecting an intended response. When a speaker makes a promise, the terms of that promise are uttered in human language and form the locution of the performative act. However, in making a promise, the speaker commits himself to act according to the terms of the promise in the locution and, thereby, performs an illocutionary act. By committing himself in promise, the speaker hopes to affect a particular response in the one to whom the promise is made. He hopes that as the hearer apprehends the locutionary and illocutionary nature of the speech-act, it will cause him to believe the promise is genuine and to live with the expectation that the promise will be kept according to the terms of the locution.[55] When this happens, perlocution has

53. In the history of speech act theory, John R. Searle and William P. Alston are prominent figures who continued to develop Austin's approach to language. See Searle, *Speech Acts*; Alston, *Illocutionary Acts and Sentence Meaning*. The application of Austin's speech act theory to the hermeneutics of literary texts has been developed in a variety of secular and biblical works. See Pratt, *Towards a Speech Act Theory of Literary Discourse*; Petrey, *Speech Acts and Literary Theory*; White, "Speech Act Theory and Literary Criticism," 1–24; White, "Value of Speech Act Theory for Old Testament Hermeneutics," 41–64; Patte, "Speech Act Theory and Biblical Exegesis," 85–102; Buss, "Contribution of Speech Act Theory to Biblical Studies," 125–34; Detweiler, "Speaking of Believing in Gen. 2–3," 135–42.

54. Austin, *How to Do Things with Words*, 4. G. B. Caird classifies what Austin terms "performatives" as a type of "commissive" use of language. See Caird, *Language and Imagery of the Bible*, 8.

55. With regard to perlocution, Caird writes, "Many performatives depend for their effectiveness (but not for their validity) on a response. An order does not produce the intended result unless it is obeyed otherwise it will only have the unintended, though possibly foreseen, effect of rendering its recipient disobedient . . ." (Caird, *Language and Imagery of the Bible*, 22). Likewise, Austin writes, "Saying something will often, or even normally, produce certain consequential effects upon the feelings, thoughts, or actions of the audience, or of the speaker, or of other persons: and it may be one with the design, intention, or purpose of producing them . . . We shall call the performance

taken place.[56] Recognizing the relationship that exists between locution, il-locution, and perlocution, Wolterstorff writes, "Illocutionary acts are related to locutionary acts by way of the *counting as* relation; perlocutionary acts are related to illocutionary acts by causality. Asserting, commanding, promising, and asking do not consist in the transmission of knowledge."[57]

Although Hirsch dealt strictly with meaning on the level of locution, speech-act theory allows the interpreter to expand his model of "willed-type" to include all three levels of meaning. Understanding an author's "willed-type" in a text, then, not only involves the apprehension of the *willed-locutionary-force* (i.e., verbal meaning) but also involves the apprehension of the *willed-illocutionary-force* (i.e., the act of promising, commanding, asserting, etc.) and the *willed-perlocutionary-force* (i.e., the production of faith, obedience, expectation, etc.).[58] When the interpreter views verbal meaning in this tertiary fashion, he opens the door to a better understanding of what is happening as he reads the biblical text.

Summary

This study will operate on the premise that language is a willed-type and constitutes an act of communication, that is, a speech act. Through the locutionary, illocutionary, and perlocutionary aspects of the willed-type, the meaning conceived by the author is recognizable and shareable through the language used in the written medium of the text. This meaning is stable and therefore preserves the possibility that the author's act of communication can be continually recognized by those who read it, even if these readers are separated by a significant period of time. In order to increase the likelihood that one will apprehend the author's intended meaning, careful attention must be paid to the literary genre of the text which will set-up certain interpretive expectations for the reader as he encounters the text.

---

of an act of this kind the performance of a 'perlocutionary' act . . ." (Austin, *How to Do Things with Words*, 101).

56. See Austin, *How to Do Things with Words*, 98–101.

57. Wolterstorff, *Divine Discourse*, 33.

58. In his dispensational biblical theology, Johnson identifies promise, prophecy, and law as three prominent types of speech-acts to be found in Scripture. See Johnson, *Dispensational Biblical Theology*, 9–10.

2

Abraham and the Interpretation of Romans 4:1–25 in the Dispensational Tradition

INTRODUCTION

To appreciate the diversity of the dispensational tradition concerning God's method of salvation, it is important to understand how Rom 4:1–25 has been interpreted within its history. Interestingly, when one takes the time to gain this historical perspective, one will at once realize that many of the misconceptions regarding dispensational soteriology arise from a narrow or incomplete view of the historical development of this aspect in its theological history. While the dispensational tradition has found a large degree of unity in the belief that salvation has always included a common *requirement* (faith), a common *object* (God), and a common *basis* (Christ's death), since the beginning of dispensationalism's "conscious self-identity" in the 1800s to the present day,[1] there has never been a single dispensational view regarding the role of faith's *content* in God's program for salvation throughout the Old and New Testaments—a so-called dispensational perspective. In fact, in historical review, it becomes apparent that while all dispensationalists see a level of discontinuity in the content of saving faith, the tradition has always been a home both to those who question whether one can discern any

1. Dispensational historian Michael J. Svigel uses the term "conscious self-identity" to refer to the birth of dispensationalism as a system during the period of Benjamin Will Newton and John Nelson Darby in the 1800s. See Svigel, "History of Dispensationalism in Seven Eras," 73.

significant continuity in the content of saving faith as well as to those who claim that belief in Messiah is a discernable point of continuity throughout Scripture.[2] As the following discussion will show, these two views do not represent an early and late development within the progress of dispensational history but, rather, strands that have coexisted throughout its history.

DISPENSATIONALISM AND DISPARITY IN THE CONTENT OF FAITH

The View of John Nelson Darby (1800–82)

John Nelson Darby is widely recognized for his contribution to the systematization of dispensational premillennialism and has been called by some "the father of modern dispensationalism."[3] Darby was born in London in 1800 to wealthy Irish parents and practiced law after receiving an education at Trinity College in Dublin. Darby would later leave the legal profession to work as an Anglican priest in Ireland until he left the Church of England in 1831 to join the Plymouth Brethren, the community in which he would make his most significant theological contributions.[4] Darby was a prolific writer during his career and authored over fifty volumes of expositional, doctrinal, and practical material for the church.[5]

Basis of Salvation

In his exposition of the book of Romans, Darby makes it abundantly clear that he believes the only basis, past or present, upon which God justifies believers is the substitutionary death of Jesus. For Darby, this common basis reflects the tremendous patience of God in his desire to save the sinner

2. This portion of the study is limited to those dispensationalists whose views on Rom 4:1–25 can clearly be established. As such, there are prominent dispensationalists who will be left out of this discussion because they either did not directly address this passage in any extant works or because their treatment of the passage did not clarify their perspective.

3. Stallard, "Interpretation of the New Covenant in the History of Traditional Dispensationalism," 74. Svigel suggests that Darby was the one to codify what would become the identifying elements of dispensational theology in his theological break from Benjamin Willis Newton over eschatology. Because of this, Svigel concludes that Darby began the era in which dispensationalism achieved its conscious identity" (Svigel, "History of Dispensationalism in Seven Eras," 73–74).

4. Balmer, "John Nelson Darby," 170–71.

5. Crutchfield, *Origins of Dispensationalism*, 7.

from wrath. Reflecting on the theological truth taught by Paul in Rom 3:25, Darby writes,

> The sin, whether of Jew or Gentile, is put away by the blood-shedding of Jesus, and God's righteousness manifested in forgiving. This righteousness is now the starting-point of faith: we have met God here. But this shewed the righteousness of God in his patience with, and forgiveness of, the sins of Old Testament believers. The patience had been shewn of old. The work of Christ shewed the righteousness ground of this patience. We, or they, are all fully justified by Christ's blood.[6]

While some may object to the language used by certain dispensational writers with respect to the basis of salvation, it is important to observe that a dispensational commitment to the common ground of salvation for Old and New Testament believers can be traced back to the father of the dispensational movement.

Requirement for Salvation

In Darby's exposition of Rom 4:9–12, he explains that the justification which God granted the sinner on the basis of Jesus' death has always been received through the "principle of faith."

> And is God only the God of a people, even of His people? Is He not God of all nations? Surely He is, and indeed now in grace, just as He is for the Jew, who needed it as much as the Gentile. For it is one and the same God who justifies the circumcision (who sought their own righteousness by law) on the principle of faith, freely by grace, and, if a Gentile had that faith, justified that Gentile by the faith that he had. This is the force of the words translated "by" and "through." "By" is on the principle of; "through" by means of, when one possessed it. The Jew sought righteousness on a wrong principle. The gospel revealed the true one—faith. If the Gentile had the faith, he had the justification which was given on that principle.[7]

Darby draws the faith principle from his understanding of Paul's use of the Abraham story in the book of Genesis: "Abraham believed God, and was reckoned righteous because of his faith. It was not that his faith had so

---

6. Darby, *Collected Writings of J. N. Darby*, 34. See also Darby, *Collected Writings of John Nelson Darby*, 257.

7. Darby, *Collected Writings of J. N. Darby: Expository No. 5*, 135.

much intrinsic value, which was put to his account, as so much righteousness; but he was esteemed or reckoned righteous for his faith."[8] In Darby's soteriology, faith is the requirement for salvation.[9]

Object of Faith

In his development of what he refers to as the "resurrection principle," Darby explains how Paul uses the Abraham story to teach a common object of faith in salvation. Comparing Abraham's faith in the God who could provide him offspring despite the deadness of his body with the faith of New Testament believers in the God who raised Jesus from the dead, Darby writes,

> In chapter 4 we have another thing, resurrection in principle. Abraham believed God. This is faith in its groundwork. God is believed. Next, in object, not only did he believe in the resurrection, but in the God that raised. So with us; we do not merely believe in Jesus, who rose from the dead, but in the God who raised Him . . ."[10]

Later in his commentary, Darby explains how Abraham could believe in the "God that raised." At the point Abraham placed his faith in God's promise of offspring, he and his wife, Sarai, were old and long past child-bearing years. Yet, despite the deadness of their bodies, Abraham believed that what God had promised he could do, bringing life from their dead (i.e., barren) bodies. In this way, Darby states that Abraham believed in a "quasi-resurrection" and, therefore, in the God who raised.[11] In Darby's soteriology, Abraham and Christians share continuity in God's method of salvation in that both have God as the common object of their faith.

---

8. Darby, *Collected Writings of J. N. Darby: Expository No. 5*, 136. In his exposition on Gen 15:6, Darby states the importance of this "faith principle" in Abram's justification. He writes, "It is the first time this great and all-important truth [righteousness by faith] is taught in Scripture, or even the word for it found; and, I doubt not, intentionally so, though we know there were believers before. But now, in the great root of the tree of promise, this fundamental truth was to be brought out. The very ground of man's blessing was laid here, but it was still meeting man's need. He could not be before God or inherit the promise without it. He had it not in himself. God counts his faith to him as such" (Darby, *Collected Writings of J. N. Darby*, 142).

9. Elsewhere Darby develops this faith principle from Paul's use of the Abraham story in a reply written to an article in the *British and Foreign Evangelical Review*, February 7, 1862. For the text of this letter see, Darby, *Collected Writings of John Nelson Darby*, 349–87.

10. Darby, *Collected Writings of J. N. Darby: Expository No. 5*, 34–35.

11. Darby, *Collected Writings of J. N. Darby: Expository No. 5*, 137–38.

Content of Faith

Although Darby believes that Abraham and New Testament believers share a large degree of continuity when it comes to God's method of salvation—both share a common basis, requirement, and object of faith—Darby believes that the content of saving faith is a discontinuous element of a biblical soteriology. Reflecting on Paul's teaching at the end of Rom 4, Darby writes, "[O]ur faith, though in principle the same, has in one very important respect a different character from that of Abraham. He believed that God was able to perform what He had said. We believe that He has raised Christ from the dead."[12] While the specific content of the Christian's faith is made abundantly clear—belief in God's resurrection of Jesus Christ—his language describing the content of Abraham's belief is a bit ambiguous. What was it that Abraham "believed that God was able to perform?" Darby answers this in his expositional comments on Gen 15.

> As a man upon this earth, Abram wanted a son to continue his name, and posterity to inherit and enjoy the promises. God was fully minded to give this. The natural wish and desire of Abram, Abram connects with the testimony of divine favour. God had, in the revelation which Abram had received when in the land, promised a seed to Abram connected with the inheritance of the land. Abram naturally wished to associate the promised blessing and glory with his own descendants.[13]

Darby sees a distinction between the content of Abraham's faith and that of the Christian. Whereas Abraham believed that God was able to fulfill the promise of numerous descendants to enjoy the land given to him through promise, the Christian believes that God has raised Jesus from the dead for the forgiveness of sins.[14]

---

12. Darby, *Collected Writings of J. N. Darby: Expository No. 5*, 138.

13. Darby, *Collected Writings of J. N. Darby: Expository No. 1*, 141. See also Darby, *Collected Writings of John Nelson Darby*, 328.

14. Elsewhere, it is clear that Darby understands Jesus to have been anticipated in the promises of Gen 3:15 and 12:3. However, particularly with Gen 12:3, he gives no indication that Abraham had a conscious recognition of this knowledge. "Now, from the beginning, the coming of Christ was intimated in the judgment pronounced on Satan; and then, when God began to deal with man in the new world when it had wholly departed from Him into idolatry, in the promise of the Seed in whom the nations should be blessed, to Abraham called out from it. But the promise was never fulfilled till Christ came . . ." (Darby, *Collected Writings of John Nelson Darby*, 348). For his exposition on Gen 12, see Darby, *Collected Writings of J. N. Darby: Expository No. 1*, 122–33.

Summary

In Darby's exposition, the elements of continuity and discontinuity emerge to form his soteriology. In Darby's view, the elements of continuity in God's method of salvation are found in a common basis, requirement, and object of faith. The *basis* is the substitutionary death of Christ, the *requirement* is faith, and the *object* of faith is the God of the resurrection. The element of discontinuity is found in the *content* of faith. While Abraham's belief was future oriented, including belief in God's ability to bring life from dead bodies and his provision of a posterity to enjoy the land, Christians believe that God has raised Jesus from the dead for the forgiveness of sins. Although Abraham and the Christian believe in the same God and his ability to bring life from the dead, Abraham did not express faith in Messiah making the content of faith largely discontinuous.[15]

The View of Lewis Sperry Chafer (1871–1952)

Lewis Sperry Chafer was born in 1871 in Rock Creek, Ohio, to a pastor of a Congregational Church. Receiving a collegiate level education at Oberlin College, Chafer spent much of his early life as a musician with the YMCA. In 1896, Chafer became an assistant pastor of a congregational church like his father and ministered in Painesville, Ohio, and then in Buffalo, New York. In 1901, Chafer moved to Northfield, Massachusetts, where he traveled as an itinerate preacher and evangelist. During this time, Chafer also worked as a musician for the Northfield Bible conferences. While in Northfield, Chafer met C. I. Scofield, who introduced him to dispensational theology. Because of the influence of Scofield, Chafer moved to New York in 1915 to work as an extension teacher at Scofield's correspondence school. Chafer would later assume the pastoral role at Scofield's church in Dallas, Texas, where he would found the Evangelical Theological College which was later renamed Dallas Theological Seminary, a prominent evangelical and dispensational graduate institution.[16] As a writer, Chafer is perhaps best known for

15. Some might be tempted to suggest that Darby does see a continuous component in the content of faith for he suggests that both Abraham and Christians believe not simply in God but the God of the resurrection. Should not resurrection, then, be held as a point of continuity in the content of faith? If Abraham and Christians placed their faith in the same type of resurrection, then such a suggestion would hold some validity. However, the term as used by Darby possesses two different senses. In the case of Abraham, resurrection means "life from barrenness" and is, therefore, used in a reproductive sense. In the case of Christians, resurrection means "bodily resurrection from the dead." This is not belief in the same type of resurrection.

16. Balmer, "Lewis Sperry Chafer," 120–21.

his eight-volume *Systematic Theology*, which functioned to further codify dispensational thought in a systematic form.[17]

Basis of Salvation

In the development of his soteriology, Chafer suffered from a lack of clarity with regard to the basis upon which God justified Old and New Testament believers. In 1936, Chafer wrote *Dispensationalism*, in which he tried to clarify dispensational theology in light of criticism from other theological traditions. In one section, Chafer explained what he believed to be the basis on which people achieved a right standing before God.

> Whatever may have been the divine method of dealing with individuals before the call of Abraham and the giving of the law by Moses, it is evident that, with the call of Abraham and the giving of the law and all that has followed, there are two widely different, standardized, divine provisions, whereby man, who is utterly fallen, might stand in the favor of God, namely, (a) by physical birth into Judaism or (b) by spiritual birth into Christianity or the kingdom of God.[18]

Taken at face value, this explanation by Chafer appears to contrast the "physical birth" of Jews and the "spiritual birth" of Christians as two separate bases of salvation. However, in 1945, Chafer penned an article defending dispensationalism against covenant theologians who claimed that the system taught two different ways of salvation. In his fiery defense, Chafer emphatically asserts that "God never saved any one person or group of persons on any other ground than that righteous freedom to do so which the Cross of Christ secured. There is, therefore, but one way to be saved . . ."[19] Here Chafer clearly communicates his belief in a single basis of salvation.

In 1946, Chafer wrote an editorial on the doctrine of justification and drew on Paul's teaching in Rom 4 to help explain his theology. Unfortunately,

17. Stallard, "Interpretation of the New Covenant in the History of Traditional Dispensationalism," 95.

18. Chafer, *Dispensationalism*, 41. Later in the same section, Chafer explains that Israel became a permanently redeemed people by "power and blood" during the exodus and cites Isa 63:1. He notes that the Passover lamb, an anticipation of "God's perfect lamb," allowed God to redeem the nation forever (Chafer, *Dispensationalism*, 42) With regard to the spiritual birth of Christians, Chafer described it as being "individually redeemed by the blood of Christ, born of the Spirit into a relationship in which God becomes their Father and they become His legitimate sons and heirs—even joint-heirs with Christ" (Chafer, *Dispensationalism*, 43–44).

19. Chafer, "Inventing Heretics through Misunderstanding," 1.

his doctrinal treatise in this work only added more confusion to the precise nature of basis upon which people are justified in his understanding.

> In justification God does not legalize a fiction or make-believe. He must have, and does have, a righteous ground on which to justify the ungodly (cf. Rom. 4:5). A distinction must be observed between *just men* of the Old Testament and the justified according to the New Testament. According to the Old Testament, men were *just* because they were true and faithful in keeping the Mosaic law . . . Men were therefore *just* because of their own works for God, whereas New Testament justification is God's work for man in answer to faith (Rom. 5:1).[20]

In this editorial, Chafer appears to believe that people in the Old Testament were considered righteous on the basis of works under the Mosaic covenant while Christians are considered righteous on the basis of God's work for them received by faith.[21] While he does not reference this passage, it is possible that he found validity for his theology in Deut 6:25.

It is difficult to evaluate how these various statements made by Chafer existed together in his understanding of this important point of soteriology. Rather than elevate one statement as normative of his thinking over another, it seems best to allow the seeming contradictions to stand in Chaferian thought. However, the fact that he, at times, did promote a single basis of salvation to be found in the substitutionary death of Christ is a fact that cannot be overlooked.

Requirement for Salvation

Chafer's thought becomes a bit clearer when it comes to the requirement for salvation, although it does not come without nuance. Here, Chafer asserts unequivocally that the requirement for salvation is faith. In his comments on Rom 4:5 Chafer states that "the ungodly may be counted righteous on the ground of faith in Christ."[22] For him, Paul's use of the Abraham story proves that faith is the requirement placed upon those who were to receive

---

20. Chafer, "Editorials: Justification," 130. Emphasis his.

21. In his exposition of Rom 3:23–26, Chafer intimates, although does not state explicitly, that the substitutionary death of Christ is the common basis upon which men are saved as foreshadowed by the "sweet savor offerings" (Chafer, *Systematic Theology*, 201–2). In his volume on Soteriology, Chafer states that the sacrifice of Christ was the basis upon which God could defer the judgment for sin in every age. See Chafer, *Systematic Theology*, 102–3.

22. Chafer, *Systematic Theology: Soteriology*, 83.

God's gift of salvation. In his comments on Rom 4:13–16, Chafer states, "In Abraham's case, as is the case of all who exercise Abrahamic faith, the promise of imputed righteousness is (1) by faith (nothing on man's part—cf. vs. 5), that it might be by grace (everything on God's part), to the end that the promise might be *sure*."[23] Yet, for Chafer, Paul's use of the Abraham story is a model only for those who existed before and after the Law. Drawing this theology from Rom 4:17–18, Chafer writes, "Let it be restated that Abraham is the pattern of a Christian under grace and not of a Jew under the law. The character of his faith, as defined in verses 17–22, is worthy of most careful consideration. But righteousness received by faith is not alone the heritage of Abraham; it is 'for us also.'"[24] What, then, would Chafer claim is the requirement placed on the Jew to be saved? Is it different than the requirement placed on Abraham and the New Testament believer? Chafer answers this question in his editorial defense of dispensational soteriology.

> Regarding the nation and her promised salvation, it will be seen that they are to be saved because of the covenant Jehovah made with them to this end. When they are saved it will be because One died for that nation and on that righteous ground alone, which death for them they will then be moved by the Holy Spirit to accept by faith.[25]

In Chafer's soteriology, while the Jew possesses a covenant privilege guaranteeing his salvation in the end, the requirement placed on the Jew for salvation is still faith.

23. Chafer, *Systematic Theology: Soteriology*, 84.

24. Chafer, *Systematic Theology: Soteriology*, 84.

25. Chafer, "Inventing Heretics through Misunderstanding," 4. While Chafer believed that salvation for Jews under the Law was guaranteed by virtue of their covenant position, an individual Israelite could forfeit his position in the kingdom and be cut off from his people. "Thus it is disclosed that the salvation of an Israelite, who lived in the Mosaic age, which age will be completed in the coming Tribulation, was guaranteed by covenant; yet the individual could, by failing to do God's revealed will as contained in the Mosaic Law, sacrifice his place in the coming Kingdom and be cut off from his people . . ." (Chafer, "Inventing Heretics through Misunderstanding," 4–5). In light of Chafer's emphasis in this editorial on faith as the requirement for Abraham, the believer, and the Jew, one would assume that "God's revealed will" would include faith, although this is not something that Chafer himself unpacks. See also Chafer, *Systematic Theology: Soteriology*, 105–6.

Object of Faith

A clearer point in Chafer's understanding of God's method of salvation arrives when he describes what he believes Paul teaches regarding the object of saving faith.

> That God has assigned different human requirements in various ages as the terms upon which He Himself saves on the ground of the death of Christ, is a truth of Scripture revelation and is recognized as true by those who receive their doctrine from the Sacred Text rather than from manmade creeds. Nevertheless, when the various human requirements of the different ages are investigated it is found that they come alike in the end to the basic reality that faith is exercised in *God*. And that one basic element of trust in God doubtless answers that which in every case God must require.[26]

Chafer connects his understanding of God as the common object of faith to Paul's use of the Abraham story in Rom 4:23–24, where Paul relates the object of Abraham's faith to that of the New Testament believer. "[B]oth have a promise of God on which to rest and both believe *God*."[27]

Content of Faith

In his writings, Chafer was quite clear that the precise content of faith was an element of discontinuity in God's method of salvation. In his comments on Rom 4:23–24, Chafer says,

> God imputes righteousness to those in this age who believe, which righteousness is the foremost feature of salvation, on the one demand that they believe; but this belief is not centered in a son which each individual might generate, as in the case of Abraham, but in the Son whom God has given to a lost world, who died for the world and whom God has raised from the dead to be Saviour of those who do believe. In Romans 4:23, 24 it is written, "Now it was not written for his sake alone, that it was imputed to him; But for us also, to whom it shall be imputed, if we believe on him that raised up Jesus our Lord from the dead." From this it will be seen that, though the specific object

---

26. Chafer, "Inventing Heretics through Misunderstanding," 2. Emphasis his. It is important to understand that when Chafer speaks of "different human requirements" as the different terms of salvation, he is specifically speaking about the content of faith.

27. Chafer, "Inventing Heretics through Misunderstanding," 3. Emphasis his.

of faith—Isaac in the case of Abraham and Jesus Christ in the
case of those becoming Christians—varies, both have a promise
of God on which to rest and both believe in God.[28]

To avoid confusion, Chafer immediately emphasizes that it "does not
follow that men of all ages may be saved by believing any promise of God; it
is only such promises as God has Himself made to be the terms upon which
He will save."[29] For Chafer, then, there is a large degree of discontinuity to be
found in the content of saving faith in the Bible. The specific revelation to be
believed at the point of salvation is determined by God but need not possess
any essential components in various expressions of faith.

Summary

In Chafer's exposition, the elements of continuity and discontinuity emerge
to form his soteriology. For Chafer, the elements of continuity in God's
method of salvation are found in a common requirement for salvation, object of faith, and possibly in the basis of salvation. The *requirement* is faith,
and the *object* of faith is God, and at least in some of his articulations, the
basis is found in the substitutionary death of Jesus. The element of discontinuity rest in the *content* of faith. While Abraham believed in God's promise
of Isaac, an immediate heir, Christians believe in Jesus Christ. For Chafer,
the important aspect of the content of faith is that it is a content designated
by God at the point of salvation rather than a set of continuous elements in
varying expressions of saving faith.

The View of Charles C. Ryrie (1925–2016)

It is quite possible that no dispensational theologian in the twentieth
century had a more significant impact on the dispensational movement
than Charles C. Ryrie. Ryrie was born in St. Louis in 1925 and became a
Christian at the age of five through the influence of his father. Ryrie became acquainted with dispensational thinkers early in life. After graduating
from high school at sixteen, Ryrie spent a semester at Stony Brook School
in Long Island under the leadership of Frank E. Gaebelein, the son of Arno
C. Gaebelein. After transferring to Haverford College in Philadelphia, Ryrie
attended Tenth Presbyterian Church where he sat under the teaching of
Donald Grey Barnhouse. During this time, Ryrie befriended Lewis Sperry

28. Chafer, "Inventing Heretics through Misunderstanding," 2.
29. Chafer, "Inventing Heretics through Misunderstanding," 3.

Chafer who, in 1943, led him to dedicate his life to ministry. Ryrie would go on to receive both his master's and doctoral degrees at Dallas Theological Seminary where he would later teach as a professor of systematic theology.[30] Throughout his career, Ryrie was a prolific writer and defender of dispensational theology and helped introduce important revisions to the dispensational system.[31]

In light of his prolific writing, it is no surprise that Ryrie's view regarding the continuity and discontinuity in God's method of salvation found expression in his written works. In the 2007 version of his work *Dispensationalism,* Ryrie sought to clarify how dispensationalists could maintain one method of salvation while distinguishing the dispensations of Law and grace. For Ryrie, the elements of continuity that maintained a single method of salvation were to be found in a *common basis* (Christ's death), a *common requirement* (faith), and a *common object of faith* (God). Because these elements were transdispensational, they allowed dispensationalists to claim one method of salvation.[32] The element of discontinuity related to the *content of faith*. In the same work, Ryrie explains in what way the content of faith is discontinuous when he writes,

> In examining salvation under the Mosaic Law, the principal question is simply, How much of what God was going to do in the future did the Old Testament believer comprehend? According to both Old and New Testament revelation, it is impossible to say that he saw the same promise, the same Savior as we do today. . .[T]he content of faith depends on the particular revelation God was pleased to give at a certain time.[33]

Like many of the dispensationalists before him, Ryrie does not believe that content of faith possesses any necessary elements of continuity in its various expressions so long as the sinner believes the specific revelation God gave at the time. While Ryrie summarizes his position quite clearly in *Dispensationalism,* in his earlier writings he attaches the various elements of his view to the Abraham story and Paul's use of it in Rom 4.

---

30. Enns, "Charles C. Ryrie," 366–67.

31. Based his participation in these revisions, the most notable of which was the rejection of the dualism present in earlier dispensationalism, Craig A. Blaising and Darrell L. Bock categorize Ryrie as a "revised dispensationalist." See Blaising and Bock, *Progressive Dispensationalism,* 31–46.

32. Ryrie, *Dispensationalism,* 134.

33. Ryrie, *Dispensationalism,* 140.

Basis of Salvation

In his work *Biblical Theology of the New Testament*, published in 1959, Ryrie understands Paul to be teaching that redemption through justification by grace is for all mankind (Rom 3:23–25).[34] He describes this divine action as "an act of grace on God's part; it is made possible on the basis of the sacrifice of Christ."[35] For Ryrie, there is one basis for salvation, the sacrificial death of Christ.

Requirement for Salvation

In Ryrie's soteriology, faith was held to be the single requirement placed upon the sinner to receive God's gracious gift of salvation. He understands this to be one of the great lessons Paul teaches in Rom 4. "In Romans 4, Paul illustrates from the life of Abraham that all a man must do is believe in order to gain God's righteousness."[36] Therefore, he emphatically states that that "the human requirement is faith."[37]

Object of Faith

In his study Bible, Ryrie claims that Paul's use of the Abraham story in Rom 4:16–25 claims that the object of Abraham's faith was God. He titles this passage, "Abraham's faith was in God."[38] In his note on verse 19, where Paul speaks of Abraham's age and Sarah's barrenness as human obstacles to the promise of God, Ryrie observes that "Abraham fully faced the difficulty, yet believed God."[39]

Content of Faith

With respect to the content of Abraham's faith and the faith of the New Testament believer, it is here where Ryrie acknowledges the disparity in

---

34. Ryrie, *Biblical Theology of the New Testament*, 185.

35. Ryrie, *Biblical Theology of the New Testament*, 186. See also Ryrie, *So Great a Salvation*, 130.

36. Ryrie, *Biblical Theology of the New Testament*, 187. See also Ryrie, *So Great a Salvation*, 133.

37. Ryrie, *Biblical Theology of the New Testament*, 186.

38. Ryrie, *Ryrie Study Bible*, 1548.

39. Ryrie, *Ryrie Study Bible*, 1548, note on 4:19.

the contents of belief. He notes that Abraham's faith was placed in God's promise of numerous descendants, while the content of faith for the New Testament believer is found in the death and resurrection of Jesus Christ.[40] In his note on Rom 4:24, Ryrie writes, "Saving faith is faith in the Giver of miraculous life, demonstrated in the resurrection of Jesus."[41] For Ryrie, the first part of his explanation provides the common element in God's method of salvation. Abraham believed that God could do the miraculous and bring life—numerous descendants—from his old body. The Christian, however, believes that God did the miraculous when he raised Jesus to life.

Summary

In Ryrie's soteriology, the elements of continuity in God's method of salvation are found in a common basis, requirement, and object of faith. The *basis* is the substitutionary death of Christ, the *requirement* is faith, and the *object* of faith is God. The element of discontinuity is found in the *content* of faith. While Abraham believed in God's ability to bring life, that is, fulfill the promise of numerous descendants, Christians believe in the resurrected Jesus. Abraham, therefore, did not express faith in Messiah making the content of faith largely discontinuous.

The View of David K. Lowery (1949–Present)

David K. Lowery served as a professor of New Testament studies at Dallas Theological Seminary, founded by Lewis Sperry Chafer in 1924. He received his master of theology degree (ThM) from Dallas Seminary in 1975, completed his doctorate at the University of Aberdeen in 1987, and pursued postdoctoral work at Tübingen University. Lowery has made numerous written contributions to theological journals and multi-author volumes in New Testament studies.[42]

---

40. In his comments on the content of Abraham's belief, Ryrie points the reader to Gen 15. In his note on 15:6, Ryrie observes that Abraham's belief was an "amen" to the promise of numerous offspring in the preceding verse. Ryrie, *Ryrie Study Bible*, 27, note on 15:6.

41. Ryrie, *Ryrie Study Bible*, note on 4:24.

42. Dallas Theological Seminar, "David K. Lowery."

Basis of Salvation

Commenting on the significance of Paul's theology in Rom 3:22–24, Lowery emphasizes that Jesus' resurrection from the dead is the only basis upon which people may be saved. "With the coming of Christ a new era in the history of salvation dawned. Jesus' death and resurrection made redemption possible for all people, Jew or gentile. As Paul sees it, the present reality of this redemption is that the declaration of righteousness is given to those who believe (Rom 3:22–24)."[43]

Requirement for Salvation

For Lowery, the common requirement for salvation is faith. He understands this to be one of the principle features of Paul's use of the Abraham story in Rom 4. Drawing on the theology taught in Rom 4:18–22, Lowery states, "Faith is the recurring medium in salvation history."[44] Faith, however, is not a passive response to the gospel but one that requires a holistic response on the part of the individual.

> [P]aul regarded faith as a response of the whole person to the gospel, a response of the mind, emotions, and will that manifests itself in speech and action. This is not to say that Paul believed salvation was in any way earned, gained, or merited by particular behavior. His brief statement to the Romans summed up his view: "to the man who does not work but trusts God who justifies the wicked, his faith is credited as righteousness" (4:5).[45]

Object of Faith

Drawing upon the analogy of Abraham developed by Paul, Lowery understands the common object of faith in God's method of salvation to rest in God. This was true for Abraham and is true for the New Testament believer. "Paul finds in Abraham an example of faith in God and his Word (Rom 4:18–22) . . ."[46] For Lowery, Paul elevates the history of Abraham as a nor-

43. Lowery, "Christ, the End of the Law in Romans 10:4," 243. See also Lowery, "Theology of Paul's Missionary Epistles," 270.

44. Lowery, "Christ, the End of the Law in Romans 10:4," 247. See also Lowery, "Theology of Paul's Missionary Epistles," 248.

45. Lowery, "Theology of Paul's Missionary Epistles," 281–82.

46. Lowery, "Christ, the End of the Law in Romans 10:4," 247.

mative example in God's method of salvation. As Abraham believed God, so too do Christians place their faith in God. God is the *object* of faith and his word provides the *content* of faith.

Content of Faith

Although Abraham and the New Testament believer share a common object of faith, Lowery sees a changing focus in the content of faith in the progress of history. "In the progress of salvation history the focus of faith changes. Abraham accepted as true that God would fulfill the promise of descendants. With the coming of Christ, faith finds its focus in what he said and did."[47] In Lowery's soteriology, there is discontinuity to be found in the content of saving faith. Abraham was responsible to believe God's promise of a posterity for his justification. With the coming of Jesus, the requirement for justification centers on a different content, his words and works.

Summary

In Lowery's view, the elements of continuity in God's method of salvation are found in a common basis, requirement, and object of faith. The *basis* is the death and resurrection of Christ, the *requirement* is faith, and the *object* of faith is God. The element of discontinuity is found in the *content* of faith. While Abraham's believed God's promise of posterity, Christians believe in the words and works of Jesus. Abraham, then, did not express faith in Messiah making the content of faith discontinuous.[48]

DISPENSATIONALISM AND CONTINUITY IN THE CONTENT OF FAITH

The View of William Kelly (1821–1906)

In the history of dispensationalism, the significant role of William Kelly cannot be overlooked. As a contemporary of John Nelson Darby, Kelly translated many of Darby's works into English since Darby wrote in a variety

47. Lowery, "Christ, the End of the Law in Romans 10:4," 247.

48. Although they do not specifically address Rom 4:1–25, dispensationalists Allen P. Ross and John S. Feinberg align themselves with Lowery's view regarding the continuity in God's one plan for salvation. See Ross, "Biblical Method of Salvation," 171–72; Feinberg, *Continuity and Discontinuity*, 61.

of different languages. During his life, Kelly collected and edited Darby's writings.[49] In the words of one writer, "[Kelly] is viewed as close to a clone of Darby as is possible among human beings. Only minor differences between them occurred. In a real sense, Kelly took the dispensational baton from Darby (i.e., among the Brethren) and handed it to the next generation."[50] Clones though they may have been, Kelly differed from Darby in a significant way with respect to God's one method of salvation.

Basis of Salvation

In the development of his soteriology, Kelly was abundantly clear that the only basis on which an individual was saved, past or present, is the substitutionary death of Jesus. The difference, though, was dispensational. Forgiveness in the past was granted in anticipation of Christ's finished work while forgiveness in the present age is based on the completion of Christ work. In his comments on Rom 3:23–26, Kelly writes,

> Hence it [justification] is wholly apart from the law, whilst witnessed to by the law and prophets; for the law with its types had looked onward to this new kind of righteousness; and the prophets had borne their testimony that it was at hand, but not then come. Now it was manifested, and not promised or predicted merely. Jesus had come and died. Jesus had been a propitiatory sacrifice; Jesus had borne the judgement of God because of the sins He bore. The righteousness of God, then, could now go forth in virtue of His blood . . . There is the vindication of God in His ways with the Old Testament believers. Their sins had been passed by.[51]

For Kelly, justification was never to be found through Law. Rather, it was something to which the Law bore witness, communicating the reality that a right standing before God was to be found outside the Law. It was this righteousness that the prophets anticipated and predicted would be fulfilled in Jesus. The completed work of Jesus through his substitutionary death fulfilled this Old Testament anticipation and vindicated God's righteousness.[52]

49. Stallard, "Interpretation of the New Covenant in the History of Traditional Dispensationalism," 83.

50. Stallard, "Interpretation of the New Covenant in the History of Traditional Dispensationalism," 83.

51. Kelly, *Lectures Introductory to the Study of the Epistles of Paul the Apostle*, 16–17, 19.

52. "It [justification] is quite independent of law, on the wholly different principle of

Requirement for Salvation

In Paul's use of the Abraham story in Rom 4, Kelly finds validation that the
only requirement for salvation is faith. While Judaism held Abraham in high
regard, the apostle's development of Abraham proved his theology. Faith is
the only means by which a person, Jew or gentile, could receive God's gracious gift of salvation. Thus, he can write, "Abraham is the proof of the value
of faith in justification before God."[53] That Abraham was justified before the
giving of the Law and his own circumcision proved Paul's soteriology.

> Not only was Abraham justified without law, but apart from that
> great sign of mortification of the flesh . . . The [Jews] appeal to
> their own inspired account of Abraham turned into a proof of
> the consistency of God's ways in justifying by faith, and hence
> in justifying the uncircumcised no less than the circumcision.[54]

Object of Faith

In his exposition of Rom 4:3, Kelly explains that the faith by which Abraham
was justified was in God. "Abraham believed God, and it was counted to him
for righteousness. There was no law there or then; for Abraham died long
before God spoke from Sinai. He believed God and His word, with special
approval on God's part; and his faith was counted as righteousness (ver. 3)."[55]
That Kelly views God as a common object of faith in his one method is
confirmed when he comments on the similarity between the faiths of Abraham and the New Testament believer in Rom 4:24. "[W]e believe *on Him
that raised up* Jesus our Lord from the dead."[56] Both Abraham and the New
Testament believer share a common object of faith in salvation. Both believe
in God.

---

grace, though the law as well as the prophets bore an anticipative witness to it. Law (not
in types, but in its proper character) appeals to the individual's own obedience, knows
nothing of a substitute. Grace always supposes the intervention of God Himself in His
Son, who in the cross establishes the right of God to bless him that believes in Jesus. It
is not simply His prerogative of mercy, it is His righteousness. For the blood of the only
acceptable victim is shed, the sacrifice is offered, the judgment of the sins has fallen on
Him, He has accepted it all" (Kelly, *Notes on the Epistle of Paul,* 43).

53. Kelly, *Lectures Introductory to the Study of the Epistles of Paul the Apostle,* 20.

54. Kelly, *Lectures Introductory to the Study of the Epistles of Paul the Apostle,* 21.

55. Kelly, *Lectures Introductory to the Study of the Epistles of Paul the Apostle,* 20.

56. Kelly, *Lectures Introductory to the Study of the Epistles of Paul the Apostle,* 22.

Content of Faith

Commenting on Rom 4, William Kelly explains the relationship between Abraham's faith and the Christian faith in Paul's doctrine of justification. For Kelly, the relationship goes deeper than simply a common object of belief.

> But the apostle takes care to point out the difference as well as the analogy. The faith not of Abraham only but of all Old Testament saints was exercised on promise. They all in a large sense waited for the accomplishment of what God held out, sure that He could not lie, and was able also to perform. But in the great ulterior object of their hope they were expecting One who was only promised and not yet come.
>
> It is not so with the Christian; for though he, like the elders, obtains a good report by faith, and has his faith reckoned for righteousness, yet the personal object of hope is come, and has wrought the infinite work of redemption.[57]

The dispensational change in Kelly's soteriology is found in promise and fulfillment. Abraham and Old Testament believers were justified as they believed in God's revelation of Messiah, although he had not yet come. Like Old Testament saints, New Testament believers are justified by faith in Messiah, but in the progress of history, that Messiah has been revealed to be the crucified and resurrected Jesus.[58]

Summary

In Kelly's view, the elements of continuity in God's method of salvation are found in a common basis, requirement, object of faith, and content. The *basis* is the propitiatory sacrifice of Jesus, the *requirement* is faith, the *object* of faith is God, and the *content* of faith includes belief in God's Messiah. In his model, the element of discontinuity is found in the distinction between promise and fulfillment. In the Old Testament, believers were justified as

---

57. Kelly, *Notes on the Epistle of Paul*, 54.

58. Elsewhere, Kelly describes the relationship when he writes, "And this leads us to see not only where there was an analogy with those who believe in a promised Saviour, but also to a weighty difference. And this lies in the fact that Abraham believed God before he had the son, being fully persuaded that what He had promised He was able to perform; and therefore it was imputed to him for righteousness. But we believe on Him that raised up Jesus our Lord from the dead. It is done already. It is not here believing on Jesus, but on God who has proved what He is to us in raising from among the dead Him who was delivered for our offences, and raised again for our justification" (Kelly, *Lectures Introductory to the Study of the Epistles of Paul the Apostle*, 22).

they believed in God's promise of Messiah. But as promise, it was an anticipated provision of God, not an historical reality. After the arrival and sacrifice of Jesus in the New Testament, faith still includes belief in Messiah, but that Messiah, in the progress of revelation, is revealed to be Jesus. The faith of the New Testament believer is more detailed than the faith expressed by Old Testament saints, but they find a continuity in expression through faith in Messiah.

The View of Arno C. Gaebelein (1861–1945)

Arno C. Gaebelein was born in Thuringia, Germany, in 1861. Feeling a deep call to the ministry, Gaebelein emigrated to the United States in 1879 where he worked as an ordained minister in the Methodist Church, serving congregations in Maryland, New York, and New Jersey. While in the United States, Gaebelein became acquainted with the work of John Nelson Darby and quickly became an enthusiastic supporter of dispensationalism. In 1894, Gaebelein began to work for the New York branch of The Hope of Israel Mission and founded a periodical, *Our Hope*, through which he publicized his dispensational interpretations to the broader population.[59] As a Jew, Gaebelein held strong opinions on the importance of national Israel. In his early career, Gaebelein was emphatic that it remained necessary for Jewish converts to maintain strict observance to the Law, however he would later revise this view to promote freedom from the Law.[60] This revision is evident in his exposition of Romans with respect to Pauline soteriology.

Basis of Salvation

In his commentary on the book of Romans, Gaebelein strongly promoted the idea that Christ substitutionary death was the only basis upon which God has ever justified the sinner. In his comments on Paul's theology in Rom 3:23–26 he writes,

> The sins that had taken place before, does not mean the sins committed before the conversion of an individual believer. It means the sins of believers before Christ had come and died. When sins were forgiven in Old Testament times God's gracious

59. Balmer, "Arno C. Gaebelein." For a good summary of the life and ministry of Gaebelein see Stallard, *Early Twentieth-Century Dispensationalism of Arno C. Gaebelein*, 11–60.

60. Stallard, *Early Twentieth-Century Dispensationalism of Arno C. Gaebelein*, 30–32.

forbearance was manifested, but when Christ had paid the great redemption price, when His blood had been shed, then God's righteousness was made manifest in having declared righteous believers, who lived before Christ had died.[61]

In light of Paul's teaching, "Gaebelein asserts that righteousness cannot be bestowed by the Law in any sense of the word."[62] Continuity in God's one method of salvation has always included a common basis, the substitutionary death of Jesus.

Requirement for Salvation

In his exposition of Paul and his use of the Abraham story in Rom 4, Gaebelein observes that the history of Abraham demonstrates faith to be the only requirement placed upon the sinner who is justified. Commenting on the theology found in 4:1–5, Gaebelein says, "Faith was reckoned to him [Abraham] for righteousness."[63] As he develops this theology in verses 9–12, he concludes that "ordinances, or sacraments so called by man, have no part in bestowing salvation upon man."[64] As demonstrated in the life of Abraham, God's method of salvation possesses a common requirement, faith.

Object of Faith

In Paul's development of Abraham, Gaebelein notes that the object of Abraham's faith was God. "How then was Abraham counted righteous before God? . . .Abraham simply believed God when He gave him a promise (Gen xv: 5–6) and God said, you have no righteousness, but I take your faith instead of righteousness."[65] Expressing the continuity between Abraham's faith and the faith of the New Testament believer taught by Paul in 4:23–25, Gaebelein states that "we believe on Him [God] also."[66] For Gaebelein, God's method of salvation contained continuity in the object of faith. It always included faith in God.

---

61. Gaebelein, *Epistle to the Romans*, 25. See also Gaebelein, *Gaebelein's Concise Commentary on the Whole Bible*, 900.

62. Gaebelein, *Epistle to the Romans*, 23.

63. Gaebelein, *Epistle to the Romans*, 26.

64. Gaebelein, *Epistle to the Romans*, 28.

65. Gaebelein, *Epistle to the Romans*, 26.

66. Gaebelein, *Epistle to the Romans*, 29.

Content of Faith

In his exposition of Rom 4:13–25, Gaebelein understands Paul to be moving toward a climax in his use of the Abraham story. He saw a deep continuity between the content of Abraham's faith and the faith of New Testament believers. While Gaebelein acknowledges that Abraham believed that God would give him an heir in the immediate provision of Isaac, Gaebelein understood there to be a connection between the promised heir and the ultimate fulfillment of the Abrahamic promises so that the heir God promised was more than Isaac.

> The promised seed was *more than Isaac*, it was Christ; so that Abraham believed the God who raised the Lord Jesus from the dead. And we believe on Him also. Our Lord was delivered for our offences and has been raised for our justification. His resurrection is the blessed and positive proof that our sins are completely put away. For this reason the resurrection of Jesus, our Lord is the justification of the believer.[67]

Gaebelein explains the manner in which Isaac tokens Christ in his hermeneutic when he deals with the content of Abraham's faith in Gen 15. "The connection with the previous chapter [Gen 14] is extremely precious. Abram had honored the Lord and now the Lord honored him. Then the seed is promised. That seed promised is Isaac; Christ is typified by him."[68] In Gaebelein's thought, the continuity in the content of faith rests in typology. Abraham believed God would provide him an heir through whom the promises would be fulfilled. In his historical context, Isaac represented an immediate heir. However, as Isaac did not fulfill all that God had promised, Isaac's arrival as an immediate heir anticipated God's provision of a future heir, Jesus Christ.[69]

Summary

For Gaebelein, the elements of continuity in God's method of salvation are found in a common basis, requirement, object of faith, and content. The *basis* is the death of Jesus through which redemption was made, the *requirement* is faith, the *object* of faith is God, and the *content* of faith included belief in Messiah. In his model, the element of discontinuity is found in the

67. Gaebelein, *Epistle to the Romans*, 29.

68. Gaebelein, *Gaebelein's Concise Commentary on the Whole Bible*, 28.

69. Since Gaebelein connects his typology in Genesis with divine promise in Rom 4, it is reasonable to assume that Gaebelein understood typology as prophetic.

hermeneutics of typology. In the Old Testament, Abraham was justified as he placed his faith in God's provision of an heir through whom the covenant promises would be fulfilled. The immediate fulfillment of this promise was Isaac, but Isaac functioned only as a token of God's promise of Christ. What Abraham believed in promise New Testament believers understand has been fulfilled in Jesus.

The View of H. A. Ironside (1876–1951)

H. A. Ironside was born in 1876 to a Plymouth Brethren household in Toronto, Canada. Although Ironside was self-educated, throughout his career and ministry he published more than forty books. After converting to Christianity at the age of fourteen, Ironside served in the Salvation Army in California where he quickly became known as "the boy preacher from Los Angeles." In 1896, Ironside joined the Plymouth Brethren and worked as an itinerate preacher until accepting the pastorate at Moody Memorial Church in Chicago in 1930. Throughout his career, Ironside dedicated his life to dispensational expositions of the Scripture, many of which have been preserved in writing for future generations.[70]

Basis of Salvation

With respect to God's method of salvation, Ironside was unequivocal in his belief that the substitutionary death of Jesus was the only basis upon which God had ever justified the sinner, past or present. In his comments on Rom 3:25, Ironside wrote,

> Till the Lord Jesus suffered for sins, the Just for the unjust, to bring us to God, the sin-question was not really settled . . . Old Testament saints therefore were all saved 'on credit,' as we say. Now that Christ has died the account is closed, and God declares His righteousness in pretermitting sins down through the past ages when men turned to Him in faith.[71]

In his soteriology, then, Ironside believed that Old and New Testament believers shared a common basis for salvation. It has always been based on the death of Christ.

70. Balmer, "H. A. Ironside," 298.
71. Ironside, *Lectures on the Epistle to the Romans*, 52.

Requirement for Salvation

In his exposition of Rom 4, Ironside believed that Paul utilized the Abraham
story to show the common elements in the salvation experience. For him,
the common requirement for salvation is faith. "To earn salvation by works
would be to put God in man's debt. He would owe it to the successful worker
to save him . . . It is his faith that is counted for righteousness. To this then
Abraham bears testimony."[72] Because of Paul's teaching, Ironside refers to
the requirement for salvation as "faith-righteousness."[73]

Object of Faith

In development of Pauline theology, Ironside understood Paul to be teaching that saving faith finds a common object in God. It is faith in God that
saved Abraham, and it is faith in God that saves the New Testament believer.
For Ironside, this connection is made by Paul in Rom 4:23–25. Regarding
this common feature, Ironside writes, "[A]braham believed God and it was
imputed to him for righteousness. In the same way we are called upon to
believe on Him who raised up Jesus our Lord from the dead . . ."[74]

Content of Faith

In his soteriology, Ironside saw a common element present in the content of
salvation as Paul developed the story of Abraham. He believed that the seed
which God promised and the seed in which Abraham believed was Jesus. In
his comments on Rom 4:13–17, Ironside writes,

> The promise of blessing through the Seed—which is Christ—is
> of faith that it might be by grace. And so it is "sure" to all the seed,
> that is, to all who have faith. All such are "of the faith of Abra-
> ham." He is thus the father of us all, who believe in Jesus. And
> so the word is fulfilled which said, "I have made thee a father of
> many nations." This comes in parenthetically. The words, "Before
> Him whom he believed," properly follows the words, "The father
> of us all." That is to say, Abraham, though not literally our father
> by natural generation, is the father of all who believe, in the sight
> of God. The same faith characterizes them all.[75]

72. Ironside, *Lectures on the Epistle to the Romans*, 54.

73. Ironside, *Lectures on the Epistle to the Romans*, 55.

74. Ironside, *Lectures on the Epistle to the Romans*, 57.

75. Ironside, *Lectures on the Epistle to the Romans*, 56.

Ironside believes that God's promise to Abraham meant more than simply the immediate seed which God would provide. Understanding the promise of an offspring in the context of the covenant given to him (Gen 12:3), Ironside believes that God had promised Abraham a seed, through whom the promise of blessing would be fulfilled. As Abraham believed in God and his promised seed, he was justified. As New Testament believers place their faith in Jesus, the promised seed, they become children of Abraham in the faith and are, likewise, justified before God.[76] The discontinuity, then, is to be found in what could be known of Christ. In his historical context, Abraham believed in Messiah as the seed promised by God. His full identity had not yet been revealed in history. With the advent of Jesus, believers in the present age know that the seed promised to Abraham has been revealed. The content of faith for New Testament believers is more specific but it is not a qualitatively different content than that believed by Abraham.[77]

CONCLUSION

The interpretation of Paul's use of the Abraham story in Rom 4:1–25 within the dispensational tradition evidences a diversity in the movement. Although widespread agreement has existed with respect to the continuity found in the basis of salvation, requirement for salvation, and the object of faith, there has never been a consensus on whether any common components are to be found in the content of faith. Since its beginning, there have existed those, like Darby, who have maintained that the efficacious nature of saving faith has only ever required faith in God as a common object. However, there have also existed dispensationalists, like William Kelly, who believed that God's method of salvation involves more than a common object but also includes a content that finds continuity in Messiah.

The debate within the tradition hinges on what the interpreter believes was capable of being shared through the language of the original text. To use literal interpretation consistently, one must go no further than to assign

---

76. Ironside, *Lectures on the Epistle to the Romans*, 56.

77. Although only briefly treating Paul's use of the Abraham story in Rom 4, dispensationalist Elliott E. Johnson (1936–present) shares the belief that the continuous element of saving faith is found in Messiah. "In distinction to finding covenant promises made to Israel having some fulfillment with the Church, continuity is found in promise concerning the Seed of the woman (Gen 3:15), the Seed of Abraham (Gen 12:36), the Son of David (2 Sam 7:12–16). These promises find fulfillment in Jesus Christ. Further, as believers were blessed by faith through the promised One (Gen 15:6; Ps 32:1–2), so believers are blessed by faith once the Promised One has come (Rom 4:1–8, 22–24; Gal 3:6–9)" (Johnson, *Dispensational Biblical Theology*, 8–9). See also 419–20.

meanings capable of being expressed in the historical context in which a passage was written. To read New Testament meanings back into an Old Testament context is to depart from the literal method of interpretation demanded in the dispensational tradition.[78] Ross warns of this type of interpretation when he notes the dilemma posed by the content of faith in God's one message of salvation.

> While we may all agree that salvation in the OT world was by grace through faith, there is a difference of opinion on the content of faith prior to the incarnation of Jesus Christ. What exactly did Abram believe? What did OT believers know about the provision of salvation?
>
> Many biblical scholars have stressed the uniformity of the method of salvation to such an extent that they make NT revelation the necessary content of the faith of OT believers.[79]

Dispensationalists who believe that the content of Abraham's faith in Gen 15:6 looked no further than a belief in God's provision of Isaac or a multiplicity of offspring must necessarily see the content of Abraham's faith to be essentially different than the faith of the New Testament believer, for the Christian does not place his faith in Isaac or a multiplicity of offspring for salvation but in the person and work of Christ. However, those dispensationalists who see the faith of Abraham to look beyond God's immediate provision of Isaac, or numerous descendants, to an ultimate fulfillment of covenant promise through his seed open the door to a continuity in the content of faith through each dispensation. The question to which the discussion will now turn is this: what was it that Abraham believed in Gen 15:6? While the proposed reading of the account of Abraham's faith in Gen 12–15:6 will attempt to demonstrate the validity of the dispensational tradition that has held Messiah to be an essential element of saving faith, the proposed reading is simply one way to establish that Abraham's faith was in God's promised seed and heir, Messiah. If one were to establish this same content of faith in a manner different from the way proposed in this study, it would not alter the validity of the thesis which this study seeks to establish.

78. Ryrie observes that the consistent use of a literal hermeneutic is an essential component of dispensationalism (Ryrie, *Dispensationalism*, 93).

79. Ross, "Biblical Method of Salvation," 169.

3

The Faith of Abraham in Genesis 15:6

INTRODUCTION

IF ONE WISHES TO understand the content of Abraham's faith in Gen 15:6, it is first necessary to understand the theology and argument of the book on the whole. Only this sense of the whole provides the appropriate context within which to exegete particular elements of the text. When one takes the time to understand what the author of Genesis is doing as he develops the argument of the book, one will quickly observe that the author not only intends to provide Israel with her heritage in the redemptive plan of God, but he also intends to provide her with a stewardship rooted in the message of Messiah who was to arise from the nation.

LITERARY GENRE AND HISTORICITY OF GENESIS

At the outset of this discussion, it is necessary, at least in a preliminary fashion, to establish the basic genre of the book as a whole, for doing so will alert the reader to the basic interpretive expectations he is to hold as he encounters this text of Scripture. Should the reader expect a literal or non-literal use of language?[1] Are the things to which the author refers to be taken as

1. G. B. Caird observes that literal versus non-literal language is not the same as the true versus false. Literal vs. non-literal language need only refer to the type of relationship that exists between the words used and the entities to which they refer. See Caird, *Language and Imagery of the Bible*, 131. In his book, *Anatomy of Criticism*,

real, historical entities, or are they imagined constructs referring to an imaginary, fictional realm? These interpretive questions are answered at the level of genre, and so it is imperative that the study address this issue to ensure that the conclusions reached are consistent with the type of literature the book itself claims to be. While an in-depth discussion the literary genre and historicity of Genesis would go far beyond the bounds of the current study, the basic elements upon which this study will assume these features will be presented. Should the reader wish to investigate these issues more fully, footnotes will be provided where such further study might be accomplished.

When attempting to establish the literary genre of a work, it is important to consider the textual clues that lead one to a particular conclusion. Yet, attempting to impose an overarching genre on a book does not come without difficulty, since most literature contains a variety of genres which, being thatched together, comprise the whole.[2] The difficulty in establishing the basic genre of Genesis can be easily seen by observing the variety of views that have been presented concerning the type of literature it is intended to be. Writing at the end of the nineteenth and into the twentieth centuries, Hermann Gunkel held that Genesis should largely be taken as an example of "legend," with some mythic elements.[3] As legend, Gunkel believed that Genesis was not a clear historical account of Israel's history but, rather, a literary work combining elements from surrounding cultures through a long oral tradition. "Legend—the word is employed in none other than the generally acknowledged sense—is a popular, long-transmitted, poetic account dealing with past persons or events."[4] In his view, the mythic elements of Genesis were "narratives about gods, in contrast to legends whose agents are human."[5]

Northrop Frye places an author's use of language in terms of a continuum of allegory. On the one end of the continuum is what would be an author's literal use of language, "anti-allegorical." On the other end would be a highly figurative use of language. Frye's observation highlights the importance for the interpreter to establish an author's use of language as he reads the text. Literary genre is one of the primary keys to identifying his use. See Frye, *Anatomy of Criticism*, 91.

2. Hoffmeier, "Genesis 1–11 as History and Theology," 27. Recognizing the variety of genres within Genesis itself, Kenneth Matthews writes, "Genesis is a complex literary composition with symmetrical unity but a diversity of genres (e.g., narrative, genealogy, and lyric poetry)" (Mathews, *Genesis 1–11:26*, 25).

3. Gunkel, *Genesis*, xvi, xlviii. While Gunkel believed that the Noah narrative and Gen 12–50 were to be read as legends, he held that the creation account was an example of ancient Near Eastern myth like those one might find in Babylonian literature (Gunkel, *Genesis*, 25–52). See also Gunkel, *Schöpfung und Chaos in Urzeit und Endzeit*, 3–16.

4. Gunkel, *Genesis*, viii.

5. Gunkel, *Genesis*, xii.

Others, like Bernard Batto, believe that the Israelites incorporated a number of mythic elements in the composition of Genesis, particularly in the creation account in Gen 1. As such, the composition, or at least elements within it, is not meant to be viewed as history in the same way that modern historiography would envision it.[6] Still others, like Sigmund Mowinckel, understand Genesis through an etiological lens and believe that its purpose is to tie various cultural practices to some imagined historical basis—a mythic history so to speak.[7] In light of the proliferation of views, what are the textual clues that alert the reader to the type of literature Genesis is intended to be? In response to this important question, it seems that the *tôledôt* structure and genealogical emphasis of the book provide the literary clues to suggest that the book of Genesis was intended to be read as *narrative history*.[8]

6. Batto writes, "[B]iblical ideas of creation are grounded in the cultural context of the ancient Near East, including mythic conceptions of the origins of humankind and the world that humankind inhabits." See Batto, *In the Beginning: Essays on Creation Motifs in the Ancient Near East and the Bible*, 11. It is important to note, however, that a variety of disagreement exists on the nature of *myth* in the ancient Near East. See George, *Epic of Gilgamesh*, xxxiii. De Wette defined myth as the means by which primitive people "clothed" abstract realities (De Wette, *Critical and Historical Introduction to the Canonical Scriptures of the Old Testament*, 23). See also Gaster, *Myth, Legend, and Custom in the Old Testament*, xxxiii–xxxvii. Carmino J. De Catanzaro suggests that myth provided the ancients with a means to describe things in the natural realm that they did not yet understand through science (De Catanzaro, "Man in Revolt," 285). However, James Barr argues that myth should not be understood primarily as symbolism but a holistic way of perceiving reality in an ancient society (Barr, "Meaning of 'Mythology' in Relation to the Old Testament," 3–5). See also Thordarson, "Mythic Dimension," 212–20.

7. "Die ätiologische Sage baut immer auf eine Wirklichkeit auf. Diese Wirklichkeit ist aber kein Ergeignis, geschweige denn ein geschichtliches Ereignis, sondern ein Zustand, etwas Daseiendes, ein topographisches, ethnologisches, kultisches, gewohnheitsmassiges usw. Datum permanenter Art. Das Aition will Ursprung und Existenz dieses immer daseienden Faktums erklären."

["The etiological legend is always based on a reality. However, this reality is not an event, let alone a historical event, but a state, something existing, a topographical, ethnological, cultic, habitual, etc. datum of a permanent nature. The *aition* wants to explain the origin and existence of this always existing fact]" (Mowinckel, *Tetrateuch-Pentateuch-Hexateuch*, 81).

8. The nomenclature of "narrative history" has been used and debated for some time. See White, "Question of Narrative in Contemporary Historical Theory," 1–33. In the present discussion, "narrative history" has been chosen over "historical narrative" because of its emphasis on the literary design of the text as a means to communicate historical reality. See Long, *Art of Biblical History*, 58–76. Adele Berlin describes narrative as "a form of representation." See Berlin, *Poetics and Interpretation of Biblical Narrative*, 13.

The Narrative Design of Genesis

As Tremper Longman notes, a narrative is a story that, at its most basic level, includes a plot, characters, and the narrator or point of view. The way in which these basic elements are combined may differ from culture to culture, or from author to author, yet they, nevertheless, are essential components of a narrative design.[9] Of these basic ingredients, plot is the component that provides cohesion and gives meaning to each particular element within the narrative framework. Recognizing the importance of plot, Peter Brooks writes, "Plot is, first of all, a constant of all written and oral narrative, in that a narrative without at least a minimal plot would be incomprehensible. Plot is the principle of interconnectedness and intention which we cannot do without in moving through discrete elements—incidents, episodes, actions—of a narrative."[10] Because the narrative books of the Bible *are not* "mere compilations of unconnected stories, but as is well-known, are made up of sequences of narratives [episodes], which combine to constitute wider structures"[11] *biblical narratives* are to be *sharply distinguished from episodic narratives* wherein narrative episodes exist, to a large extent, in isolation from each other or are minimally connected without coordinating to develop a central plot action.[12]

In the book of Genesis, the protagonist—as with the whole of the biblical story—is God who, in history, partners with fallen human agents to resolve the conflict initiated in the fall of mankind. The antagonist is Satan (i.e., the serpent) who, through deception, seeks to disrupt the *mediatorial rule of God* through his human representatives so that they bear his image

---

9. Longman III, "Biblical Narrative," 71.

10. Brooks, *Reading for the Plot*, 5. Like Brooks, Tremper Longman III believes that plot provides the framework that gives meaning to the elements within the story. He writes, "This narrative trait of plot is so pervasive that readers will automatically attribute causation between narrative episodes even if they are not explicit in the text itself . . . One way of proceeding is to identify the central plot conflict of a book and then see how the different episodes of the story fit into the progression toward the resolution of the conflict" (Longman, "Biblical Narrative," 71). For a good discussion of plot in narrative design, see Bar-Efrat, *Narrative Art in the Bible*, 93–140.

11. Bar-Efrat, *Narrative Art in the Bible*, 132.

12. Leland Ryken defines an episodic narrative as a story in which "the events succeed each other but do not form a cause-effect chain in which one event produces the next." See Ryken, *How to Read the Bible as Literature and Get More Out of It*, 45. Unfortunately, Ryken suggests that such disconnected, episodic narratives are to be found in the Bible. See Ryken, *How to Read the Bible as Literature and Get More Out of It*, 45.

(i.e., become his offspring) rather than God's image on the earth God created.[13] The narrative structure of Genesis could be outlined as follows:[14]

I. Setting (Gen 1–2)

II. Conflict (Gen 3)

III. Rising Action (Gen 4–21)

IV. Climax (Gen 22)

V. Falling Action (23–36)

VI. Resolution (Gen 37–48)[15]

VII. Denouement (Gen 49–50)

Genesis as History

Establishing the historical nature of the Genesis narrative is an important task and holds important implications for the theology of the book. Yet, as Meir Sternberg importantly observes, the fictional or historical intention of the author cannot be discerned by the narrative form of the book alone.

> There are simply no universals of historical vs. fictive form. Nothing on the surface, that is, infallibly marks off the two genres. As modes of discourse, history and fiction make *functional* categories that may remain constant under the most assorted *formal* variations and are distinguishable only by their overall sense of purpose.[16]

While narrative form may not be adequate alone to distinguish between the historical or fictional intention of an author, such intention can be established by paying careful attention to the details embedded in the

---

13. Alva J. McClain made an important contribution when he distinguished between the universal and mediatorial kingdom of God in Scripture. While the universal rule of God has never nor could ever be challenged, it is God's mediatorial rule through people that is at issue in the biblical story. See McClain, *Greatness of the Kingdom*, 21.

14. For a similar narrative outline of the book, see pages 193–213 of the working manuscript by Charles P. Baylis. Charles P. Baylis, "Creation of the Nation Israel (Jacob) to Represent God (27–50)"

15. Although the book of Genesis leaves the ultimate resolution of the conflict begun in chapter 3 unresolved, chapters 37–48 does provide resolution to the conflict faced by the family of Israel in the land of Canaan.

16. Sternberg, *Poetics of Biblical Narrative*, 30.

narrative text itself.[17] The first, and perhaps most significant, textual clue with which the reader can identify the historical purpose of Genesis is found in its *tôledôt* structure. This phrase, which is frequently translated as "these are the generations" (RSV, ESV, KJV) or "this is the account of" (NIV) is found eleven times throughout the book (Gen 2:4; 5:2; 6:9; 10:1; 11:10; 11:27; 25:12, 19; 36:1, 9; 37:2). As early as 1899, Franz Delitzsch used the repetition of the *tôledôt* formula to structure his commentary on the book.[18] Many scholars since have recognized the importance of this formula to the macro-structure of Genesis.[19] While some, such as Julius Wellhausen, have suggest that the *tôledôt* formulas should be understood as colophons that conclude units within the text,[20] the word is derived from the *hiphil* form of the Hebrew verb, *yālad* ("to beget"), and is better understood to function as a heading that refers to the product or result of its subject.[21] In an attempt to identify the macro-structure and thematic trajectory of Genesis as a whole, T. D. Alexander notes that the *tôledôt* headings serve two primary functions. First, they function like chapter headings, which either introduce major narrative sections of the book related to the history of particular individuals (2:4; 6:9; 11:27; 25:15; 37:2) or genealogical material tracing a central lineage or ancestry peripheral to this main line of descent (5:1; 10:1; 11:10; 25:12; 36:1, 9).[22] Second, the *tôledôt* formulas function like the "zoom-lens" on a camera. They focus the reader's attention on particular individuals and their immediate children.[23]

> In this way Genesis highlights the lineage which, beginning with Adam, is traced through Adam's youngest son Seth to Noah, the father of Shem, Ham and Japheth. The next stage of the line takes us from Shem to Terah, the father of Abraham,

17. See Long, *Art of Biblical History*, 65–67.

18. Delitzsch, *New Commentary on Genesis*, 58–59.

19. For examples, see Richelle, "La structure littéraire de l'histoire primitive (Genèse 1,1–11,26) en son état final," 3–22; Thomas, *These are the Generations*, 6; Ross, *Creation and Blessing*, 65; Alexander, "Genealogies, Seed and the Compositional Unity of Genesis," 255–70; Woudstra, "*Toledot* of the Book of Genesis and Their Redemptive-Historical Significance," 184–89.

20. Wellhausen, *Die Composition des Hexateuches und der historischen Bücher des Alten Testaments*, 3–5. See also Eissfeldt, *Die Genesis der Genesis*, 13–14; Wiseman, *Clues to Creation in Genesis*, 34–37; Harrison, *Introduction to the Old Testament*, 543–47.

21. For a good defense of this position, see DeRouchie, "The Blessing-Commission, the Promised Offspring, and the *Toledot* Structure of Genesis," 222–29; Ross, *Creation and Blessing*, 69–74.

22. Alexander, "Genealogies, Seed and the Compositional Unity of Genesis," 258–59.

23. Alexander, "Genealogies, Seed and the Compositional Unity of Genesis," 259.

Nahor and Haran. We then move from Abraham to Isaac, from Isaac to Jacob, and, finally, to Jacob's twelve sons.[24]

Whether through narrative or genealogy, the literary function of the *tôledôt* formulas concerns itself with history. Therefore, the presence of these formulas as an organizing principle behind the composition of Genesis lends validity to the view that the book was intended to be read as narrative history.[25] Recognizing the "historical-genealogical framework" behind Genesis, Hoffmeier concludes that "the narratives are dealing with real events involving historical figures . . ."[26] While the present discussion is focused on the literary clues present in Genesis and cannot devote adequate space to background studies, it is important to note that Kenneth Kitchen has argued for the veracity of narrative history in Genesis by comparing the biblical historiography with those of surrounding nations both before and after the time of the flood. Based on this study, Kitchen has demonstrated that historical and genealogical record keeping—dating back to even prediluvian times—can be found in other Mesopotamian civilizations and therefore should not be quickly dismissed as ahistorical in Genesis.[27]

The present study will operate under the assumption that the book of Genesis was intended to be read as an historical account. Identifying the genre as narrative history sets up certain interpretive expectations for the reader. As history, the people, records, and accounts the author relates in narrative form represent real history as opposed to an imagined reality intended to create some mythic identity for ancient Israel.

EXPECTATION OF THE SEED AND THE "INTRINSIC GENRE" OF GENESIS

Having discussed the basic genre of Genesis, it is important to go beyond this generic descriptor to examine the various ways that the author of Genesis has particularized the genre to set up additional interpretive expectations

24. Alexander, "Genealogies, Seed and the Compositional Unity of Genesis," 259.

25. See Kaiser Jr., *Promise-Plan of God*, 35.

26. Hoffmeier, "Genesis 1–11 as History and Theology," 32. Historical records in the ancient Near East have largely been taken seriously by scholars and not dismissed as fictional. For examples, Hoffmeier, "Historiography: King Lists," 68; Ritner, "Denderite Temple Hierarchy and the Family of Theban High Priest Nebwenenef," 205–26

27. In his defense, Kitchen shows that the extreme ages found in the Genesis account do not necessarily undermine its historical nature. For a full discussion of his defense of the historical nature of Genesis, see Kitchen, *On the Reliability of the Old Testament*, 421–47. See also Pritchard, *Ancient Near Eastern Texts Relating to the Old Testament*, 265.

for the reader—what Hirsch referred to as the "intrinsic genre" of a work.[28] By pinpointing these additional textual clues, the reader increases the likelihood that communication will transpire between him and the author through the text he wrote. This additional level of description, broadly speaking, provides the framework within which the reader can validate the interpretation of individual elements, since a valid interpretation must fit what the author is attempting to do on the whole.

A careful observation of the book of Genesis reveals that the author is not simply satisfied to trace the history of Israel within God's program for humanity, although this is certainly accomplished in the work. More than this, the author has carefully crafted the book to highlight the lineage of, and expectation for, *a coming individual.* This expectation of a *Coming One* is accomplished through the oracle of judgment in Gen 3:14–15, the author's use of linear genealogies in 5:1–32 and 11:10–26, the individual focus of the narratives in chapters 12–36, and the use of poetry in chapter 49 to summarize the key elements of his narrative argument.[29]

The Future Seed of Gen 3:15

The expectation of a coming seed in Genesis begins as early as 3:15 in an oracle of judgment which the Lord God (יְהֹוָה אֱלֹהִים) pronounces on the serpent for his role in Adam and Eve's fall into sin. While much could be said about this verse, the concern of the present discussion is merely to establish the beginning of the expectation of a coming individual in the book of Genesis as a whole. Therefore, much of what could be said about this verse will be omitted since its contribution is tangential to the goal of the current discussion.

While some have argued that the verse should be understood within an ancient Near Eastern *Sitz im Leben* and function as an etiological description of the ancients' fear of snakes,[30] the Jewish tradition preserved

---

28. Hirsch Jr., *Validity in Interpretation*, 78. The term "intrinsic genre" has been previously defined and can be found on page 17 of this study.

29. Noting the particular way in which the author of Genesis has particularized his use of historical narrative, DeRouchie develops the following statement as his idea of the whole: "The means by which God's blessing-commission of kingdom advancement will be fulfilled in a cursed and perverted world is through an ever-expanding God-oriented, hope-filled, mission-minded, community, climaxing in a single kin in the line of promise who will perfectly reflect, resemble, and represent God and who will definitively overcome all evil, thus restoring right order to God's kingdom for the fame of his name" (DeRouchie, "Blessing-Commission," 247).

30. See Chisholm Jr., *From Exegesis to Exposition*, 59–60; Von Rad, *Genesis.*

in the LXX and various Christian interpreters—as early Irenaeus—have understood the passage as a *protoevangelium*.[31] Although the designation of this passage as a first-gospel was largely assigned on the basis of New Testament revelation, certain elements of this verse lend credibility to the view that it was originally intended to refer to a promised male-descendant of the woman who would be God's agent of judgment on the serpent.

The oracle of judgment is communicated through the Hebrew parallelism of 3:15:

1. One synonymous bicolon (3:15a)
      "I will put enmity between you and the woman
      And between your seed and her seed"

2. One antithetical bicolon (3:15b)
      "He shall bruise you on the head
      And you shall bruise him on the heel"[32]

In the context of Gen 3, this oracle of judgment is God's solution to the conflict introduced by the serpent who had successfully challenge God's mediatorial rule in his temptation of Adam and Eve.[33] The conflict would be resolved through a human agent, a future descendant of Eve, who would judge the serpent on behalf of God through personal conflict (3:15b).[34]

Some, such as Walter Kaiser, have sought to find a basis for a coming singular seed in the author's use of pronouns.[35]

> That is the most striking thing that happens in verse 15—the
> suffix on the Hebrew word "heel" is singular ("his"). This suffix

---

Referring to Genesis 3:15, Ludwig Köhler writes, "[T]he passage is therefore a piece of aetiological myth—a story to explain an existing state of affairs. To regard it as 'protoevangelium' is unscriptural" (Köhler, *Old Testament*, 157).

31. See Martin, "Earliest Messianic Interpretation of Genesis 3:15," 425–27; Irenaeus, *Against the Heresies*, 108–9. For more recent interpreters who hold this position, see Davis, *Paradise to Prison*, 93; Kaiser Jr., *Messiah in the Old Testament*, 37–42.

32. This translation is taken from the NASB.

33. Alva J. McClain made an important contribution when he distinguished between the universal and mediatorial kingdom of God in Scripture. While the universal rule of God has never nor could ever be challenged, it is God's mediatorial rule through people that is at issue in the biblical story. See McClain, *Greatness of the Kingdom*, 21.

34. For a thorough discussion on the theology of Gen 3:15, see the work done by Afolarin Olutunde Ojewole in his PhD dissertation at Andrews University (Ojewole, "Seed in Genesis 3:15"). While the identity of the serpent and nature of the judgment is important, it goes beyond the scope of the current discussion, which is focused on establishing the expectation of a coming seed.

35. See also Waltke and Fredricks, *Genesis*, 93.

cannot refer to the woman, since any reference to her must be feminine; nor can it refer to the serpent, since he will be the object of this male's attack.[36]

However, others such as Robert Chisholm argue that the use of the masculine singular in 3:15b should not be taken to indicate an individual descendant.

> Proponents of this messianic interpretation should not argue their case from the presence of the singular noun, "seed, offspring," because this noun, while sometimes referring to an individual descendant, frequently refers to one's offspring or descendants in a collective sense . . . The use of the third-person singular pronoun ("he"/"his") to refer to the "seed of the woman" in the second half of the verse does not militate against this collective interpretation, for modifiers of collective nouns and pronouns referring to collectives are often singular.[37]

Since the noun "offspring" (זֶרַע) is grammatically singular in 3:15a, it is possible that the masculine singular pronouns used in 3:15b were chosen simply to agree with the previous noun. Therefore, one must go beyond the use of pronouns to establish the singular intent of Gen 3:15. To this end, it is important to observe that the image used to describe the judgment on the serpent is that of a personal conflict. If the serpent in the image is a real serpent that will experience a real judgment, then it is logical to surmise that the heel used to strike his head depicts a real person who will exact this judgment upon the serpent. The personal nature of this image to depict a real judgment provides a context in which to see the promise of a future individual to be actualized.[38]

John H. Sailhamer has observed that in the broader structure of the Pentateuch, the author will frequently return to earlier themes to build upon their theology.[39] Significantly, in Num 24:17, the author writes the following with regard to the future, messianic star of Jacob. "I see him, but not now; I behold him, but not near; A star shall come forth from Jacob, And a

---

36. Kaiser, *Messiah in the Old Testament*, 39.

37. Chisholm, *From Exegesis to Exposition*, 59–60. He cites Gen 16:10, 22:17, and 24:60 as examples.

38. Walt Kaiser recognizes the influence of this image in his interpretation of Gen 3:15. "Moreover, the reference to 'his heel' bears out the correctness of understanding Hebrew *hû'* as a singular masculine pronoun in the phrase 'he will crush your head'" (Kaiser, *Messiah in the Old Testament*, 35).

39. See Sailhamer, *Pentateuch as Narrative*, 405–6; Sailhamer, *Meaning of the Pentateuch*, 335–41.

scepter shall rise from Israel, *And shall crush through* [מָחַץ] *the forehead of Moab*, And tear down all the sons of Sheth."[40] Although the verb "to crush" (מָחַץ) used in Num 24:17 is not the same verb used in Gen 3:15 (שׁוּף), they occupy the same field of meaning and create a parallel image which might provide another layer of evidence to help understand the intended meaning of Gen 3:15.

Further validity for the proposed interpretation of Gen 3:15 can be found in the Septuagint's translation of this important text. In rendering this verse, the translators of the LXX used the masculine singular pronoun (αὐτός) in 3:15b to refer back to σπέρματός in 3:15a instead of using the neuter form, which would be required for grammatically agreement. It reads, καὶ ἔχθραν θήσω ἀνὰ μέσον σου καὶ ἀνὰ μέσον τῆς γυναικὸς καὶ ἀνὰ μέσον τοῦ σπέρματός σου καὶ ἀνὰ μέσον τοῦ σπέρματος αὐτῆς αὐτός σου τηρήσει κεφαλήν καὶ σὺ τηρήσεις αὐτοῦ πτέρναν.[41] In this way, the translators of the LXX appear to provide a messianic interpretation of this text, an interpretation which would provide further evidence for the legitimacy of the proposed reading.[42]

Although the messianic expectation in Gen 3:15 remains a legitimate center of debate, a case can be made that the author of Genesis intended to communicate the expectation of a future descendant of the woman who would be God's agent of judgment on the serpent to resolve the conflict initiated at the fall. This expectation sets up what G. B. Caird referred to as a "situation vacant" anticipation in which the author or speaker "describes in

---

40. Emphasis mine. This translation has been taken from the New American Standard Bible.

41. See Wevers, *Septuaginta*, 92–93.

42. Regarding the Septuagint's translation of Genesis 3:15, R. A Martin writes, "It seems unlikely that this is mere coincidence or oversight. First of all, the quality of the Greek translation of the Pentateuch is, generally speaking, higher than that of the other parts of the OT. Second, in all other instances where such literalness would have resulted in violence to agreement in Greek between the pronoun and antecedent the translator avoided such literalness and used the required feminine or neuter pronoun. The most likely explanation for the use of αὐτός in Genesis 3:15 to refer ack to σπέρμα is that the translator has in this way indicated his messianic understanding of this verse." See Martin, "The Earliest Messianic Interpretation of Genesis 3:15," 427. See also Kaiser, *Messiah in the Old Testament*, 40. For further reading on this important verse, see DeRouchie, "Blessing-Commission," 228. See also DeRouchie and Meyer, "Christ or Family as the 'Seed' of Promise?" 38–40. On the basis of the author's use of singular verb inflections, adjectives, and pronouns, Jack C. Collins and T. Desmond Alexander argue that author of Genesis is able to specify collectivity or singularity in his use of the term "seed." See Collins, "Syntactical Note (Genesis 3:15)," 139–48; Alexander, "Further Observations on the Term 'Seed' in Genesis," 363–67.

some detail a person whose identity is not yet known . . ."[43] Although God did not disclose the identity of the promised descendant, the description concerning what this descendant would accomplish provided Adam and Eve—along with the reader—the details necessary for his identification. The promised descendant would be identified when he resolved the conflict by exacting God's judgment on the serpent.[44]

While more will be said about the nature of performative statements later in the chapter, in terms of its function as a speech-act, the intent of Gen 3:15 can be fleshed out based on its locutionary, illocutionary, and perlocutionary forces.[45] In its *willed-locutionary-force*, God reveals that the conflict initiated at the fall will be resolved when a future descendant of the woman exacts judgment on the serpent. In its *willed-illocutionary-force*, the commissive nature of God's pronouncement obligates him to fulfill the terms of the locution in his governance of history. This governance of history is a necessary implication of God's promissory speech-act. Without such governance, there can be no assurance that what God has promised will come to pass. In its *willed-perlocutionary-force*, God's pronouncement is intended to validate the certainty of judgment on the serpent and move Adam and Eve to an expectant faith in God's provision of this future descendant.[46]

In light of the commissive nature of Gen 3:15, the oracle of judgment functions as a sort of lens through which Adam, Eve, and the serpent might exegete history. Literarily, the performative speech act provides the reader the lens through which to interpret the remainder of the historical narrative.[47] Although God had initially told Adam that eating from the forbidden tree would bring death (2:16–17), in his pronouncement of judgment, he reveals a delay in the physical aspect of this penalty to allow Eve a posterity through which the promised descendant might come. Through his use of linear genealogies (5:1–32; 11:10–26) and the genealogical narratives of the patriarchal period (12–50), the author of Genesis focuses attention on Eve's posterity with particular concern for *individual male descendants*. While to the modern reader, this observation could be explained as a mere patriarchal

---

43. Caird, *Language and Imagery of the Bible*, 57.

44. The nature of this conflict is a legitimate point of study but would take this discussion beyond its intended purpose.

45. These terms have been previously defined on pages 19 and 20 of this study.

46. For more on intended perlocutions for various illocutionary acts, see Caird, *Language and Imagery of the Bible*, 7–8.

47. While the reader has the benefit of the author's perspective and can see the historical connections made through the author's use of narrative history, this does not necessarily mean that every character in the narrative account were aware of all of these same details.

convention of ancient Near Eastern societies, its function in the outworking of God's governance of history argues that it must be related to God's decree defining the course of human history revealed in 3:15.[48] Gen 3:15, therefore, provides the interpretive framework within which to analyze the lives of each chosen male descendant in the sequence of the narrative history. As each male character is introduced in the story, one is right to wonder, "Has God provided Eve the promised descendant?"

The Use of Linear Genealogies in Gen 5:1–32 and 11:10–26[49]

In his study of biblical genealogies in their ancient Near Eastern context, Robert R. Wilson distinguishes between two basic types of genealogical material found in the Old Testament. He notes that in some instances, a genealogy will trace more than one lineage from a single ancestor and refers this type of genealogy as a "segmented genealogy."[50] At other times, he observes that an author will trace only a single lineage through an ancestor and refers to this kind as a "linear genealogy."[51] Recognizing the development of a single lineage unifying the book as a whole, Desmond Alexander notes the way the author of Genesis uses the two types of genealogies to establish this main line of descent. He observes that "to ensure that the main line of descent in Genesis is clearly established, segmented genealogies are never used in relation to it; only linear genealogies are employed (5:1–32; 11:10–26)."[52] Upon closer examination, however, the linear genealogies in Gen 5 and 11 not only contribute to the development of this central lineage in the book,[53] connecting the primeval history (1–11) to the patriarchal nar-

---

48. When one realizes the promissory nature of God's speech-act-judgment in Gen 3:15, one understands that God is obligating himself to perform what he has promised. The nature of the God's commitments in Gen 3:15—providing a descendant of Eve who will be God's agent of judgment on the serpent to resolve the conflict initiated at the fall—necessitates a sovereign God who can and will control history to accomplish what he has promised. Without this divine governance of history, there is no guarantee that what God has promised will in fact come to pass.

49. Since the purpose of this section is to help establish the expectation of a future seed as part of the intrinsic genre of the book, the discussion of these two genealogies will not deal with all of the issues and debate surrounding their form and function. For a good discussion on these issues, see Clark, "Genealogies of Genesis Five and Eleven"; Wilson, *Genealogy and History in the Biblical World*; Hess, "Genealogies of Genesis 1–11 and Comparative Literature," 241–54; Green, "Primeval Chronology," 285–303.

50. Wilson, *Genealogy and History in the Biblical World*, 9.

51. Wilson, *Genealogy and History in the Biblical World*, 9.

52. Alexander, "Genealogies, Seed and the Compositional Unity of Genesis," 259.

53. See Fishbane, *Text and Texture*, 28; Ross, *Creation and Blessing*, 172.

ratives (12–50), but they also contribute to the expectation of a coming male descendant initiated in 3:15.

The Genealogy in 5:1–32

In analyzing the form of the genealogy in Gen 5, which is introduced with a *tôledôt* heading, the reader will immediately be struck by the recurring pattern through which the author traces the lineage of Adam to Noah through ten generations:

> And PN_1 lived x years and begot PN_2
> And PN_1 lived, after he begot PN_2, y years
> And he (PN_1) begot sons and daughters
> All the days of PN_1 were x + y years and he died.[54]

For the purpose of this discussion, it is important to notice that, through Adam, the genealogy highlights a *single male descendant of Eve* in each of the ten generations listed.[55] While each of these male descendants has "other sons and daughters," the additional offspring are not named or given attention in the list. In fact, their presence in this anonymous and generic form suggests that the named individual is, in some sense, a preeminent figure in his generation.[56] This is consistent with the function of ancient Near Eastern genealogies which were designed to trace the inheritance of a privileged status or office through the members included in the genealogy.[57]

As a speech-act, the commissive pronouncement by God in Gen 3:15 obligated God to provide a future descendant of Eve to be his agent of

54. This is the form articulated by Richard S. Hess. See Hess, "Genealogies of Genesis 1–11 and Comparative Literature," 243. Enoch and Noah are two exceptions to this general pattern in 5:1–32 as neither mention their deaths. Since, Noah concludes the genealogy and becomes the main character of the next few chapters, the omission of his death is understandable as the author attempts to connect the lineage to the narrative that follows. Being seventh in genealogy, however, the omission of Enoch's death is a bit more mysterious. While the purpose of this omission cannot be ascertained with certainty, it certainly communicates that "death is not the irrevocable and invariable last word for all." See Waltke and Yu, *Old Testament Theology*, 272. See also Ross, *Creation and Blessing*, 174–75.

55. The genealogy traces the line of Adam through Seth who is said to be Eve's replacement son for Abel (4:25).

56. An exception to this is the conclusion of the genealogy where Noah's three sons, Shem, Ham, and Japheth, are mentioned by name (5:32). Literarily, the break from the general pattern is understandable since these sons will be characters in the subsequent narrative. The order of the sons' names is significant as the future preeminence of Shem is hinted at by listing his name first.

57. See Hess, "Genealogies of Genesis 1–11 and Comparative Literature," 247–48.

judgment on the serpent. The perlocutionary force of the speech-act functioned to validate the certainty of judgment on the serpent and to move Adam and Eve to an expectant faith in God's provision of the descendant God had promised. Although God's initial provision came at the birth of Cain and Abel (4:1–2), the history of their lives disqualified both from being the promised individual. Cain and his line were disqualified when he murdered his brother, Abel, and was cursed by God (4:9–11, 17–24).[58] Although Abel was righteous, he died without having accomplished God's judgment on the serpent and, therefore, demonstrated that he was not the seed that God would ultimately provide.[59] With her first two sons disqualified, the commissive nature of God's promise required him to provide Eve another offspring through which the promise of 3:15 might stay alive. This provision came at the birth of Seth (4:25).[60] However, as the history of Seth is summarized in the genealogy (5:6–8), he died without accomplishing God's judgment on the serpent and, thereby, showed that he was not the promised seed. With each subsequent generation, the commitment of God to his pronouncement in 3:15 was seen in his continued provision of descendants. However, the author's repetitive use of the refrain "and he died," showed that none of them were the promised seed to come.[61]

At the conclusion of the genealogy, Lamech expressed personal hope that his son, Noah, would be the one to give humanity "rest" (נחם) from the ground which God had cursed (5:29).[62] This allusion to the judgment

58. Additionally, it is not Cain's line that forms the genealogical continuity in the book but Seth's lineage.

59. While a discussion concerning the nature of this judgment would certainly be a worthy enterprise, the current discussion will keep the meaning at the level of "judgment" to maintain the overall focus on the expectation of a coming individual in the book as a whole, which is the overall goal of the present discussion.

60. In her statement at the birth of Seth, Eve recognized that Seth was a seed of God's provision to replace Abel. "God has appointed me another offspring (זֶרַע) in place of Abel" (4:25).

61. In the progress of revelation, Jesus is revealed to be the promised descendant of Eve. Unlike the individuals in the genealogy, Jesus's death did not disqualify him since he defeated death in his resurrection. This is something that none of those in Genesis ever did.

62. While the allusion to oracles of judgment in Gen 3 may not at first seem obvious, the author has included details to help the reader make this connection. Lamech specifically references the ground which God had cursed (5:29) and reuses the term "toil/pain" (עִצָּבוֹן) from 3:16 17. It is in the context of the divine curse that Lamech expresses the hope that his son, Noah, would bring "rest" (נחם). This term "rest" can mean the removal of the stated situation which has caused the grief. See H. J. Fabry and H. Simian-Yofre, "נחם," in Bottweck et al., *Theological Dictionary of the Old Testament*, vol. 9, 340–55. Mathews, *Genesis 1–11:26*, 317. In his master's thesis, Don Soula argues that "rest" in the Old Testament was always to be administered through God's anointed

oracle in 3:17–19 provides textual support for the view that the genealogy was intended to be read in light of Gen 3.[63] Nevertheless, given God's commissive speech-act in 3:15, it is at least safe to suggest that by highlighting *a single male descendent* in each generation, the genealogy in 5:1–32 continues the expectation of the promised descendant to come through the Sethite line.[64] Though each individual dies without accomplishing judgment on the serpent, God's continued provision of a posterity (זֶרַע) to Eve confirms his continued commitment to the promise of judgment on the serpent and, ultimately, to its fulfillment through the future provision of the promised seed (3:15).[65]

The Genealogy in 11:10–26

In Gen 11:10–26, the author uses another linear genealogy to connect the Sethite line to Abram through Noah's son, Shem. Like the genealogy in 5:1–32, the Shemite genealogy, introduced with a *tôledôt* heading, highlights *a single male descendant* in each of the ten generations listed. While each male descendant is said to have "other sons and daughters," these additional offspring are not mentioned by name.[66] Through its connection with the Sethite genealogy (5:1–32), and its emphasis on single male descendants, the lineage in 11:10–26 continues the expectation carried through the Sethite line from Shem to Abram.[67] Yet, as the generations quickly pass, none of the named male descendants accomplish God's word of judgment on the

---

ruler. For his argument, see Soula, "Meaning of 'I Will Give You Rest,'" 10–20.

63. See Johnson, *Dispensational Biblical Theology*, 64–65.

64. See Waltke and Fredricks, *Genesis*, 187.

65. Cain's genealogy (4:17–24) is also linear and demonstrates the degradation of humanity through Cain. Genesis chapters 4 and 5, then, trace two parallel lineages, one through Cain and the other through Seth. While God's judgment in the flood would wipe ultimately wipe out both lineages, God preserves the possibility of fulfilling his promise in Gen 3:15 through the preservation of Noah and his family.

66. Again, see Hess, "Genealogies of Genesis 1–11 and Comparative Literature," 247–48. The linear genealogy in 11:10–26 differs slightly from that found in 5:1–32. Unlike the Sethite genealogy, the line in 11:10–26 omits the total age of each patriarch and the statement "and he died." Waltke suggests that these omissions serve two basic functions in the text. First, they demonstrate the effects of the flood on humanity. The antediluvian patriarchs lived full lives, but in contrast the postdiluvian patriarchs lived shorter periods of time. Second, the omission of these facts in the Shemite genealogy cause the reader to "speed read" to Abram, who will be the principal character in the narrative that follows. See Waltke and Fredricks, *Genesis*, 187.

67. The fact that Joshua reveals that Terah and his family worshiped pagan God's (Josh 24:3) suggests that while this Shemite genealogy continues the lineage of the coming seed—and therefore his expectation—not everyone listed was necessarily a believer.

serpent and, thereby, show that none of them is the seed God promised would come (3:15).

The Individual Focus in the Patriarchal Narrative of Gen 12–50

Having arrived at Abram, the pace of the historical narrative slows dramatically as the author focuses on the history of Abram and his immediate descendants. The lack of additional linear genealogical material at this point in the narrative should not be taken as a cessation of the expectation of a coming male individual, for this focus continues as the narrative highlights a linear line of descent through the *tôledôt* of Isaac (Gen 25:19—35:29) and Jacob (37:2—50:26), with particular emphasis on Judah, one of Jacob's twelve sons (49:10; cf. Num 24:17), and his lineage through Perez (Gen 38:29; 46:12). As Wilson observes, ancient Near Eastern genealogies were not always given in list form. Sometimes these genealogies were framed in narrative form and, therefore, should be understood as *genealogical narratives*. "The genealogy itself, and thus the expression of the kinship relationships, may be either in narrative form or in list form. If it is in narrative form, then the focus of the narrative will be on the kinship relationship expressed . . ."[68] This emphasis on kinship relationships is precisely what one discovers as one reads the patriarchal narratives in Genesis (12–50). As with the linear genealogies in the primeval era (5:1–32; 11:10–26), the linear ancestry of the patriarchal narratives highlights *a single male individual*, although each patriarch sires multiple offspring.[69]

Having announced and ratified the terms of the Abrahamic covenant with Abram (12:1–3, 7, 15:7–21),[70] a covenant that anticipated worldwide blessing through him, it is Abraham's son, Isaac, who is chosen to continue the covenant line of blessing to the exclusion of Ishmael (17:18–19; 26:1–5). Although Isaac fathers Esau and Jacob, it is Jacob who is selected to continue the covenant line of blessing to the exclusion of Esau (27:27–29; 28:4, 13–15; 35:9–12). Although Jacob fathered twelve sons who would become the founding fathers of the federated tribes of Israel, it is Judah—through

---

68. Wilson, *Genealogy and History in the Biblical World*, 9.

69. This selection of a single male descendant to the exclusion of other offspring is the narrative equivalent of the repeated phrase "and he had other sons and daughters" in lineage genealogies of the primeval era.

70. A full discussion of the precise terms and nature of God's covenant promises to Abraham will be undertaken later in this chapter.

Perez (38:29; 46:12)—who is given preeminence as the father of a future administrative ruler of this covenant nation (49:10).[71]

Although the lineage in the patriarchal narratives contains the added revelation of the covenant promises to Abraham, its connection with the linear genealogies in the primeval era (5:1–32; 11:10–26) continues to develop the expectation begun in 3:15. The line from Abraham through Judah (and Perez) in the genealogical narrative continues God's provision of a posterity to Eve through which the promise of the seed might be fulfilled (3:15). Although each of the individuals in the narrative dies without having fulfilled God's word of judgment on the serpent—or, now, worldwide blessing through Abraham—God's continued provision of offspring to Eve vindicates his commitment to the judgment of the serpent (3:15) and to the promise of worldwide blessing through Abraham (12:3) though this promised seed had not yet come.

The Summarizing Function of Poetry and Gen 49:10[72]

It has long been recognized that one of the functions of poetry within Hebrew narrative is to "summarize" and "heighten" important elements of the preceding story.[73] If the expectation of an individual in the book of Genesis is so central to the intrinsic genre of the book, as is being suggested, then one would expect to find this element present in the Testament of Jacob (49:1–28), a prophetic poem which Jacob uttered over his twelve sons at the end of Genesis.[74]

71. See Alexander, "Genealogies, Seed and the Compositional Unity of Genesis," 255–70; Alexander, "From Adam to Judah," 5–19. While Joseph receives significant attention in Gen 49—and Joseph and Levi in Deut 33—their omission in this discussion is simply due to the fact that the purpose of the current section is to maintain focus on the expectation of the seed whose lineage is traced through Judah, not Joseph or Levi.

72. For a thorough analysis of this poem's history of interpretation and exegesis, see Pehlke, "Exegetical and Theological Study of Genesis 49:1–28."

73. Alter, *Art of Biblical Poetry*, 29; Pröbstle, "Lion of Judah," 25.

74. Discussing the summarizing function of poetry on a broader level in the Pentateuch, Sailhamer observes than in concluding poems, like the Testament of Jacob, frame "narrative text of the past are presented as pointers to future events" (Sailhamer, *Pentateuch as Narrative*, 37). Similarly, James W. Watts recognizes the proleptic force of this concluding poem when he writes, "The book of ancestral history thus closes not with a retrospective review of its main characters (like 1 Samuel does), but with contemporary and proleptic portraits of the tribal nation yet to come—a suitable conclusion to a story centered around promises of descendants and land" (Watts, *Psalm and Story*).

While there is much to say regarding this important unit in Genesis, a few observations stand out that directly bear on the discussion at hand. As Jacob begins to describe what will become of his twelve sons in "future days" (בְּאַחֲרִית הַיָּמִים; 49:1), the majority of the poem is dedicated to the fortunes of only two sons, Judah and Joseph. Out of the poem's twenty-five verses, ten are dedicated to blessing of these two (49:8–12, 22–26). The prominence of Judah and Joseph in the poetic prophecy of Israel summarizes the pre-eminent role each played in the preceding patriarchal narratives.[75] Although he was sold into slavery, Joseph had been used by God to preserve his family in Egypt (37–48), securing him a special place in the Testament of Jacob. While Judah had convinced his brothers to sell Joseph into slavery (37:26–28) and succumbed to sexual sin in the Tamar account (38:1–30), he later demonstrated self-sacrificial repentance when he offered himself as a substitute slave for his brother Benjamin (44:18–34). Because of the important role these two played in the patriarchal narratives, the blessing, which according to societal norms would have normally gone to the firstborn, Reuben, was divided between Judah and Joseph.[76] Significantly, Jacob's blessing on Judah both continues and develops the expectation of a coming individual who would arise from his tribe. Although Joseph receives a preeminent place in the Testament of Jacob, where he receives the blessing of God and protection of God from his enemies (49:22–26), the current discussion will highlight Judah since it is through him that the lineage and expectation of the promised seed continues.

In 49:8, Jacob transfers the right of rulership which Joseph had exercised in the Genesis narrative (37:5–10) to Judah. "Judah, your brothers shall praise you; Your hand shall be on the neck of your enemies; Your father's sons shall bow down to you" (NASB). The administration of this rulership anticipated a future king to come, a *male descendant* who would represent the apex of Judah's dynasty. "The scepter shall not depart from Judah, Nor the ruler's staff from between his feet, Until Shiloh comes, and to him shall be the obedience of the people" (49:10).[77] While a variety of interpretations

---

75. Pröbstle, "'Lion of Judah,'" 28; Wenham, *Genesis 16–50*, 468–70. For a good overview of the allusions in this poem to the history of Jacob's twelve sons in the patriarchal narratives, see Mathews, *Genesis 11:27—50:26*, 883–915.

76. Regarding this custom in the ancient world, Kass notes, "When a society is well established and running smoothly, preferences are usually given to the firstborn, for the firstborn is the one who, naturally, guarantees a next generation; in arranging for perpetuation, custom follows and ratifies the natural order of succession" (Kass, *Beginning of Wisdom*, 643). Analysis of the Testament of Jacob reveals that Reuben disqualified himself (35:22; 49:3–4).

77. This translation has been taken from the NASB.

have been given concerning best rendering of the verse,[78] many scholars have argued for its expectation of a coming ruler. Kaiser represents the view well when he writes,

> The meaning of "until Shiloh comes" can be best explained if the pointing of the vowels is changed from *šîloh* to *šelloh* or *šeloh*, a form supported by thirty-eight Hebrew manuscripts. In that case *šeloh* is a compounded word from *še*, the shortened form of the so-called relative particle *ʾašer* ("which, whose"), *le* ("belonging to"), and the suffix *ôh* for *ô*, ("him"). This accords perfectly with the longer form that is spelled out more distinctly in Ezekiel 21:27 [32], "until he comes to whom it rightfully belongs."[79]

It seems at least valid to suggest that the pronouncement of Jacob in 49:10 envisions the arrival of a Judahite king whose rule would represent the zenith of Judah's royal lineage.[80] That this expectation is found in the summative Testament of Jacob and validates the notion that the expectation of a coming individual is indeed an important aspect of the book as a whole.

Summary

The analysis of Genesis demonstrates a significant emphasis on the expectation of a coming individual. Beginning in Gen 3:15, God's pronouncement of judgment on the serpent promised a seed through Eve who would execute God's judgment through a personal conflict with the serpent. Though Eve's first two sons, Cain and Abel, were disqualified, God's commitment to his word of judgment guaranteed Eve another offspring through whom the promise of judgment might remain alive, or ultimately be fulfilled. This provision came at the birth of Seth; however, Seth and the line he sired (5:1–32; 11:10–26) all experienced death without accomplishing God's judgement on the serpent.

Beginning with Abraham, the lineage begun through Seth continued through the patriarchal period with added revelation. The seed which would be God's agent of judgment on the serpent (3:15) would also be God's agent

---

78. For a good overview of the interpretive options, see Pröbstle, "Lion of Judah," 36–43; Moran, "Gen 49,10 and Its Use in Ez 21, 32," 405–25.

79. Kaiser, *Messiah in the Old Testament*, 51–52. See also Pehlke, "Exegetical and Theological Study of Genesis 49:1–28," 169–75; Baron, *Rays of Messiah's Glory*, 258–62; Mathews, *Genesis 11:27—50:26*, 892–96. In the development of the narrative, Joseph is originally function as a ruler (Gen 37:7–10). However, in the Testament of Jacob, this rulership is handed over to Judah (49:8b).

80. Pehlke, "Exegetical and Theological Study of Genesis 49:1–28," 169.

of worldwide blessing (12:3). As the lineage continued through the patriarchal period, none of the patriarchs accomplished what God had promised and, thereby, demonstrated that they were not the promised seed to come. Yet, even in the age of the patriarchs, the continuation of the lineage begun through Seth, demonstrated God's commitment to the promise of this seed in his governance of history and, therefore, kindled the hope that the promised seed would someday arrive. As the lineage moved from Abraham to Isaac, from Isaac to Jacob, and from Jacob to the twelve sons of Israel, the expectation of a coming individual was not lost. Providing a poetic summary of the patriarchal period (49:1–26), Jacob prophesied that the tribe of Judah would produce a line of kings through which a future ruler would arise (49:10). The presence of this expectation of a future seed/ruler in the concluding poem validates its place in the intrinsic genre of the book as whole. As such, the book's focus on a coming seed becomes an important part of the interpretive expectation that the author designed on the whole and, therefore, forms a broad basis upon which validity in interpretation can be established. Only interpretations that are consistent with the intrinsic genre[81] of the book can claim to have validity.

THE FAITH OF ABRAM IN GEN 15:6

Having addressed the preliminary issues related to the intrinsic genre of the book, it is now possible to examine the faith of Abram in the early chapters of the patriarchal narratives (12:1—15:6). Although the Abrahamic narrative is connected, literarily, to the expectation of a coming seed in Gen 3:15, historically it is impossible to say how much of this pre-history Abram knew at the time of his calling (12:1–3).[82] Therefore, the present discussion of Abram's faith will be limited to his own dealings with the Lord leading to God's declaration of his righteousness (15:6).

81. The term "intrinsic genre" has been previously defined and can be found on page 14 of this study.

82. Joshua 24:3 observes that Abram came from a pagan family; however it is not possible to know the exact spiritual state of Abram at the time of his calling. However, the fact that Terah, Abram's father, is listed in the genealogy of the coming seed suggests that not all listed in the lineage were believers. What Abram's generation knew of God through the witness of individuals from previous generations, in a tight chronology, cannot be ascertained with certainty.

Gen 12:1–3, 7 as Abrahamic Promise

In 1954, George E. Mendenhall published a groundbreaking article in which he attempted to compare ancient Near Eastern covenant forms to the Bible, specifically the Mosaic Law in the Decalogue and its renewal in Josh 24.[83] Soon, other scholars began to make additional contributions to this study as they, too, began to see significant parallels between ancient Near Eastern suzerainty treaties and the various expressions of the Mosaic Law in Scripture.[84] As scholarly interest in exploring these covenant parallels grew, it became apparent that other types of covenants in Scripture—the Abrahamic and Davidic—were not receiving enough attention.[85] In 1970, Moshe Weinfeld attempted to fill this void when he compared the Abrahamic and Davidic covenants to parallel texts in the ancient Near East.[86] Based on his comparative studies, Weinfeld identified two basic types of biblical covenants. A covenant, according to him, could be either "obligatory" or "promissory."[87] Obligatory covenants were "treaties" in which a suzerain placed certain obligations on a vassal as a legal means by which the master could protect his rights. Promissory covenants, on the other hand, were "grants" in which a master committed himself in promise to provide (i.e., "grant") a servant rewards for past loyalty. Whereas the nature of obligatory covenants protected the rights of the master, promissory covenants protected the rights of the servant to whom the covenant promises were made.[88] Importantly, Weinfeld concluded that obligatory covenants were conditional whereas promissory covenants were unconditional.

83. Mendenhall, "Covenant Forms in Israelite Tradition," 50–76. In a later work, Mendenhall would expand his application to include the book of Deuteronomy as a whole in terms of its relationship to Hittite suzerainty treaties. See Mendenhall, *Law and Covenant in Israel and the Ancient Near East*, 21–23.

84. For significant contributions in this area see McCarthy, *Treaty and Covenant*; Kline, *Treaty of the Great King*; Baltzer, *Das Bundesformular*; McCarthy, "Covenant in the Old Testament"; McCarthy, *Old Testament Covenant*; Dumbrell, *Covenant and Creation*; Altman, *Historical Prologue of the Hittite Vassal Treaties*; Johnston, "Revisiting Moshe Weinfeld's Comparative and Traditio-Historical Analysis."

85. Cleon Rogers levels this criticism against the works of Mendenhall, Baltzer, and McCarthy. Rogers Jr., "Covenant with Abraham and Its Historical Setting," 241–42.

86. Weinfeld, "Covenant of Grant in the Old Testament and in the Ancient Near East," 184–203.

87. Weinfeld, "Covenant of Grant in the Old Testament and in the Ancient Near East," 184.

88. Weinfeld, "Covenant of Grant in the Old Testament and in the Ancient Near East," 185. Weinfeld notes that the granting of land, found in the Abrahamic covenant, and provision of a dynasty, as found in the Davidic covenant, were the two most common rewards in the Hittite royal grants (Weinfeld, "Covenant of Grant in the Old Testament and in the Ancient Near East," 189).

In contradistinction to the Mosaic covenants, which are of an obligatory type, the covenants with Abraham and David belong to the promissory type. God swears to Abraham to give the land to his descendants, and similarly promises to David to establish his dynasty without imposing any obligations on them. Although their loyalty to God is presupposed, it does not occur as a condition for keeping the promise.[89]

In Weinfeld's writings, one can discern a tension between what he perceived to be the unilateral and unconditional nature of the promissory covenants and certain instances where such promissory royal grants were conditioned. In his discussion of the land grant made by *Muršiliš II* to *Abiraddaš*, Weinfeld himself acknowledged,

> Similarly we find that the Hittite suzerain *did not always grant land unconditionally*. In a land grant of Muršiliš II to Abiraddaš, the Hittite suzerain guarantees the rights of DU-Tešup, Abimardaš' son, to throne, house and land, only on condition that DU-Tešup will not sin (*uaštai-*) against his father. The unconditional promise is therefore a special privilege and apparently given for extraordinary loyal service.[90]

Weinfeld acknowledged that certain passages related to both the Abrahamic (17:1) and Davidic (1 Kgs 2:4; 8:25; 9:4–10) covenants appeared to condition the promises which originally had been framed as unconditional. Nevertheless, he saw these passages to be later additions to the original covenant formulations out of Israel's necessity to reinterpret these covenants in a manner consistent with the nation's history after the fall of the northern and southern kingdoms.

> The exile of Northern Israel and the destruction of Jerusalem and disrupting of the dynasty refuted, of course, the claim of the eternity of the Abrahamic and Davidic covenants and therefore a reinterpretation of the covenants was necessary by putting in the condition, i.e., the covenant is eternal only if the donee keeps his loyalty to the donor.[91]

Based on his commitment to Wellhausen's documentary hypothesis, Weinfeld considered the conditional elements of the Abrahamic covenant

---

89. Weinfeld, "Berîth," 270.

90. Weinfeld, "Covenant of Grant in the Old Testament and in the Ancient Near East," 193. Emphasis mine.

91. Weinfeld, "Covenant of Grant in the Old Testament and in the Ancient Near East," 195.

(Gen 17:1–2) to be a later addition of the priestly source whereas the covenant form in Gen 15 expressed the original unconditional nature of the covenant.[92]

Although many scholars have adopted Weinfeld's belief in the unilateral and unconditional nature of promissory covenants,[93] recent scholarship has questioned his interpretation of specific ancient Near Eastern texts and his application of these to the Abrahamic and Davidic Covenants found in Scripture. Gary N. Knoppers argues that the ancient Near Eastern texts on which Weinfeld based his understanding of the unilateral and unconditional nature of promissory covenants was flawed and demonstrates that a full contextual reading of these documents shows that certain obligations were placed on the recipient conditioning the grant made in promise.[94] Likewise, Gordon H. Johnston argues that "Weinfeld created a false dichotomy between promise and obligation in ancient Near Eastern grants."[95] He observes that treaty texts between *Hatti* and *Arzawa* in the Hittite corpus show examples of royal grants being given in seemingly unconditional terms yet requiring certain obligations in the subsequent grant treaties which fleshed out their original intent.[96]

While it does seem likely that the Abrahamic covenant is ultimately contextualized in a royal grant type of covenant (15:7–21), Erhard Gerstenberger notes, in his review of McCarthy's *Treaty and Covenant*, that attempting to identify the biblical covenants with their ancient Near Eastern counterparts is not always easy, especially if what one seeks is a perfect formal identity between them.[97] Additionally, when one discusses biblical

---

92. Weinfeld, *Deuteronomy and the Deuteronomic School*, 74–75. For a further analysis of Weinfeld's critical views and their implications for his understanding the nature of promissory covenants, see Johnston, "Revisiting Moshe Weinfeld's Comparative and Traditio-Historical Analysis of the Promissory and Obligatory Passages Related to the Abrahamic Covenant," 3–5.

93. For examples, see Loewenstmm, "Divine Grants of Land to the Patriarchs," 509–10; Levenson, "On the Promise to the Rechabites," 508–14; Levenson, "Davidic Covenant and Its Modern Interpreters," 205–14; Ben-Barak, "Meribaal and the System of Land Grants in Ancient Israel," 73–91; Mullen Jr., "Divine Witness and the Davidic Royal Grant," 207–18; Mullen Jr., "Royal Dynastic Grant to Jehu and the Structure of the Book of Kings," 193–206; Mendenhall and Herion, "Covenant," 1:1188–90; Waltke and Yu, *Old Testament Theology*, 148.

94. See Knoppers, "Ancient Near Eastern Royal Grants and the Davidic Covenant," 670–97.

95. Johnston, "Revisiting Moshe Weinfeld's Comparative and Traditio-Historical Analysis," 6.

96. Johnston, "Revisiting Moshe Weinfeld's Comparative and Traditio-Historical Analysis," 7. For the text of these Hittite treaties to which Johnston refers, see Beckman, *Hittite Diplomatic Texts*, 69–93.

97. Gestenberger, "Book Review," 198.

covenants, one must always be aware of the fact that biblical covenants are distinct from their ancient Near Eastern counterparts in that God is party to the covenant. As Rogers observes, this covenant partnership between God and man finds no equivalent in ancient Near Eastern society.[98] Therefore, while recognizing its ancient Near Eastern context, one must allow the Bible to determine the nature of its promissory covenants.

How, then, is one to understand the promissory and obligatory elements in the development of the Abrahamic covenant in Genesis? While it is given, on the one hand, as an irrevocable commitment by God in promise (12:2–3; 15:8–21; 18:18–19; 22:16–18), the experience of the covenant blessings, on the other hand, is conditioned on the obedience of Abraham and his descendants after him (17:1–2; 18:19).[99] In light of the tension created by these promissory and obligatory elements, it seems that a distinction must made between the *existence* of a covenant and its *function*.[100] Upon ratification[101] the covenant comes into existence and, assured by God's commitment in promise, will ultimately be fulfilled. However, the experience of these covenant blessings in history comes only as those party to the covenant fulfill the terms required for its function. In the case of the Abrahamic covenant, the promissory and obligatory elements of the covenant are revealed in stages. While the covenant is ratified and comes into existence in Gen 15:7–21, where God promises Abraham the land (cf. 12:1–3, 7),[102] the

98. Rogers writes, "It is obvious that Israel's covenants with God are somewhat different because the surrounding nations had no covenants with their gods" (Rogers, "Covenant with Abraham and Its Historical Setting," 250).

99. In Gen 17:1, God's command to Abraham that he "walk before him and be blameless," (הִתְהַלֵּךְ לְפָנַי וֶהְיֵה תָמִים) introduces a covenant obligation. The nature of this blameless walk is clarified in 18:18–19 when God says, "Abraham will surely become a great and mighty nation, and in him all the nations of the earth will be blessed? For I have chosen him, in order that he may command his children and his household after him *to keep the way of the LORD by doing righteousness and justice*; in order that the LORD may bring upon Abraham what He has spoken about him" (NASB). Emphasis mine. For a good overview of the word "blameless" (תָּמִים) used in 17:1, see Kedar-Kopfstein, *tāmîm*, 699–711.

100. This distinction comes from Johnson, *Dispensational Biblical Theology*, 80–81. Here, Johnson follows Weinfeld's use of the term "promissory covenant" to describe the Abrahamic covenant; however, unlike Weinfeld, Johnson recognizes obligatory elements in the covenant formulation and, in light of this, posits a distinction between the existence and function of a covenant.

101. For a discussion regarding the ancient Near Eastern background related to the cutting of animals in the ratification of a treaty, as found in Gen 15, see McCarthy, *Treaty and Covenant*, 54–55; Beyerlin, *Near Eastern Religious Texts Relating to the Old Testament*, 260.

102. This covenant in Gen 15 commits God to provide Abram and his descendants the promised land. This is the land that God promised to show Abram in Gen 12:1 and

obligatory aspect of the covenant is revealed later when God obligates Abraham to walk blamelessly before him in order for the covenant to function in history (17:1–2; 18:19). In light of the previous discussion, this distinction would not be out of place in an ancient context.

The relationship between the promises of Gen 12:1–3, 7 and the covenant ratification in Gen 15:7–21 must be given careful consideration. If a covenant does not come into existence until its ratification by oath or sacrifice,[103] then the promises to Abram do not become *covenant promises* until the ratification ceremony in Gen 15:7–21.[104] If this is the case, then it is anachronistic to designate God's promises in Gen 12:1–3, 7 as Abrahamic covenant for the promises have not yet been incorporated into a covenant formulation. Rather, Gen 12:1–3, 7 are pre-covenant commitments and might more accurately be described as *Abrahamic promises*.[105] While the promises in their subsequent covenant formulation will reveal the condition upon which the promises will be experienced (17:1–2; 18:19), the *Abrahamic promises* of 12:1–3, 7 are *promissory locutions* that reveal the unconditional nature of the obligations assumed by God in his partnership with Abram.

Genesis 12:1–3, 7 and the Hermeneutics of Promise

In the literary design of Genesis, chapter 12 marks a pivotal change in the trajectory of the book. Prior to this point, the author has recounted the history of the primeval era (1–11), and its downward spiral, at a rapid pace. Beginning in chapter 12, however, the pace of the narrative slows tremendously as the author seeks to highlight God's program of blessing through Abram and its outworking in the subsequent patriarchal narratives (12–50). As Allen P. Ross observes, "While chapters 1–11 portrayed the race in rebellion to what God had intended, chapters 12–25 recount God's development

would be needed if Abram was to become a great nation (12:2–3). Although the land for Abram and his descendants was already promised beforehand (12:7, 13:14–16), it is in chapter 15 that God provides a covenant formulation for this promise. The land, then, is the focal point for the promises of 12:1–3 to be fulfilled. It is the locus of blessing.

103. Weinfeld, "B^{e}rîth," 262–63; Beyerlin, *Near Eastern Religious Texts Relating to the Old Testament*, 260.

104. In Gen 15:18 the narrator says, "*On that day* the LORD made a covenant with Abram, saying, 'To your descendants I have given this land, From the river of Egypt as far as the great river, the river Euphrates'" (NASB). Emphasis mine.

105. Regarding the promises of Gen 12:1–3 Dumbrell writes, "What we have in this passage is a summary of the relationships begun by God with Abram to which the title b^{e}rît is later given in Genesis 15 (Dumbrell, *Covenant and Creation*, 64).

of the promised blessing through Abram."[106] Following the genealogy of Shem (11:10–26), which connected Abram to the Sethite line from which God's provision of the seed would come (5:1–32), the Lord's (יְהוָה) word of promise came to Abram while he resided in Ur of the Chaldeans (11:28–31; cf. Acts 7:2) to enact additional element of his plan for history. This word of promise included a series of commands (12:1) followed by promises that were to define the partnership the Lord would make with Abram (12:2–3):

Gen 12:1–3[107]		
Command (12:1): "Go forth . . ."	From your country, relatives, and father's house to the land I will show you	Imperative: לֶךְ־לְךָ
Promise 1 (12:2a): "I will . . ."	Make you a great nation	Cohortative in Function: וְאֶעֶשְׂךָ
Promise 2 (12:2b): "I will . . ."	Bless you	Cohortative in Function: וַאֲבָרֶכְךָ
Promise 3 (12:2c): "I will . . ."	Make your name great . . . so you will be a blessing	Cohortative: וַאֲגַדְּלָה שְׁמֶךָ Result (Indirect Volative): וֶהְיֵה בְּרָכָה
Promise 4 (12:3a): "I will . . ."	Bless those who bless you	Cohortative: וַאֲבָרֲכָה מְבָרְכֶיךָ
Promise 5 (12:3b): "I will . . ."	Curse the one who esteems you lightly	Cohortative: וּמְקַלֶּלְךָ אָאֹר
Promise 6 (12:3c): "In you . . ."	All the families of the earth will be blessed.	Result: וְנִבְרְכוּ בְךָ כֹּל מִשְׁפְּחֹת הָאֲדָמָה

Abram was to leave his country and familial relations so that he could see the land where God would bless him and untold his plan of blessing. As promise, the commitments of God held absolute performative force. Nevertheless, the assurance of God's promises did not dispense with Abram's responsibility. As G. B. Caird observed, "In the Bible predestination is never confused with determinism. God's appointments have absolute performative force, but this causal power never dispenses with human response."[108] The command of God in 12:1 was, for Abram, a call to a partnership through

---

106. Ross, *Creation and Blessing*, 80–81.

107. This chart summarizes the commands and promises in Gen 12:1–3 and, though largely from the NASB, includes some translation choices of the author.

108. Caird, *Language and Imagery of the Bible*, 24.

which God's redemptive plan would unfold. The ultimate purpose of this partnership was not only revealed by the scope and grandeur of this promise but also by the grammar of Gen 12:1–3. As Hans Walter Wolf observed, the sudden shift in the final clause of 12:3 to the perfect tense, revealed the final clause to be the overall purpose or goal of the whole oracle of blessing, what one might term the *principal promise.*

> The predominance of the promise [12:2–3] is clear. Still, at what does it really aim? We observed in the chain of promises a syntactical change in the last clause 3b. Here the series of five imperfect-cohortative consecutive clauses is interrupted by a clause with a perfect consecutive. This, verse 3b is clearly set off as the sequel to the consequences (vss. 2–3a) of the departure of Abraham (vs. 1); it is the real result and it is, therefore, confirmed definitively by the perfect. The abrupt change in the final clause is further clarified by the fact that in verse 3b the subject is no longer Yahweh but "all the families of the earth." In so doing, it is set down conclusively whom Yahweh's action, already manifoldly described, ultimately concerns and what this action is to accomplish for them.[109]

The *principal promise,* then, is the Lord's commitment to bless all the nations of the earth through Abram (12:3). This is the ultimate goal of their partnership. Although the nations of the earth had been formed and scattered through divine judgment at Babel (11:1–9; cf. 10:1–32), these same nations—all of humanity—could now experience blessing through a relationship with Abram according to the Lord's divine word of promise.

Literarily, two important features must be noted about this promised blessing. First, as Abram is himself connected to the lineage of the coming seed, the promise of worldwide blessing in 12:3 is now connected to the expectation of the coming one. The one who will be God's agent of judgment on the serpent (3:15) will also be the one through whom God will bless the nations of the earth (12:3). While the phrase "in you" necessitates that Abram will mediate this blessing in some fashion, it introduces a level of ambiguity as originally uttered. By "in you," did God mean to identify Abram as the promised seed, or did the phrase refer to another in Abram's lineage? This ambiguity is quickly clarified in the early chapters of the Abraham narrative where God reveals that the promised seed of blessing will be Abram's own offspring and heir (12:7 13:14; 15:4).

---

109. Wolff, "Kerygma of the Yahwist," 138. See also Miller Jr., "Syntax and Theology in Genesis XII 3a," 472–75; Kaiser, *Promise-Plan of God,* 55.

Second, it is important to observe that the promise of blessing is a response to the proliferation of sin described in Gen 3–11. Although the flood gave mankind a new beginning through Noah (6:1—9:18), it did not deal with the problem of sin (cf. 9:19–29; 11:1–9). In response to sinful humanity's failures, God responds with a promise of blessing for this same humanity through Abram, that is, through his seed. As a response to the sin cycle (3–11), the promise of worldwide blessing must include a remedy for sin. In the progress of revelation, the original meaning of this promise of blessing is clarified to be justification through faith in Messiah (Gal 3:8–11; cf. Gen 15:3–6).[110] The New Testament, then, brings clarity, not a new meaning, to God's original intent. Although deserved, judgment could never fix sinful humanity's problem, only a magnificent blessing of God—a blessing wholly unmerited as Gen 3–11 revealed—could provide the remedy needed for the reclamation of God's mediatorial reign of the earth.[111]

The oracle itself in Gen 12:1–3 anticipated two responses: blessing and disregard. Those who blessed Abram would themselves be blessed (בָּרַךְ). Those who disregarded (קָלַל) Abram would be cursed (אָרַר). Though the original oracle implied the inheritance of a land (12:1)—a requirement necessary to establish a nation—this provision of the land is only specified after Abram enters Canaan, for it is here that the Lord promises to give Abram's seed (זֶרַע) the land (12:7; 13:14–15). The revelation of a seed (זֶרַע) to inherit the land, then, is added to the promises of 12:2–3 as an additional commitment of God. Importantly, however, the Lord does not clarify the sense in which this "seed" (זֶרַע) was to be understood. In promising a seed, did the Lord mean a collective posterity? Or, did he mean that he would provide Abram with a seed who would inherit the land? To understand the faith of Abram in these early chapters of the patriarchal narrative, it is essential to examine these commitments by the Lord in terms of their intended locutionary, illocutionary, and perlocutionary forces.

110. It is again important to distinguish between what God originally meant as understood through the literary development of Genesis and what Abram understood and believed in his historical situation. In its use of the Old Testament, the New Testament can clarify and affirm the literary meaning of an Old Testament text, but this is not the same as affirming a character's historical knowledge of this meaning, particularly if the character did not have access to the literary composition under consideration. Unless the New Testament specifically speaks to a historical character's knowledge, such knowledge must be ascertained by looking at the particular details the author provides as these individuals interact with the revelation of God in the narrative account.

111. In his work *Covenant and Creation*, William Dumbrell observes that the oracle 12:1–3 is given in response to the sin cycle in 3–11 and implies that God's promised blessing through Abram will deal with the problem of sin. See Dumbrell, *Covenant and Creation*, 67–75.

Locutionary Force

In the Lord's promises to Abram, he formed a locution by uttering the words that formed the basis, or terms, of his performative action.[112] In its "willed type," the locution is simply what the Lord meant by what he spoke. The locutionary scope of Gen 12:1–3, 7 can be summarized as follows:

The Locutionary Force of Gen 12:1–3, 7[113]	
Passage	**Locutionary Acts**
12:1a	Go forth from your country, and from your relatives and from your father's house, to the land I will show you
12:2a	I will make you a great nation
12:2b	I will bless you
12:2c	And make your name great so you shall be a blessing
12:3a	I will bless those who bless you
12:3b	The one who esteems you lightly I will curse
12:3c	In you all the families of the earth shall be blessed
12:7	To your seed I will give this land

Illocutionary Force

In terms of its speech action, the Lord performed certain actions by uttering the locution. The *uttering* of the words in the locution *counts as* the Lord's performance of the speech actions in his revelation to Abram. In his philosophical work *Divine Discourse*, Nicholas Wolterstorff discusses the relationship between an illocutionary and locutionary act when he writes,

> It was by uttering the words, "the jewels are buried in the garden" that the old man asserted that the jewels are buried in the garden; his uttering those words, which is the locutionary act in this case, *counts as* his asserting that proposition, this latter being the illocutionary act . . . Illocutionary acts are related to locutionary acts by way of the *counting as* relation . . .[114]

112. Since a speech act always occurs in a context, Jeannine K. Brown argues that locutions are always part of an utterance. "An *utterance* is a speech act with a context. In relevance theory, a communicative act assumes a context. Thus, we might understand an utterance as consisting of both *linguistic expression* and *assumed context*" (Brown, *Scripture as Communication*, 35, emphasis hers).

113. This largely NASB translation includes some translation choices of the author.

114. Wolterstorff, *Divine Discourse*, 33. Emphasis his. See also Vanhoozer, *Is There a Meaning in This Text?* 209.

To understand the hermeneutics of the Lord's revelation to Abram, it is necessary to discern what actions he performed by uttering the locutions in revelation:

The Illocutionary Force of Gen 12:1–3, 7[115]		
Passage	**Locutionary Action**	**Illocutionary Action**
12:1a	Go forth from your country, and from your relatives and from your father's house, to the land I will show you	Command
12:2a	I will make you a great nation	Promise
12:2b	I will bless you	Promise
12:2c	And make your name great so you shall be a blessing	Promise
12:3a	I will bless those who bless you	Promise
12:3b	The one who esteems you lightly I will curse	Promise
12:3c	In you all the families of the earth shall be blessed	Promise
12:7	To your seed I will give this land	Promise

After the initial command to "go forth" to the land the Lord would show him, the Lord *commits himself in promise* to accomplish the terms of the locution. The utterance of the locutionary promises *count as* the Lord's performance of these commitments and, necessarily, implies a governance

115. This largely NASB translation includes some translation choices of the author. The purpose of this chart is to examine Gen 12:1–3 in terms of its function as a series of speech-acts. Speech-act theory looks at language from the speaker's point of view, not the hearers. It is the speaker who is doing things by what he says. The divine imperative to "go forth" in 12:1 establishes this verse as a command in terms of its function as a speech-act. To be sure, Abram was responsible to obey this command for only by doing so would he be able to experience the promised blessings in the land God would show him. But the force of God's speech is that of a command. The repeated use of "I will . . ." throughout 12:2–3 set up the subsequent speech-acts as acts of promise from the perspective of the speaker. In the broader narrative, it becomes clear that God's intention was to bless Abram despite his failings. In other words, God's promises were bigger than Abram's weaknesses. This is demonstrated by a number of elements early in the narrative. Although Abram left the land where God had called him to sojourn when he traveled to Egypt, God both protected and blessed Abram despite this act of disobedience (12:10–20). Although God had told Abram to depart from his father's house (12:1 בֵּית אָבִיךָ), a separation that referred to the individual members of Terah's household (cf. 24:7; Josh 7:16–18), Abraham brought Lot with him to Canaan (12:5). Though this act of disobedience caused problems for Abram in the land (13:5–11), it did not nullify God's plan to bless Abram according to his promises (12:7; 13:14). Therefore, both in terms of language and the narrative context, it seems legitimate to view the statements of God in 12:2–3 as promissory speech-acts. For a good discussion on the complete separation required by God in his call of Abram, see Mathews, *Genesis 11:27—50:26*, 110–11.

of history—the means—to accomplish for Abram what he here commits to do for him in promise, the ultimate commitment being to bless all the nations of the earth through Abram (12:3c). It is this very commitment to govern the means that distinguishes *promise* from *prediction.*

Willis J. Beecher observed an important distinction between promise and prediction. He noted that, whereas a prediction requires nothing more than a simple prognostication of some future event, a promise, however, necessarily includes a commitment to bring about what was promised. Therefore, the promise not only involves a knowledge of a future event (i.e., a prediction) but also a commitment to govern the means that leads to the accomplishment of the commitment made in promise.

> From some points of view there is no difference between performing something that has been promised or threatened and the coming to pass of something that has been foretold; but from other points of view there is a great difference. For example, when we think of a promise and its fulfillment, we think of the means employed for that purpose. The promise and the means and the result are all in mind at one, and our conception of each is modified by our conception of the others . . .Every fulfilled promise is fulfilled prediction; but it is exceedingly important to look at it as a promise, and not as mere prediction.[116]

By performing the illocutionary act of promise, the Lord not only predicts a future for Abram—and through him a prediction concerning worldwide blessing—but *he commits himself* to fulfill the obligations made in history (i.e., the means).[117] The nature and scope of the promises made to Abram necessitate God's sovereign control of history. Without such control, there is no basis to expect that God can accomplish what he has promised to do. As these promises must be fulfilled in history, God must control and orchestrate the events of history to ensure that what he has promised he is able to perform.

Therefore, from the moment the Lord utters the words of promise (i.e., the locution), his providential governance of history begins until what he commits to do comes to pass. A promise, then, involves a process of "fulfilling" (i.e., the historical means) as well as an ultimate "fulfillment" (i.e., the

116. Beecher, *Prophets and the Promise,* 376.

117. Regarding this distinction, Walter C. Kaiser writes, "Whereas systematic theology generally separates prediction from promise, omitting references to the threatening aspect of the promise and the judgments of God as well as the historic *means* that God used to keep his word alive and ultimately to bring his word to pass, biblical theology insists on keeping both the threatening aspects and the predictions of hope together as alternative parts of the same promise-plan" (Kaiser, *Promise-Plan of God,* 18).

final result). These illocutionary commitments of the Lord provide the lens through which Abram might exegete history thereafter. Literarily, these illocutionary actions provide the interpretive framework within which the author narrates the patriarchal history as the Lord's governance of history begins through Abram and the family he would sire.[118]

Elliott E. Johnson observes another important distinction between promise and prediction. In a prediction, meaning is expressed with such specificity that it limits itself to a single, future referent when fulfilled in history. A promise, on the other hand, is more broadly defined and, therefore, potentially opens itself to multiple fulfillments in history before it is ultimately fulfilled.

> [T]he meaning of the prediction is specified so explicitly in context that it allows for only one reference in the future . . . The promise is a broader commissive statement in the sense that it does not necessarily specify one historical reference . . . the broader scope, involving fewer necessary components, in the statement of a promise does not specify the circumstances of fulfillment so completely while at the same time affirming the fact of commitment to act. Therefore a promise is potentially capable of multiple partial fulfillments before reaching a final realization of the commitment.[119]

As promise, then, the revelation of the Lord to Abram is not so specific in its expression as to provide Abram with a detailed knowledge of its future fulfillment in history, although these details are certainly present in the Lord's divine intent. Yet, at the same time, the terms of the promise are clear enough to create what Caird referred to as a Situation Vacant advertisement in which the author "describes in some detail a person whose identity is not yet known to the writer."[120] In the Lord's revelation to Abram, the historical referent is included in God's divine intent—though he is unrevealed in the locution of the promise—and can be identified in history when he fulfills

---

118. Allen Ross, commenting on this passage, refers to the promissory commitments of Yahweh as "foundational promise of blessing" and note that they help to establish the "pattern" for the narrative history of the patriarchs which follows. See Ross, *Creation and Blessing*, 259.

119. Johnson, *Expository Hermeneutics*, 162–63. Because of this difference, Beecher observes that while the Bible contains many promises, it contains fewer predictions. "The proposition that the Old Testament contains a large number of predictions concerning the Messiah to come, and that these are fulfilled in Jesus Christ, may be scriptural in substance, but it is hardly so in form. The bible offers very few predictions save in the form of promises or threatenings" (Beecher, *Prophets as Promise*, 178).

120. Caird, *Language and Imagery of the Bible*, 57.

the terms of the Lord's commitments to Abram, the principal promise being to bless all the nations of the earth through him (12:3c). The generic nature of promise as a speech act focuses Abram's attention on the *commitments* of the Lord rather than on the *circumstances* surrounding their fulfillment as is the case in a prediction. In this way, the person of the Lord is brought to the fore as he begins a partnership with Abram in his governance of history.

John R. Searle discusses the requirements necessary for a genuine performative illocutionary speech act to occur. Among those relevant to this discussion are the requirements that (1) a speaker expresses the true contents of the promise in uttering the locution, (2) by expressing the contents of the promise, the speaker sincerely predicates his future action(s), (3) it is not obvious that the speaker's promise would occur in the normal course of events without the speaker's commitment, (4) the speaker sincerely intends to fulfill the promise, (5) the speaker intends that the utterance of the locution will place him under an obligation to fulfill the promised action(s), and (6) the speaker intends to produce in the hearer the knowledge that the utterance of the locution places the speaker under an obligation to fulfill the promise.[121] As a speech act, then, the Abrahamic promises of Gen 12:1–3, 7 place God under obligation to Abram and give Abram the right to hold God accountable for what he has promised.

Perlocutionary Force

In communication, the purpose of a speaker's illocutionary action is to produce a particular response in the one to whom he speaks.[122] This is what William P. Alston describes as the "perlocutionary intention" of the speaker.[123] To be sure, the nature of the Lord's illocutionary actions in Gen 12:1–3, 7 required more than simple mental cognition on the part of Abram. The type of illocutionary action performed was intended to produce a specific response in Abram who received the revelation. Through his command (12:1), the Lord sought to produce obedience. This obedience involved Abram's departure from his homeland and separation from his kinsmen in his travel to the land that God would show him. Through his promises (12:2–3, 7), he sought to produce *expectant belief* as Abram possessed the

---

121. Searle, *Speech Acts*, 57–61.

122. Austin, *How to Do Things with Words*, 101.

123. "The act of affecting H [a hearer] in some way—getting H to believe that p [a proposition] or to form the intention to do D [a directive]—is a perlocutionary act. And so the intention to affect A [an action] in some way can be termed a 'perlocutionary intention'" (Alston, *Illocutionary Acts and Sentence Meaning*, 37).

right to hold him accountable for the commitments made in his governance
of history:

The Perlocutionary Force of Gen 12:1–3, 7[124]			
Passage	**Locution**	**Illocution**	**Perlocution**
12:1a	Go forth from your country, and from your relatives and from your father's house, to the land I will show you	Command	Obedience
12:2a	I will make you a great nation	Promise	Expectant Faith
12:2b	I will bless you	Promise	Expectant Faith
12:2c	And make your name great so you shall be a blessing	Promise	Expectant Faith
12:3a	I will bless those who bless you	Promise	Expectant Faith
12:3b	The one who esteems you lightly I will curse	Promise	Expectant Faith
12:3c	In you all the families of the earth shall be blessed	Promise	Expectant Faith
12:7	To your seed I will give this land	Promise	Expectant Faith

To grasp the causative force of an illocutionary act, it is essential to
recognize *apprehension* as the necessary basis for a speech act to have the
intended perlocutionary affect. For this reason, Jeannine K. Brown observes
that "[u]nderstanding is the characteristic perlocution, because it precedes
and grounds all other hearer responses."[125] If a hearer fails to grasp the illocutionary force in the saying of a locution, he will likely fail to apprehend
the corresponding perlocution which the speaker hopes to affect. One might
very well tell a child to clean his room, however if the child fails to understand the sense of the locution, or its illocutionary force as a command, he
will likely fail to obey, which is the perlocutionary intent of the speech act.

In practice, speech acts often produce both *intended* and *unintended*
perlocutions.[126] When an *unintended perlocution* occurs, it may be that the
hearer has failed to apprehend some aspect of the performative speech act—
locutionary or perlocutionary—or the unintended behavior might betray

---

124. This largely NASB translation includes some translation choices of the author.

125. Brown, *Scripture as Communication*, 33. Nicholas Wolterstorff recognizes the
essential role of apprehension when he writes, "It may be added that perlocutionary
actions, as Austin understood those, occur only if one's auditor apprehends or thinks he
apprehends an illocutionary action that one has performed, and only if that apprehension (or purported apprehension) evokes the effect in question" (Wolterstorff, *Divine
Discourse*, 76).

126. See Brown, *Scripture as Communication*, 33.

the fact that the hearer does not yet fully trust the speaker to perform what he has promised to do. As this trust develops, the original speech act *gains causative power* as the original commitment of the speaker persuades the hearer to exhibit more of the *intended perlocutions.*

The beginning chapters of the patriarchal narratives reveal that Abram exhibited both *intended* and *unintended* perlocutionary responses to the revelation of God (12:1–3, 7). In obedience to the divine command (12:1), Abram migrated to the land of Canaan where the Lord had promised to bless him (12:5–6). When the Lord committed himself in promise to give the land of Canaan to Abram's seed (12:7a), Abram responded by building an altar to him (12:7b). All of these were *intended perlocutions* and demonstrate that Abram did possess genuine faith in the Lord, a fact to which the New Testament bears witness (cf. Heb 11:8).[127] However, the narrative also relays certain aspects of Abram's response that could only be described as *unintended perlocutions.* These *unintended perlocutions* reveal that Abram has either failed to grasp the full sense of the Lord's illocutionary commitments, or they demonstrate a lack of trust in the Lord's ability or willingness to perform what he had promised. Although the Lord had originally commanded Abram to separate (לֶךְ־לְךָ)[128] from his "relatives" (מוֹלֶדֶת) and "father's house" (וּמִבֵּית אָבִיךָ) in his migration to Canaan (Gen 12:1), it was Terah, Abram's father, who led Abram and his nephew, Lot, to settle in Haran—not Canaan—until Terah's death (11:31).[129] After the death of his father, Abram traveled to Canaan with Lot, a partnership that would cause problems for Abram while in the land (13:1–12). Although the Lord had commanded Abram to sojourn in Canaan, where he promised to bless him, Abram moved his family to Egypt to escape a famine and lied about his relationship with Sarai, his wife, in an attempt to preserve his own life (12:10–20). Yet, in his governance of history according to the commitments made in promise, the Lord orchestrates the circumstances of Abram's life—despite these *unintended perlocutions*—to protect and preserve his commitments to him.

---

127. A discussion concerning the testimony of Heb 11:8 to the faith of Abram will be pursued later in the chapter.

128. In 12:1, לֶךְ־לְךָ connotes the sense of separation. See Brown, Driver, and Briggs, *Hebrew and English Lexicon of the Old Testament*, 231.

129. In Acts 7:4 Stephen explains that it was God who moved Abram from Haran into Canaan after his father's death.

The Faith of Abram in Gen 15:1–6

In terms of its function as a speech act, it has been established that the performative commitments of the Lord in his revelation to Abram (12:2–3, 7) placed him under obligation to fulfill his promises, the principal of which was to bless all the nations of the earth through Abram (12:3c). The magnitude of this promise made it clear that such blessing would not occur naturally in the normal course of history and, therefore, was a necessary and genuine commitment of the Lord. As a genuine speech-act, the Lord's illocution placed him under obligation to govern the means—history—and gave Abram the right to hold the Lord accountable to fulfill what he had committed to do in promise. In function, the Lord's speech-act provided Abram the lens through which to exegete history. All the events in Abram's life must, therefore, relate to the "fulfilling" of the commitments made until they are finally "fulfilled" in history. Recognizing the force of the Lord's speech-act holds an important implication for the hermeneutics of the Abraham story in Genesis (12:1—25:10) and the whole of the patriarchal narratives (25:11—50:26). As the Lord had decreed history in promise (12:2–3, 7), a proper interpretation of any events within history must relate these events to the illocutionary commitments of God. Literarily speaking, it requires the reader to relate any interpretation within the patriarchal history to the promises of Gen 12:2–3, 7 since they form the narrative, literary account of the Lord's governance of history according to promise.

In the Abraham story, Gen 15 exists as an important development of the promises announced in 12:2–3, 7 for it is here that the Lord clarifies important elements of his promissory commitments, and it is here that the promises previously announced are formally ratified in a covenant formulation.[130] The chapter can be divided into two separate dialogues between Abram and the Lord.[131] The first of these dialogues concerns Abram's reward and heir (15:1–6) while the second involves the inheritance of Abram's future posterity in the land of promise. Recognizing the relationship between chapter 15 and the original promises of God (12:2–3, 7), Coats refers to this chapter as "promise dialogue."[132] While the topic of these dialogues in-

130. Recognizing the importance of this chapter, Walter Brueggemann writes, "This chapter [Gen 15] is pivotal for the Abraham tradition. Theologically, it is probably the most important chapter of this entire collection. It has been judged by many scholars to be the oldest statement of Abrahamic faith, from which the others are derivative" (Brueggemann, *Genesis*, 140). Kenneth A. Mathews writes, "It [Gen 15] provides a theological commentary on the promises foundational to the theme of the Abraham narrative" (Mathews, *Genesis 11:27—50:26*, 157).

131. See Ross, *Creation and Blessing*, 305; Waltke and Fredricks, *Genesis*, 238.

132. Coats, *Genesis*, 122–23. Coats outlines these dialogues as follows: "(1)

cludes explanations of the Lord's promissory commitments, the underlying question in the account relates to Abram's faith in God and his Word. For Abram, the question underlying the first dialogue is simple. Would God truly provide him an heir?

In Gen 15, the word of the Lord came to Abram in a command (15:1a),[133] an assurance (15:1b), and a promise (15:1c):

Gen 15:1[134]			
15:1a	Do not fear Abram	אַל־תִּירָא אַבְרָם	Command
15:1b	I am a shield to you	אָנֹכִי מָגֵן לָךְ	Assurance
15:1c	Your reward shall be very great	שְׂכָרְךָ הַרְבֵּה מְאֹד	Promise

As Meredith Kline notes, the revelation of the Lord in 15:1 was likely a divine response to the events which transpired in the previous chapter.[135] After Lot had been captured in the siege of Sodom (14:1–12), Abram put together a rescue party consisting of 318 men and rescued Lot along with those who had been taken captive (14:14–17). Abram's fear of retaliation was, likely, the contextual impetus for the revelation of the Lord in 15:1. In response to Abram's fear, the Lord commanded Abram not to be afraid (15:1a) and assured him that he himself would protect Abram as his divine "shield" (מָגֵן; 15:1b; cf. Ps 84:7–12). Because the Lord was Abram's protection, he could both protect Abram and promise the future security of Abram's great "reward" (שָׂכָר).

In response to the word of the Lord (15:1), Abram revealed a lack of trust in the Lord, a deficiency that had put him in danger of committing yet another *unintended perlocution*. Although the Lord had promised to make Abram into a great nation and to give the land of Canaan to his seed (12:2, 7), Abram, according to the custom of the ancient Near East, was left with his servant, Eliezer, as his heir because he had not been given a son (15:2–3).[136] As God had not given Abram a natural heir, Abram would be forced

---

self-revelation speech (v. 1 par. v. 7); (2) Abram's complaint ([2] 3 par. 8); (3) instructions speech (5a par. 9); and (4) promise speech (4, 5b par. 13–16, 18–21)" (Coats, *Genesis*, 123).

133. Although the verb "to fear" (יָרֵא) is here used as a jussive, in instances where the jussive stands alone, as is the case in 15:1, the verb frequently carries the force of a command. See Kautzsch, *Gesenius' Hebrew Grammar*, 321.

134. The text comes from the NASB.

135. Kline, *Kingdom Prologue*, 238.

136. In light of ancient Near Eastern records, Moshe Weinfeld observed that it was customary for the father to have the right to designate his heir. "As is now known to us from Nuzi, Alalaḫ, Ugarit and Palestine the father had the right to select a 'first born' as

to preserve his own inheritance through the appointment of Eliezer, a man with whom he had no biological relationship (15:2–3). Abram's complaint revealed that he did not yet understand how to trust that the Lord would provide him a *natural heir* through which his illocutionary commitments would be fulfilled (12:2–3, 7). That this appointment would be an *unintended perlocution* is confirmed in the Lord's response to Abram's admission. "This man will not be your heir [לֹא יִירָשְׁךָ זֶה]; but one who shall come forth from your own body, he shall be your heir" (15:4). It was not the Lord's intent to bless the nations of the earth through Eliezer. Rather, when the Lord had originally announced his commitments in promise (12:2–3, 7), he had intended them to be fulfilled through *a natural offspring* of Abram. In his dialogue with Abram, God provided clarity and assurance to Abram. While Abram's *heir* would be *a natural, male offspring* (15:4), the "nation" would include a *natural posterity* as numerous as the stars in the sky (15:5; cf. vv. 7–21). It was at this juncture that the narrator concluded the first dialogue (15:1–6) by revealing something important about Abram. "Then he [Abram] believed in the Lord; and He reckoned it to him as righteousness" (15:6).[137]

The syntactical relationship of 15:6 to the preceding dialogue (15:1–5) has engendered some debate. Although Hebrew narrative typically relays sequential events by using the *wayyiqtol* form to develop a narrative progression,[138] the author used the *weqatal* form (וְהֶאֱמִן) in 15:6 to introduce the narrative statement of Abram's faith and the Lord's reckoning it to him as righteousness. Following the parenthetical function of the *weqatal* form in Gesenius' *Hebrew Grammar*,[139] many commentators understand the syntax

---

well as making all his heirs share alike, and was not bound by the law of primogeniture." Weinfeld, "Covenant of Grant in the Old Testament and in the Ancient Near East," 194. M. J. Selman adds to the understanding of the ancient custom of inheritance when he notes that Babylonian records show that in the event a man had no son, he could name a servant as heir. See Selman, "Comparative Customs and the Patriarchal Age," 126–27.

137. Kenneth A. Mathews writes, "[T]he righteousness that Abram receives is not due to conformity to a covenant standard. Rather, this righteousness is extrinsic to Abram and is solely bequeathed by God's gracious declaration" (Mathews, *Genesis 11:27—50:26*, 168). The Septuagint translates the verb "to believe" (אמן) in 15:6 with the Greek verb πιστεύω. As R. W. L. Moberly observes, the *hiphil* form of the verb, as occurs in 15:6, most closely approximates the meaning of this Greek counterpart and, therefore, carries the sense of "accepting what someone says as true." See Moberly, "*āmēn*," 431. See also Jepsen, "*āman*," 298–300; Healey, "Faith," 744–49.

138. For the function of *wayyiqtol* forms and their sequential function in narrative literature, see also Kautzsch, *Gesenius' Hebrew Grammar*, 132–33; Chisholm, *From Exegesis to Exposition*, 119–20.

139. Kautzsch, *Gesenius' Hebrew Grammar*, 336–37. Bill T. Arnold and John H. Choi write, "The *waw* conjunctive employed with the verbal idea is also used in

of 15:6 to provide supplemental information related to the preceding dialogue (15:1–5).[140] For them, the *waw* is disjunctive rather than consecutive in function. According to this view, the syntax of 15:6 simply reminds the reader that faith was *the normal response* of Abram to the revelation of God and should not be understood sequentially to indicate that his justification occurred *because of his belief* in the content of the Lord's revelation (15:4–5). However, other commentators hold that the declaration of Abram's faith and subsequent justification should be seen as the resolution to the dialogic conflict (15:1–3) and result of the Lord's revelation (15:4–5). Therefore, they see a consecutive function in the syntax of 15:6 and hold it to be the climactic event in this first dialogue.[141]

In his study of *weqatal* forms in Hebrew prose, Robert E. Longacre observed that Hebrew grammarians have failed to sufficiently account for isolated occurrences of the *weqatal* form in Hebrew narrative literature. In such literature, Longacre suggested that the use of an isolated *weqatal* form marked a climactic event or result in a narrative sequence (e.g., Judg 3:20–23; 2 Sam 13:1–21, note verse 18; 1 Kgs 20:1–21; 2 Kgs 14:8–14; 24:10–16, note verse 14). The change in form was the author's way of highlighting a particular event grammatically in a way that set it apart from the preceding narrative sequence.

> Properly speaking, *wqtl* forms have no proper place or function in narrative. But such isolated occurrences of *wqtl* in narrative context do occur, and when they occur they can be considered to be highly marked. We are provoked as analysts to say to such a form when it occurs in a narrative context "What are you doing here?" I do not believe that any such unusual occurrences of isolated *wqtl* forms imply repeated action or frequentative . . . Rather, an isolated *wqtl* form in a narrative is pivotal or climactic in the story.[142]

narrative texts to present an idea that is strongly disjunctive from the *waw* consecutives in context" (Arnold and Choi, *Guide to Biblical Hebrew Syntax*).

140. For examples of scholars who hold this view, see Von Rad, *Genesis*, 184; Wenham, *Genesis 1–15*, 329; Sarna, *Genesis*, 113; Sailhamer, "Genesis," 129; Ross, *Creation and Blessing*, 309; Mathews, *Genesis 11:27—50:26*, 166.

141. For examples of scholars who hold this view, see Kidner, *Genesis*, 214; Westermann, *Genesis 12–36*, 222; Waltke and Fredricks, *Genesis*, 242; Walton, *Genesis*, 421; McKeown, *Genesis*, 90; Arnold, *Genesis*, 152; Kaiser Jr., "Is It the Case That Christ Is the Same Object of Faith in the Old Testament? (Genesis 15:1–6)," 294; Kuruvilla, *Genesis*, 190; Johnson, *Dispensational Biblical Theology*, 96.

142. Longacre and Bowling, *Understanding Biblical Hebrew Verb Forms*, 624. Elsewhere, Longacre writes, "As we saw in previous sections, a sequence of *weqatal* forms in narrative regularly marks the inclusion of a how-it-was-done (our routine sequence)

While a complete discussion of isolated *weqatal* forms in Hebrew narrative cannot be dealt with here, a couple of examples should be adequate to illustrate Longacre's assertion. In Judg 3:20–23, the author narrates the assassination of Eglon by Ehud. The narrative relays the sequence of events through the use of ten *wayyiqtol* clauses followed by a single, terminal *weqatal* clause:

Judges 3:20–23[143]		
Clause	**Text and NASB Translation**	**Syntax**
1 (3:20)	And Ehud came to him וְאֵהוּד בָּא אֵלָיו	Introductory disjunctive clause
2	While he was sitting alone in his cool roof chamber וְהוּא־יֹשֵׁב בַּעֲלִיַּת הַמְּקֵרָה אֲשֶׁר־לוֹ	Circumstantial disjunctive clause
3	And Ehud said, "I have a message from God for you." וַיֹּאמֶר אֵהוּד דְּבַר־אֱלֹהִים לִי אֵלֶיךָ	Consecutive *wayyiqtol* clause
4	And he arose from his seat וַיָּקָם מֵעַל הַכִּסֵּא	Consecutive *wayyiqtol* clause
5 (3:21)	And Ehud stretched out his left hand וַיִּשְׁלַח אֵהוּד אֶת־יַד שְׂמֹאלוֹ	Consecutive *wayyiqtol* clause
6	Took sword from his right thigh וַיִּקַּח אֶת־הַחֶרֶב מֵעַל יֶרֶךְ יְמִינוֹ	Consecutive *wayyiqtol* clause
7	And thrust it into his belly וַיִּתְקָעֶהָ בְּבִטְנוֹ	Consecutive *wayyiqtol* clause
8 (3:22)	The handle also went in after the blade וַיָּבֹא גַם־הַנִּצָּב אַחַר הַלַּהַב	Consecutive *wayyiqtol* clause
9	And the fat closed over the blade וַיִּסְגֹּר הַחֵלֶב בְּעַד הַלַּהַב	Consecutive *wayyiqtol* clause

procedural discourse. But even granting N + *qatal* forms as a secondary storyline and some uses of *weqatal* in which the *waw* is conjunctive, we still are left with a stubborn residue of *weqatal* forms in narrative that do not seem to fit any of these functions. My suggestion is this: an isolated *weqatal* in the narrative framework marks a climactic or at least a pivotal event" (Longacre, "*Weqatal* Forms in Biblical Hebrew Prose," 71. Robert B. Chisholm recognizes this function of the *weqatal* form when he writes, "Sometimes the *waw* + perfect construction formally marks the end of a scene or the final action in a series of events" (Chisholm, *From Exegesis to Exposition*, 132).

143. This example comes from Longacre's discussion. See Longacre, "Weqatal Forms in Biblical Hebrew Prose," 71–72.

Judges 3:20–23[143]		
Clause	**Text and NASB Translation**	**Syntax**
10	For he did not draw the sword out of his belly כִּי לֹא שָׁלַף הַחֶרֶב מִבִּטְנוֹ	Explanatory noun clause
11	And the refuse came out וַיֵּצֵא הַפַּרְשְׁדֹנָה	Consecutive *wayyiqtol* clause
12 (3:23)	Then Ehud went out into the vestibule וַיֵּצֵא אֵהוּד הַמִּסְדְּרוֹנָה	Consecutive *wayyiqtol* clause
13	And shut the roof chamber behind him וַיִּסְגֹּר דַּלְתוֹת הָעֲלִיָּה בַּעֲדוֹ	Consecutive *wayyiqtol* clause
14	And locked the door וְנָעָל	Final *weqatal* clause

In this passage, the final *weqatal* form cannot be parenthetical or supplemental to the sequence of events in the preceding narrative but must relay the final event in a series of consecutive actions. This example may indicate that Longacre overstated his case when he called each isolated occurrence a climactic or pivotal event—since locking a door would not seem to be climactic or pivotal—yet it does illustrate the consecutive, non-disjunctive, nature of such isolated *weqatal* forms.

In 1 Kgs 20:1–21, the author narrates the defeat of the Syrians and Ben-hadad by Israel. While the narrative of this defeat begins in 20:1, the conclusion to the account is relayed in 20:21:

1 Kings 20:21[144]		
Clause	**Text and NASB Translation**	**Syntax**
1	And the king of Israel went out וַיֵּצֵא מֶלֶךְ יִשְׂרָאֵל	Consecutive *wayyiqtol* clause
2	And he struck the horses and chariots וַיַּךְ אֶת־הַסּוּס וְאֶת־הָרָכֶב	Consecutive *wayyiqtol* clause
3	And killed the Arameans with a great slaughter וְהִכָּה בַאֲרָם מַכָּה גְדוֹלָה	Final *weqatal* clause

Here again, the isolated use of the *weqatal* form at the end of the sequence cannot be understood as parenthetical to the preceding *wayyiqtol*

---

144. This example comes from Longacre's discussion. Longacre, "Weqatal Forms in Biblical Hebrew Prose," 72–73.

clauses but most reasonably reveals the final, climactic result to end the narrative of Israel's war with Syria.

Longacre's observation is consistent with normal Hebrew grammar which uses a *waw* + a nonverb to introduce disjunctive clauses and rarely does so with finite verbs. As Allen Ross observed, "The disjunctive clause is signaled by *wāw* + a word other than a finite verb at the beginning of the clause. Such a clause may be introduced by *wāw* + noun, pronoun, participle, *or (rarely) a verbal form that breaks the consecutive narrative sequence*."[145] However, rare disjunctive uses of isolated *weqatal* forms do exist (e.g., 2 Sam 16:5), and Longacre would do well to acknowledge such occurrences. Yet, the presence of such rare uses should not cloud the interpretive waters when the more common use makes good sense in a passage.

When one analyzes the syntactical structure of Gen 15:1–6 in light of Longacre's observations, one discovers that the author has used an isolated *weqatal* form in 15:6 to conclude Abram's first dialogue with the Lord. The structure of the dialogic unit is as follows:

---

145. Ross, *Introducing Biblical Hebrew*, 156. Emphasis mine. As Robert Chisholm notes, *weqatal* forms can be used to introduce a new narrative or shift the focus of a narrative scene (e.g., 2 Sam 16:5). See Chisholm, *From Exegesis to Exposition*, 129.

Gen 15:1–6		
Verse	**Text and NASB Translation**	**Syntax**
15:1	After these things the word of the Lord came to Abram in a vision, saying, "Do not fear, Abram, I am a shield to you; Your reward shall be very great." אַחַר הַדְּבָרִים הָאֵלֶּה הָיָה דְבַר־יְהוָה אֶל־אַבְרָם בַּמַּחֲזֶה לֵאמֹר אַל־תִּירָא אַבְרָם אָנֹכִי מָגֵן לָךְ שְׂכָרְךָ הַרְבֵּה מְאֹד	Introductory disjunctive clause
15:2	And Abram said, "O Lord God, what wilt Thou give me since I am childless, and the heir of my house is Eliezer of Damascus?" וַיֹּאמֶר אַבְרָם אֲדֹנָי יֱהוִה מַה־תִּתֶּן־לִי וְאָנֹכִי הוֹלֵךְ עֲרִירִי וּבֶן־ מֶשֶׁק בֵּיתִי הוּא דַּמֶּשֶׂק אֱלִיעֶזֶר	Consecutive *wayyiqtol* clause
15:3	And Abram said, "Since Thou hast given no offspring to me, one born in my house is my heir." וַיֹּאמֶר אַבְרָם הֵן לִי לֹא נָתַתָּה זָרַע וְהִנֵּה בֶן־בֵּיתִי יוֹרֵשׁ אֹתִי	Consecutive *wayyiqtol* clause
15:4	Then behold, the word of the Lord came to him, saying, "This man will not be your heir, but one who shall come forth from your own body, he shall be your heir." וְהִנֵּה דְבַר־יְהוָה אֵלָיו לֵאמֹר לֹא יִירָשְׁךָ זֶה כִּי־אִם אֲשֶׁר יֵצֵא מִמֵּעֶיךָ הוּא יִירָשֶׁךָ	Deictic disjunctive clause
15:5a	And He took him outside and said, "Now look toward the heavens, and count the stars, if you are able to count them." וַיּוֹצֵא אֹתוֹ הַחוּצָה וַיֹּאמֶר הַבֶּט־נָא הַשָּׁמַיְמָה וּסְפֹר הַכּוֹכָבִים אִם־תּוּכַל לִסְפֹּר אֹתָם	Consecutive *wayyiqtol* clause
15:5b	And He said to him, "So shall your descendants be." וַיֹּאמֶר לוֹ כֹּה יִהְיֶה זַרְעֶךָ	Consecutive *wayyiqtol* clause
15:6a	Then he believed in the Lord וְהֶאֱמִן בַּיהוָה	Climactic *weqatal clause*
15:6b	And He reckoned it to him as righteousness וַיַּחְשְׁבֶהָ לּוֹ צְדָקָה	Consecutive *wayyiqtol* clause

Longacre's assertion related to the isolated uses of *weqatal* forms in Hebrew narrative fits the structure of Gen 15:1–6 well and holds significant implications for the soteriology of the passage.[146] In response to the word of the Lord concerning his divine protection and reward for Abram (15:1), Abram revealed a lack of trust in God's provision of a natural heir through

---

146. Reasons for choosing this proposed reading of Gen 15:1–6 will be provided at the end of this section.

whom the obligations of God would be fulfilled (12:2–3, 7). "And Abram said, 'O Lord God, what wilt Thou give me, since I am childless, and the heir of my house is Eliezer of Damascus?' And Abram said, 'Since Thou hast given no offspring to me, one born in my house is my heir'" (15:2–3).[147] In the absence of a son, Abram would be forced to preserve his own inheritance by appointing Eliezer as his heir, a man to whom he had no biological relationship (15:2–3). However, it was not the Lord's intent to bless the nations of the earth through Eliezer but through *a natural offspring* of Abram. This *principle promise* formed the ultimate goal of the promissory partnership between God and his chosen steward (12:3). Therefore, God clarified his original intent to Abram.[148] "This man will not be your heir; but one who shall come forth from your own body, he shall be your heir" (15:4).[149] God affirmed that Abram's *heir* would be *a natural, male offspring* through whom the *principle promise* of worldwide blessing would continue and ultimately be fulfilled (12:3; 15:4). The scope of this original promise anticipated an heir unlike any other. Although Abram and his immediate offspring mediated blessing in their lives, they did not mediate blessing to all nations of the earth (e.g., 14:1–24; 20:17–18; 30:27; 39:2–6; 41:46–56). As the history of Israel unfolded, even the nation Abram would sire did not fulfill the scope of this anticipated blessing. In the progress of revelation, Paul would refer to this promise as the "gospel" fulfilled in Jesus (Gal 3:7–9). Only through him, Abram's promised heir, would all nations of the earth be blessed as they received and responded to the message of Messiah.

147. This translation has been taken from the NASB.

148. Although a commitment to provide Abram the seed was part of God's original intent (Gen 12:3; 12:7; cf. Gal 3:16), God had not clarified the sense in which the seed promise of 12:3 and 12:7 should be understood to Abram in his first revelation. By "seed," did God mean one or many? The semantic range of the word made both meanings possible. The idea of corporate solidarity, as Waltke suggests provides no solution to this dilemma because in this instance it would require that the word "seed" possess two disparate meanings. See Waltke and Yu, *Old Testament Theology*, 321 25. Something cannot be both "a" and not "a" at the same time and in the same way. In other words, the author's use of "seed" in 12:7—or elsewhere for that matter—cannot mean both a singular seed and not singular seed at the same time. In the book of Isaiah, the idea of corporate solidarity is established by relating words, each with an individual meaning, to create such a relationship. "You are my servant, Israel, in whom I will show My Glory" (Isa 49:3). The relationship between the seed of 12:7 and the promise of a seed-nation (12:2; 13:14–16) is revealed when God clarifies his intent to Abram in the first dialogue of Gen 15 (15:1–6). Here he reveals that Abram's seed-heir will be one (12:7; 15:3–4; cf. Gal 3:16), while the seed-nation will include many (12:2; 13:14–16; 15:5).

149. This translation has been taken from the NASB.

Having clarified the nature of Abram's heir, God explained that the "nation" the he had promised would include a *natural posterity* as numerous as the stars in the sky (Gen 15:5). It is at this point that the author used the *weqatal* form to highlight the climactic result of this dialogue (15:6), a result that provided resolution to the conflict between Abram and the Lord—Abram believed what the Lord had said, and the Lord counted his faith as righteousness. Only after Abram believed in God's provision of an heir—a natural male descendant through whom the nations of the earth would be blessed—did the Lord accept his faith as righteousness.[150] The use of the *weqatal* form marked this content as the basis of Abram's justifying faith and helps make the case that he had not believed this promise prior to chapter 15.[151] Although Abram did not know that the promised heir would be Jesus, in his day he knew him as the heir that God would provide. In this sense, Abram believed the gospel at the level of revelation given in his day. Paul would later affirm and clarify this truth when he recognized Jesus of Nazareth to be the promised seed and heir through whom the nations would be blessed, that is, justified through faith in him (Gal 3:8). Those who would posit that Abram had already believed in the seed prior to 15:6 must resort to a rare use of the *weqatal* form that seems unjustified since its normal use makes good sense in the passage. On a broader, literary level, Abram's faith in the Lord's provision of a future heir connected his faith to the overall expectation of a coming seed in Genesis, an expectation that began as early as Gen 3:15.[152]

---

150. That Abram was justified in 15:6 does not mean that he had reached maturity in faith but simply that the content of his faith was now sufficient for his justification. As the patriarchal narrative continues, it becomes clear that Abram's life of faith was still a work in progress. Although he believed that the heir would be his own descendant (15:6), he attempts to produce this heir through Hagar (Gen 16:1–4). Even after God clarified that this heir would be born through Sarah (17:15–17), he lies to Abimelech and admits to a habit of lying (20:1–14). Only in Gen 22 does the patriarch finally demonstrate a maturity previously unexhibited.

151. One might rightly ask whether belief in numerous posterity is also essential content as it also formed part of the content of God's revelation to Abram in 15:4–5. In response, it must be noted that the subject of the dialogue, as indicated by Abram's complaint (15:2–3), is God's provision of an heir. As this heir is the locus of Abram's complaint, it must also be the primary locus of his faith. The promise of numerous posterity is added to the promise of an heir, but it is not the primary basis for Abraham's conflict with the Lord.

152. This broader literary connection is not meant to suggest that Abram already knew of Gen 3:15. While the author connects history literarily so the reader can make broader connections, it is difficult to say with certainty how much Abram knew of this prior history.

As promise, the illocutionary commitments of God obligated him to provide Abram with an immediate heir to whom the covenant promises might pass. Yet, God had not revealed when the ultimate fulfillment of his commitments to Abram would come to pass. If delayed, the illocutionary commitments of God obligated him to provide a lineage of heirs through whom the promises might stay alive until the ultimate heir in the plan of God was revealed in history.

The second dialogue (12:7–21) provided Abram further confirmation of God's previous promise. Now that God had confirmed his promise to provide Abram an heir and descendants, would God also confirm his promise to give them the land (12:7; 13:14–16; 15:7)? The covenant ratification ceremony in 15:7–21 provided Abram the assurance he needed.[153]

While the current study cannot prove that the proposed reading is the only possible reading of the text, one can defend its legitimacy as a valid reading. First, the proposed reading of Gen 15:6 does not have to resort to a rare use of a verbal disjunctive clause as do those who propose the disjunctive nature 15:6. Since the more common consecutive nature of the proposed use of the *weqatal* form makes good sense of the passage, it does not seem necessary to resort to a rare use of the form. Second, as Longacre has demonstrated, the use of an isolated *weqatal* form to indicate a climactic event in Hebrew narrative can be attested elsewhere in the Old Testament. Third, in a dialogue that begins with Abram questioning God's provision of a natural heir (15:2–3), one would expect the narrative to resolve this tension after God affirmed his future provision of an heir for Abram (15:3–4). The proposed use of the *weqatal* form provides this direct resolution.

ABRAM'S FAITH AND HEBREWS 11:8

If it is true that use of the *weqatal* form in 15:6 is intended to reveal the climactic result of Abram's first dialogue with the Lord (15:1–6), then a few important observations must be made. First, the *weqatal* form must function as a temporal marker for Abram's justification. Second, it implies that saving faith is to be measured by both its object (God) and content (faith in Messiah). Therefore, it seems that it is possible to have faith in God without believing all that God has revealed. While God had revealed

---

153. It is important to observe that the covenant ceremony is given in response to Abram's question/request (15:7–8). This ceremony did not begin God's obligation to give Abram and his descendants the land, for God had already committed himself to do this in promise (12:7; 13:14–16; 15:7). Rather, the covenant ceremony provided Abram the assurance he needed in his walk of faith before the Lord.

that he would make Abram into a great nation (12:2) and give the land to his offspring (12:7; 13:14–16)—promises that implied an heir and natural posterity—Abram's dialogue with God in 15:1–3 revealed that he had not yet come to trust in this aspect of God's provision, as the climactic use of the *weqatal* form in 15:6 would require. However, this did not mean that Abram's faith in God began at this point. Abram's migration to the land (12:5) and worship of God (12:8) are sufficient to reveal that he did.[154] The early Abrahamic narratives (12–15) reveal a development in the content of Abram's faith. While Abram believed in God (the object of faith) in Gen 12, he did not trust that God would give him an heir (the content of faith) until Gen 15. When both the required object and content of faith were present, he was justified before God (15:6).

While the clarity of the New Testament should not be read back into the Old Testament Scriptures, the New Testament does provide a terminus that must be consistent with Old Testament revelation. Any interpretation of the Old Testament found to be inconsistent with its New Testament witness is invalid and must be reevaluated. In Heb 11:8, the author claims that Abraham's belief in God began when he was called by the Lord while in Mesopotamia. "By faith Abraham, when he was called, obeyed by going out to a place which he was to receive for an inheritance; and he went out, not knowing where he was going." In the opening verse of Heb 11 (11:1) the author explains that faith provides the assurance of things hoped for even if those things do not match the reality of one's current circumstances. "Now

154. That Abram "called upon the name of the Lord" in 12:8 after migrating to a location between Bethel and Ai, connects Abram to the godly line begun through Seth (4:26). This worship of God did not occur immediately after God's revelation (12:7)—as if it were an immediate response to God's revelation—but as a first order of business after arriving at his destination (cf. 13:4). This worship seems to necessitate that Abram possessed faith in God but would not seem to require that he had yet understood all that God had revealed. In 4:26 the phrase is used to describe men's worship of God and is connected with the godly line. The use of the phrase in the Pentateuch and, more broadly, in the Hebrew Bible make it difficult to suggest that the presence of this phrase necessarily implies a specific content of faith. In Exod 34:5, the phrase is used to describe Moses's worship of God following the second giving of the Ten Commandments. In Ps 116, the phrase is used to describe a request (Ps 116:4) and praise (116:13, 17). In 1 Kgs 18:24, the phrase is used of the petitions offered by both Elijah to Yahweh and Ahab to Baal to send fire to consume their offerings. Observing the use of the phrase in the Pentateuch, Allen Ross rightly notes that it is important to recognize that it is the name of Yahweh which is the focus of one's call and that the word "name" often refers to characteristics or attributes (cf. Isa 9:6). See Ross, *Creation and Blessing*, 169. Applying this to his understanding of the phrase in 4:26 he writes, "The idea of this line is that people began to make proclamation about the nature of the Lord ('began to make proclamation of the Lord by name')." See Ross, *Creation and Blessing*, 169. There seems to be no reason to go beyond this basic meaning when the phrase is used in the Abraham narrative.

faith is the assurance of *things* hoped for, the conviction of things not seen."[155] He goes on to say that such faith characterized the lives of Old Testament saints and obtained for them a good testimony (11:2). This introduction creates the points of emphasis the reader is to focus on as the author discusses various examples from the Old Testament. The emphasis, then, is not on *content* but on the *assurance* and *conviction* that comes through a persevering faith. In the development of the argument, the faith of these Old Testament saints is applied to the readers of Hebrews. Just as faith enabled saints in the Old Testament to gain assurance of the things for which they hoped, the readers of Hebrews gain assurance through their faith in Jesus (12:1–3). Additionally, the variety seen in the hopes of these Old Testament saints as revealed by the author of Hebrews makes it difficult to suggest that the point of the passage focuses on a common content.

In Heb 11:8, the author claims that Abraham believed God when he was called by the Lord in Mesopotamia. Because of this faith, Abraham obeyed God and traveled to the land that God would show him, even though he did not know the land where he was going. That his faith and subsequent obedience did not occur apart from the Lord's work in his life is confirmed by Stephen, who revealed that it was the glory of God shown to Abraham to which he responded, and it was the leading of God that ultimately brought him to the land (Acts 7:2–5).[156] The affirmation of Abraham's faith in Gen 12 by the author of Hebrews need not contradict the proposed reading of the Abraham narrative, for the current study has affirmed that Abraham did possess genuine faith in God at this point. As one who believed in Messiah (15:6), the author of Hebrews could use the scope of Abraham's life of faith in his relationship with God to provide an encouragement and exhortation to his audience who he hoped will follow Abraham's example in their own lives of faith.

CONCLUSION

Using the genre of narrative history, the author of Genesis developed the expectation of a coming male descendant of Eve who would be God's agent of judgment on the serpent (Gen 3:15; cf. Num 24:17). The performative

---

155. The translations for Heb 11:1 and 11:8 have been taken from the NASB.

156. Regarding this work of God in Abraham's life, J. Dwight Pentecost writes, "Stephen tells us that the God of glory appeared to Abraham when he was dwelling in his home land (Acts 7:2). The promises God gave were not themselves sufficient to move Abraham to begin a long journey when he did not know where he was going; but the revelation of glory that belonged to the God who gave promises was sufficient to bring Abraham to faith in Him" (Pentecost, *Faith That Endures*, 180–81).

nature of God's speech act in Gen 3:15 obligated God to provide Eve with this coming seed. Historically, God's illocutionary commitment provided Adam and Eve the lens through which to exegete history. Literarily, these divine commitments provide the lens through which the reader must interpret the narrative to follow. The lineage of this individual is traced from Adam through Seth (Gen 5:1–32), Shem (11:10–26), Abraham (11:31; 15:4) to a coming ruler out of Judah (49:10) through Perez (38:29; 46:12; cf. Ruth 4:18–22; Ps 72:17). Although none of the individuals in Genesis accomplished God's word of judgment on the serpent, the continued provision of offspring to Eve existed as a testimony to God's commitment to bring about the seed as he had promised.

While God had revealed that this coming seed would be his agent of judgment, God revealed that this the coming seed would also be an agent of blessing through a partnership with Abram. In a series of performative speech acts (Gen 12:1–3, 7), God obligated himself to accomplish a *principal promise* in his governance of history. Through Abram, God committed himself to bless all the nations of the earth (12:3c). Abram's response to the illocutionary commitments of God evidenced an immature faith as he exhibited both *intended* (12:5–6; 7) and *unintended perlocutions* (11:31; 12:10–20; 13:1–12) in his early response to the revelation of God. However, in his dialogue with God in Gen 15:1–3, Abram revealed that despite God's promises that he would make him into a great nation (12:2) and give the land to his offspring (12:7; 13:14–15)—promises that implied an heir and natural posterity—Abram had not yet trusted that God would indeed provide him with an heir and therefore had not yet accepted the means by which God intended to bless the nations of the earth. It was not God's intention to bless humanity through Abram's servant but through a natural heir of Abram (12:4). This future heir would be a *male descendant* that God would provide for Abram.

To highlight Abram's response to this assurance from God as the climactic event in the dialogue (15:1–6), the author shifted from the use of the *wayyiqtol* form to the *weqatal* form. In response to God's assurance, Abram believed in the Lord's word, and he reckoned his faith to him as righteousness (15:6). While the *object* of Abram's faith was God—and had been all along—the *content* of his faith now included the belief that his future heir would be *a natural male descendant* through whom God would bless the nations of the earth. Although at the time of their dialogue, the provision of this heir remained unfulfilled, Abram experienced a part of his blessing from the Lord. In response to his faith, God gifted Abram a declaration of righteousness. The blessing which Abram through his heir was to mediate was the very blessing which he himself received from the Lord.

4

Paul's Use of the Abraham
Story in Romans 4:1–25

INTRODUCTION

THE APOSTLE PAUL WROTE the book of Romans to address a problem that had arisen in the church in Rome with regard to his gospel and ministry. Paul's failure to visit the believers in Rome had caused some in that community to accuse him of avoiding the church out of shame in the gospel he preached (Rom 1:10–16; 15:22–25). Paul had preached that justification by grace through faith in the person and work of Jesus Christ was equally available to both Jew and gentile apart from works of the Law or Israelite ritual (3:24; 4:10–12). This gospel message formed the theological basis of Paul's ministry in his mission to the gentiles (1:5) and, in the book of Romans, was an essential component in his missional purpose to the believers in Rome with whom he had not yet had a personal ministry. Although Jews and gentiles could experience unity through this gospel, division had arisen between these two factions (11:13–36; 14–15).

In the gospel, Jews and gentiles were co-heirs of salvation. Neither the Law nor circumcision provided the Jew with any superior standing in the sight of God. For the Jew, Paul's gospel required a proper understanding of the role that the Law and circumcision played in Israel's history (2:17; 4:10–12; 4:1). Since neither the works of the Law or circumcision were salvific acts, the gentile believer was under no obligation to pursue righteousness through these means to attain a right standing before God. When properly understood, the role of the Law and circumcision supported Paul's gospel rather than opposed it, as he would go on to explain. The avoidance of God's wrath through justification (1:18) and unity in the body (15:7; 16:16) could only come by grace through faith in Jesus Christ.[1]

To these Jewish believers, Paul's gospel sounded like a new teaching, that is, a gospel different from what the Old Testament anticipated. It is for this reason that some believers in Rome assumed Paul to be ashamed of the message he preached (Rom 1:10–16; 15:22–25). In order to convince them that the gospel he preached was the same gospel that the Old Testament foresaw, Paul needed to demonstrate that the method of salvation by which Old Testament saints were justified was no different than the gospel he now proclaimed in Jesus. Because it was Paul's gospel that accurately represented the Scriptures, it was his gospel in which the believers in Rome needed to persevere.

In Rom 3:21–22, Paul announced that the gospel he preached, justification by grace through faith in Jesus, was the same gospel that the Law and the prophets had borne witness (cf. 1:2–4). "But now apart from the Law the righteousness of God has been manifested, being witnessed by the Law and the prophets, *even the righteousness of God through faith in Jesus Christ for all who believe*, for there is no distinction."[2] However, this announcement itself raised a series of important questions. How could the Law and prophets bear witness to a gospel including Jesus before his revelation at the advent? Did the Old Testament really preach a gospel through faith apart from circumcision and the Law? To answer these questions, Paul turned to the life of Abraham in Rom 4 to show that justification in God's one plan of salvation had always been by grace through faith in Messiah. The method of Abraham's justification made him the father of two distinct peoples in the one family of God, believing Jews and believing gentiles. Therefore, unity between Jews and gentiles in the church needed to reflect the unity of these two groups in the gospel.

The truthfulness of Paul's gospel was dependent on a real, not imagined or fabricated, continuity with the Old Testament's witness. Paul's argument, therefore, could not transform the meaning of Old Testament revelation, for to do so would be to undermine the credibility of the very thing he attempted to prove. Rather, to convince his readers that the Law and prophets bore witness to the gospel he preached, he had to show them

---

1. A couple of secondary purposes of the epistle are worth noting. Paul wanted to assure the believers in Rome of his future visit and desire to have a mutually beneficial ministry (Rom 15:22–27). He also hoped to attain help for Phoebe who was traveling to Rome (16:1–2). See Allman, *Accept One Another*, 1–6.

2. This translation is taken from the NASB. Emphasis mine.

that it did. The expectation, then, is that Paul's exposition of Abraham's life in the book of Genesis elicits a meaning capable of being shared through the divinely inspired words of Scripture in the original context rather than through *Midrash*, *Pesher*, or other methods which could be used to generate meaning from the Old Testament text.

THE NEW PERSPECTIVE ON ROM 4:1–25

Before the present study can begin to develop the thesis of this study in Paul's use of the Abraham story, it is important to frame the current discussion in terms of broader debate surrounding Pauline soteriology in general. While an exhaustive study of the current debate would take the discussion far beyond the scope of the present work, it is, nevertheless, important to acknowledge the major contributors to this aspect of Pauline theology and their understanding of Rom 4 in particular.

The New Perspective on Paul[3]

Krister Stendahl (1921–2008)

Although he preceded the movement, Krister Stendahl's ideas laid the foundations for what would become known as the New Perspective on Paul. Writing in the mid-twentieth century, Stendahl questioned the way the apostle Paul's doctrine of justification had been understood within Western Christianity. For him, Western soteriology had been overly influenced by "late medieval piety"[4] and, therefore, did not represent the doctrine as taught by Paul in his original context. Stendahl believed that this misreading began with Augustine and, through Augustine, had affected Luther's understanding so as to distort the Protestant doctrine of justification in its interpretation of Pauline soteriology. He summarized his new perspective when he wrote,

> Augustine, who has perhaps rightly been called the first truly
> Western man, was the first person in Antiquity or in Christi-
> anity to write something so self-centered as his own spiritual

---

3. For a thorough overview of the development of the New Perspective, see Erickson, "Faith Credited as Righteousness," 1–43.

4. Here he writes, "The Reformers' interpretation of Paul rests on an analogism when Pauline statements about faith and works, law and gospel, Jews and Gentiles are read in the framework of late medieval piety" (Stendahl, "Apostle Paul and the Introspective Conscience of the West," 205–6).

autobiography, his *Confessions*. It was he who applied Paul's doctrine of justification to the problem of the introspective conscience, to the question: "On what basis does a person find salvation?" And with Augustine, Western Christianity with its stress on introspective achievements started . . . Man turned in on himself, infatuated and absorbed by the question not of when God will send deliverance in the history of salvation, but how God is working in the innermost individual soul . . . And one of those who suffered most was Martin Luther, who—not by accident—was an Augustinian. In the grapplings of his introspective conscience, he picked up Paul and found in him God's answer to his problem, the problem of the West, and the problem of the late medieval piety of the West . . . The introspective conscience is a Western development and a Western plague.[5]

In Stendahl's mind, the traditional understanding of justification had been distorted from a truly Pauline doctrine into a western invention designed to fit the needs of Western Christianity's emphasis on introspective consciousness.

E. P. Sanders (1937–2022)

In a formal sense, the New Perspective on Paul, as a movement, began with E. P. Sanders who built on the foundations laid by Krister Stendahl.[6] In perhaps his most significant work, *Paul and Palestinian Judaism*, Sanders attempted to place Pauline soteriology in a second temple *Sitz im Leben* in order to understand "the basic relationship between Paul's religion and the forms of religion reflected in Palestinian Jewish literature."[7] The result of this method of interpreting Paul led to perhaps his most significant contribution, the formulation of "covenantal nomism." In this work, Sanders defined the essential elements of covenantal nomism in second temple Judaism when he wrote,

5. Stendahl, *Paul Among Jews and Gentiles and Other Essays*, 16–17. Emphasis his.

6. Concerning the significance of E. P. Sanders to the formation of the New Perspective on Paul, Cornelis P. Venema writes, "Though various forerunners contributed to the emergence of a new perspective on Paul, the most influential and pivotal is undoubtedly E. P. Sanders" (Venema, *Gospel of Free Acceptance in Christ*, 8). Likewise, Guy P. Waters writes, "His [Sander's] genius consists in synthesizing many diverse strands of Pauline anterpretation that have preceded him, and in presenting a case grounded on a fresh reading of the primary sources pertinent to ancient Judaism" (Waters, *Justification and the New Perspective on Paul*, 35).

7. Sanders, *Paul and Palestinian Judaism*, 19. See also Erickson, "Faith Credited as Righteousness," 16.

> The 'pattern' or 'structure' of covenantal nomism is this: (1) God
> has chosen Israel and (2) given the law. The law implies both (3)
> God's promise to maintain the election and (4) the requirement
> to obey. (5) God rewards obedience and punishes transgression.
> (6) The law provides for means of atonement, and atonement
> results in (7) maintenance or re-establishment of the covenantal
> relationship. (8) All those who are maintained in the covenant
> by obedience, atonement and God's mercy belong to the group
> which will be saved. An important interpretation of the first and
> last points is that election and ultimately salvation are consid-
> ered to be by God's mercy rather than human achievement.[8]

The most important theological modification in Sanders's soteriology
was the idea of the need to maintain the covenantal relationship through
the Law. Therefore, although he believed that salvation was ultimately a
gracious act of God, it was only experienced by those who maintained the
covenant relationship by the atonement provided through the Law.[9] In light
of this covenantal nomism, which he argued was present within Judaism
during the time of Paul, the student of Paul must understand his soteriology
within this historical context.

> [W]e must grant that there is a good deal to be said for the view
> that Christianity is a new covenant which, once established
> (though not established by a new exodus), does function some-
> what as does the old . . . Thus one can see already in Paul how it
> is that Christianity is going to become a new form of covenantal
> nomism, a covenantal religion which one enters by baptism,
> membership in which provides salvation, which has a specific
> set of commandments, obedience to which (or repentance for
> transgression of which) keeps one in the covenantal relation-
> ship, while repeated or heinous transgression removes one from
> membership.[10]

In Pauline soteriology, then, the doctrine of eternal security must be
discarded for, like the version present in Judaism during his time, only those
who remained in the covenant community would ultimately be saved.

8. Sanders, *Paul and Palestinian Judaism*, 422.

9. "[E]lection and salvation as such are not by works of law, although obedience is
the condition of remaining righteous" (Sanders, *Paul and Palestinian Judaism*, 423).

10. Sanders, *Paul and Palestinian Judaism*, 513.

James D. G. Dunn (1939–2020)

Building on works of those before him, James D. G. Dunn gave the ideas initiated by Krister Stendahl and developed by Sanders a name—the New Perspective on Paul.[11] Like Stendahl and Sanders before him, Dunn believed that Western Christianity had misunderstood the nature of Judaism during Paul's time and, therefore, the doctrine of salvation that Paul himself sought to preach. Criticizing the rigidly legalistic understanding of Judaism present in western Christianity, Dunn wrote,

> There can be no possibility of scholarship in the Christian tradition going back to the old portrayal of Judaism, either now or in the first century, as an arid, sterile and narrowly legalistic religion. Likewise there can surely be no going back to an interpretation of Paul's doctrine of justification which depends on sharp antitheses between Judaism and Christianity, between law and grace, between obedience and faith, and which both feeds on and perpetuates the shameful tradition of Christian anti-Judaism.[12]

While Dunn agreed with Sanders's basic conception of covenantal nomism, he believed that Sanders had not gone far enough in drawing out the implications that such a view had on understanding Pauline soteriology.[13] In an attempt to fill the gap left by Stendahl and Sanders, Dunn tried to pinpoint the precise problem in Jewish thought against which Paul wrote. In his understanding, the problem in Judaism was not the pursuit of self-righteousness through works of the Law as the reformers had imagined. Rather, the problem was an inflated sense of nationalism that had caused

11. Dunn was the first to use this name in connection to the development of the ideas begun by Krister Stendahl and developed by Sanders in an article written for the *Bulletin of the John Rylands Library*, although this article itself had been presented in the Manson Memorial Lecture delivered in 1982 at the University of Manchester and the Wilkinson Lectures at the Northern Baptist Theological Seminary. See Dunn, "New Perspective on Paul," 95–97.

12. Dunn, *New Perspective on Paul*, 96.

13. "The most surprising feature of Sanders's writing, however, is that he himself has failed to take the opportunity his own mold-breaking work offered. Instead of trying to explore how far Paul's theology could be explicated in relation to Judaism's 'covenantal nomism', he remained more impressed by the difference between Paul's pattern of religious thought and that of first-century Judaism. He quickly, too quickly in my view, concluded that Paul's religion could be understood only as a basically different system from that of his fellow Jews" (Dunn, *New Perspective on Paul*, 103).

Jews during Paul's time to exclude gentiles from participation in the covenant community.[14]

> The law thus became a basic expression of Israel's *distinctiveness* as the people specially chosen by (the one) God to be his people. In sociological terms the law functioned as an 'identity marker' and 'boundary', reinforcing Israel's sense of distinctiveness and distinguishing Israel from the surrounding nations . . . A natural and more or less inevitable converse of this sense of distinctiveness was the sense of *privilege*, precisely in being the nation specially chosen by the one God and favoured by gift of covenant and law. This comes out particularly clearly in writings which could not simply ignore and dismiss Gentiles as sinners, but which had to attempt some sort of apologetic for the claims of Israel in the face of a much more powerful Gentile world.[15]

Since the problem which Paul addressed was exclusive Jewish nationalism as opposed to self-righteous legalism, Paul's doctrine of justification—the solution to the problem—had to be modified accordingly. For Dunn, justification was not to be understood as a "once-for-all act of God" but rather the "beginning of the salvation process."[16] It was not, as the reformers would have had one believe, a legal declaration of righteousness but, rather, the simple acknowledgement that God had accepted someone into the community of faith.[17] Although God's righteousness continued without question, the issue was man's righteousness. As the believer persevered in righteousness (i.e., continued in obedience), God continued to justify him (i.e., accept him in the community of faith) until the final eschatological judgment. This mutuality in the ongoing relationship between the believer and God defined the sense in which the apostle Paul understood the term "righteousness." The believer remained righteous as he upheld his obligations, that is, continued in obedience. God was righteous as he fulfilled his covenant obligations. For this reason, Dunn believed that the righteousness of God "denotes God's fulfillment of the obligations he took upon himself in creating humankind and particularly in the calling of Abraham and the

14. "In a word, the primary answer [i.e. to the problem] seems to be not so much Jewish legalism as Jewish restrictiveness—the tendency in Judaism to restrict the covenant grace of God, covenant righteousness to Israel. This protest or reaction comes to clear expression repeatedly throughout the argument of Romans" (Dunn, *New Perspective on Paul*, 372).

15. Dunn, *New Perspective on Paul*, 146, 148. Emphasis his. See also Erickson, "Faith Credited as Righteousness," 18–20. Venema, *Gospel of Free Acceptance in Christ*, 109.

16. Dunn, *Theology of Paul the Apostle*, 386.

17. Dunn, *Theology of Paul the Apostle*, 385.

choosing of Israel to be his people."[18] It was, however, up to God to determine whether a violation of obedience necessitated the cessation of the relationship. It was on this point that one could clearly see the effects of covenantal nomism on Dunn's view of Pauline soteriology.

> But where the issue is more one of mutual obligation between partners in a relationship, there it is for the injured party to determine whether the relationship is to be ended because of the other's breach of faith or sustained despite it. It is the latter course which God in his grace follows in justifying the sinner.[19]

Because of the believer's need to preserve in his justified state, Dunn argued that the death of Christ should not be understood as a substitutionary death. Rather, it provided the believer an example of how one ought to live a life in obedience to God and, thereby, remain in a justified state before God.

> The charge of legal fiction also breaks down before our earlier finding that God's sentence of death on sin is carried through in the death of Christ. Were Paul's doctrine of atonement one of substitution (Jesus died and the sinner went scot-free) that would be more open to such a charge. But as we saw, Paul's teaching is of Christ's death as a representative death, the death of all, of sinful flesh. His gospel is not that the trusting sinner escapes death, but rather that they share in Christ's death. The cancer of sin in the human body is destroyed in the destruction of the cancerous flesh. This is the feature of the ongoing process of salvation to which we shall have to return.[20]

N. T. Wright (1948–Present)

In the history of the New Perspective, N. T. Wright was and is, perhaps, its most outspoken proponent. Although he found himself in large agreement with Sanders and Dunn in his own development of the New Perspective, Wright attempted to root the tenets of this rereading on an exegetical basis rather than on a broader religious schema as scholars before him had done.[21] As he reevaluated Paul, Wright believed that the reformation understanding of the gospel, the righteousness of God, the final judgment, and the nature

18. Dunn, *Theology of Paul the Apostle*, 342.
19. Dunn, *Theology of Paul the Apostle*, 385–86.
20. Dunn, *Theology of Paul the Apostle*, 386.
21. Wright, "New Perspective on Paul," 244–45.

of justification all needed to be refashioned to understand what Paul both thought and taught on these subjects.

> If we ask how it is that Israel has missed her vocation, Paul's answer is that she is guilty not of 'legalism' or 'works-righteousness' but of what I call 'national righteousness,' the belief that fleshly Jewish descent guarantees membership of God's true covenant people . . . Within this 'national righteousness,' the law functions not as a legalist's ladder but as a charter of national privilege . . . Over against this abuse of Israel's undoubted privileged status, Paul establishes, in his theology and in his missionary work, the true children of Abraham, the world-wide community of faith.[22]

In reexamining the nature of "the gospel" in Pauline thought, Wright argued that the traditional understanding of the gospel as a message on how to be saved was to miss Paul's own understanding. Based on his study of second temple Judaism and, in particular his reading of Josephus, Wright began to understand that Jewish thought during this time did not involve an interest in the how one was saved. Rather, this obsession was a later development that had little bearing on Jewish thinking at the time and, therefore, on Pauline thought in general.[23] Rather than a message concerning salvation, for Wright, the gospel was a person.

> My proposal is this. When Paul refers to "the gospel," he is not referring to a system of salvation, although certainly the gospel implies and contains this, nor even to the good news that there now is a way of salvation open to all but, rather, to the proclamation that the crucified Jesus of Nazareth has been raised from the dead and thereby demonstrated to be both Israel's Messiah and the world's true Lord. "The gospel" is not, "You can be saved, and here's how"; the gospel for Paul, is, "Jesus Christ is Lord."[24]

As a person rather than a method of salvation, the proclamation of the gospel was not to be viewed as an offer of salvation to the one who heard but "a royal summons to submission, to obedience, to allegiance . . ."[25]

Because the gospel was not, in its essence, a way to be saved, the notion that the sinner received God's righteousness through imputation at the moment of faith was, to Wright, an untenable position. Arguing against the

---

22. Wright, "Paul of History and the Apostle of Faith," 65.

23. Wright, *Justification*, 55–56.

24. Wright, "New Perspective on Paul," 248.

25. Wright, "New Perspective on Paul," 249.

position of the reformers, Wright believed that when Paul's conception of *dikaiosynē theou* was understood within a second temple *Sitz im Leben*, it became clear that God's righteousness referred to his covenant faithfulness.

> The main argument for taking *dikaiosynē theou* to denote an aspect of the character of God himself is the way in which Paul is summoning up a massive biblical and intertestamental theme, found not least in Isaiah 40–55, which is vital for him. God's *dikaiosynē*, God's *tsedaqah*, is the aspect of God's character because of which, despite Israel's infidelity and consequent banishment, God will remain true to the covenant with Abraham and rescue Israel nonetheless. This righteousness is a form of justice; God has bound himself to the covenant, or perhaps we should say that God's covenant is binding upon God, and through this covenant God has promised not only to save Israel but also thereby to renew creation itself.[26]

With his rejection of imputed righteousness, Wright believed that the Christian notion of the final judgment of believers needed to be reexamined accordingly. Rather than experiencing adjudication on the basis of Christ's righteousness imputed to the sinner, Wright believed that one's final adjudication would come on the basis of works.

> Paul, in company with mainstream Second Temple Judaism, affirms that God's final judgment will be in accordance with the entirety of a life led—in accordance, in other words, with works . . . He says this clearly and unambiguously in Romans 14:10–12 and 2 Corinthians 5:10. He affirms it in that terrifying passage about church builders in 1 Corinthians 3.[27]

If the believer was ultimately judged on the basis of works, to what then did the justification of the believer entail? In addressing justification, Wright emphasized that justification was what happened subsequent to joining the community of God's people and did not refer to the moment when a sinner was saved. In response to the preaching of the gospel, that is, the person of Jesus of Nazareth, a sinner experienced a "call" (cf., 1 Cor 1:26;

26. Wright, "New Perspective on Paul," 250.

27. Wright, "New Perspective on Paul," 253. It is important to note that Wright does not dismiss the security of the believer's salvation. He affirms that, although, ultimate adjudication will occur on the basis of works, God's justification—in his understanding of the term—assures the believer that he will pass this final adjudication. In response to John Piper's criticism, Wright says, "[I] agree that this sense of assurance is indeed offered by the doctrine of justification as Paul expounds it. But, as I argue in this book, Paul's way of doing it is not Piper's" (Wright, *Justification*, 11).

Gal 1:15) to which a positive response places him within the community of God's people. Justification, then, was a declaration by God that "a person is in the right."

> What, then, is this indication, this *dikaiōsis*? It is God's declaration that a person is in the right—that is, (a) that the person's sins have been forgiven and (b) that he or she is part of the single covenant family promised to Abraham . . . Paul, I believe, uses "vindication/justification" to denote God's declaration about someone, about (more specifically) the person who has been "called" in the sense described above. Vindication is not the same as call . . .We now discover that this declaration, this vindication, occurs twice. It occurs in the future, as we have seen, on the basis of the entire life a person has led in the power of the Spirit—that it occurs on the basis of "works" in Paul's redefined sense. And near the heart of Paul's theology, it occurs in the present *as an anticipation of that future verdict*, when someone, responding in believing obedience to the call of the gospel, believes that Jesus is Lord and that God raised him from the dead.[28]

The Function of Rom 4 in the New Perspective on Paul

Having outlined the New Perspective on Paul in its broad contours, it is important to address how this revision of Pauline theology has affected its interpretation of Rom 4.[29] Again, the treatment here cannot be exhaustive but exists simply as a general summary to set the development of the proposed thesis in terms of recent Pauline scholarship.

Sanders on Rom 4

While Sanders has not written any extensive commentary on the book of Romans, even a brief survey of his works reveals that Rom 3 and 4 play a pivotal role in his rereading of Pauline theology. Its importance is seen in the way that the passage has been misread by those who view Pauline soteriology according to the old paradigm. "It is this passage [Rom 3:27—4:25] which, perhaps more than any other, has served as the foundation stone for

28. Wright, "New Perspective on Paul," 260.

29. For a thorough summary on the New Perspective on Rom 4, see Visscher, *Romans 4 and the New Perspective on Paul.*

those who think that Paul opposed the Law because following it leads to pride."[30] In Paul's use of the Abraham story in Rom 4, Sanders believes that his New Perspective is vindicated because a close reading of Paul's argument demonstrates that the passage is intended to speak against the *privileged status* held by Jews to the exclusion of gentiles. As a result, Paul is not contrasting faith based righteousness with self-righteousness through the Law as previous interpreters have supposed.[31]

> The main lines of Paul's argument are thus clear. The continuation of 3:27 in vv. 29f. shows that the main point is that Jew and Gentile are to be included on the same basis, and similarly the use made of the Abraham story in 4:9–25 shows that Paul is primarily interested in the status of the Gentiles, in denying that those who are "of the law" (Jews) are privileged, and in asserting that God's righteousness in the present is on the same basis as in the past.[32]

Dunn on Rom 4

Like Sanders, Dunn believes that Paul's use of the Abraham story in Rom 4 aims to argue against the exclusive nationalism held by Jews in Paul's day. For Dunn, Paul's theology in Rom 3:28–29 lays the theological basis that frames the interpretation of Abraham in the chapter to follow.

> The unavoidable logic of 3.28–29 is that affirmation of justification by works is tantamount to saying "God is God of Jews only." "Works of the law" are what distinguish Jew from Gentile. To affirm justification by works of the law is to affirm that justification is for Jews only, is to require that Gentile believers take on the persona and practices of the Jewish people.[33]

As an outworking of 3:28–29, Dunn believes that Paul uses the Abraham story to illustrate that "works of the law," that is, an exclusive Jewish

30. Sanders, *Paul, the Law, and the Jewish People*, 32.

31. "We have concentrated thus far on the question of whether or not the objection to righteousness by the law in 3:27—4:25 is based on the supposed attitude of self-righteousness which obeying the law produces, since that is the argument which has come to the fore in recent scholarly discussion" (Sanders, *Paul, the Law, and the Jewish People*, 35).

32. Sanders, *Paul, the Law, and the Jewish People*, 34–35.

33. Dunn, *Theology of Paul the Apostle*, 364–65. See also Dunn, *Romans 1–8*, 187–93.

nationalism,[34] did not in fact prohibit gentiles from experiencing a relationship with God. In Rom 4, then, Paul is not attempting to argue against a view that salvation could be attained through a self-righteous understanding of the "works of the law" but rather attempts to break through Jewish nationalism that would exclude gentiles from joining the community of God.

> Paul picks up this theme [3:28–29] again at the beginning of Romans 4. "If Abraham was justified from works, he has something to boast about—but not before God" (4:2). The continued association of "boasting" and "works" indicates clearly that we are still in the train of thought which began at 3.27 . . . Once again it is clear that to remove "works of the law" from the equation was to remove the blockage which prevented the gospel from reaching out beyond the boundaries of Israel marked out by the law.[35]

Wright on Rom 4

Like Sanders and Dunn, Wright believes that Rom 3:27–31 provides the basic premise that Rom 4 illustrates. To understand Paul's point in Rom 3:27–31 is to understand the message of Paul's use of the Abraham story. In accordance with the New Perspective's reading of Paul, Wright understands Paul to be arguing against Jewish exclusivism rather than Jewish legalism. While he agrees with Augustine and Luther's emphasis on the free grace of God against self-righteous legalism, he believes that such a battle was reflective of Augustine's and Luther's days rather than the issue which Paul addresses.

> It is important to say that the battles of Augustine and Luther were not entirely mistaken. Paul's whole thought is characterized by the free grace of God, and any suggestion that humans, whether Jewish or Gentile, might somehow put God in their debt, might perhaps earn their good standing within God's people, would be anathema to him. This, however, is not the issue he was facing. Contemporary studies of first-century Judaism indicate that Paul's contemporaries did not think like Pelagius or Erasmus;

---

34. When Dunn refers to "works of the law," he intends to refer to the defining traits or boundaries (e.g., circumcision, food and purity laws, and the Sabbath) that gave Jews a sense of national solidarity, that is, the possession of membership in the covenant community. See Dunn, *Romans 1–8*, 158–60.

35. Dunn, *Theology of Paul the Apostle*, 364. See also Dunn, *Romans 1–8*, 198–241.

they were not bent on earning their justification, or their salvation, from scratch by performing the "works of the law."[36]

Because of this basic understanding, Wright believes that "Paul is doing something much more large-scale, much more intricately crafted, than merely 'stating a doctrine' in 3:21–31 and then 'offering a proof from scripture in chap. 4.'"[37]

> Once we recognize the main subject of the section (3:21—4:25) and its place within Paul's larger argument, we find that chapter 4 itself comes into its own. It is not simply, as it has so often been labeled, a "proof from scripture," or even an "example," of Paul's "thesis" of justification by faith in 3:21–31 . . . The chapter is, in fact, a full-dressed exposition of the covenant God made with Abraham in Genesis 15, showing at every point how God always intended and promised that the covenant family of Abraham would include Gentiles as well as Jews . . . The question Paul faces here is whether covenant membership means, after all, coming to belong to the physical family of Abraham (the question, of course, at stake in Galatians).[38]

Abraham's justification, then, in Gen 15:6 refers not to a legal declaration of Abraham's righteousness before God but, rather, his acceptance into covenant membership. Since this covenant membership was granted to Abraham prior to his circumcision, Paul argues that such covenant membership (i.e., justification) is open to gentiles as well as to Jews.[39]

Evaluation

While a thorough critique of the ideas espoused by the New Perspective on Paul cannot be accomplished here, a few general observations can be given to explain, in the first place, how these gifted thinkers have positively affected Pauline scholarship and, secondly, to provide a few criticisms that explain why this perspective will not be adopted in the development of the current thesis.[40]

36. Wright, "Letter to the Romans," 479.

37. Wright, "Letter to the Romans," 465.

38. Wright, "Letter to the Romans," 487. See also Wright, "Paul the Patriarch," 207–9. For a critique on Wright's heavy emphasis on Gen 15 as the background to Rom 4, see Lambrecht, "Romans 4: A Critique of N. T. Wright," 189–94.

39. Wright, *Justification*, 221.

40. For some good evaluations of the New Perspective on Paul, see Carson et al., *Justification and Variegated Nomism*; Westerholm, *Perspectives Old and New on Paul*; Venema, *Gospel of Free Acceptance in Christ*.

One of the positive contributions which the New Perspective on Paul has made comes through Wright's reemphasis on one's responsibility to subject his theology to the testimony of Scripture.[41] As much modern scholarship, particularly in the historical critical school, has elevated itself above Scripture, Wright's emphasis is a welcome reminder. The New Perspective has also been an advocate for the proper use of sources to illuminate the writings of the New Testament texts. As James Allman observes, "New Testament scholarship has too readily leveled Jewish material, making it all equally relevant for Paul's theology. As a result, scholars have used information from the Mishna (ca., AD 200) and even worse the Talmud (ca., AD 400) to help explain the issues addressed in, for example, Galatians and Romans."[42] Another positive contribution of the New Perspective is the clarity it has brought to the diversity of thought within Judaism during the time of the New Testament writings, though in the end it itself creates a new box within which it interprets Second Temple Judaism. The New Perspective has forced scholars—both those who agree and those who disagree with the movement—to grapple seriously with the different strains of thought found in Second Temple Judaism.

Despite these positive contributions, there are some significant criticisms of the movement that place its validity into question. The idea of covenantal nomism, specifically as advocated by Sanders, is held to be *the dominant thought* within the Judaism of Paul's day and, therefore, the proper lens through which to understand Pauline soteriology. In a real sense, it is the very heart of the New Perspective on Paul. However, as others have noted,[43] Sanders was selective in the use of sources and omitted relevant data that would have limited the prevalence of covenantal nomism to a *mere segment* of Jewish thought rather than propose it as the dominant view. More importantly, these omissions validated the notion that merit-based righteousness did in fact represent elements of Jewish thought during this period of time, an omission which lent credibility to the traditional, Reformation view of Paul. Peter T. O'Brien makes this important observation when he writes,

> Does obedience include a works-righteousness (as obviously is
> the case in the Tannaitic literature), even though there are also

41. Wright, "New Perspective on Paul," 244–45.

42. Allman, "Gaining Perspective on the New Perspective on Paul," 65. No other proponent of the New Perspective has been more helpful in this regard than E. P. Sanders. See Sanders, *Paul and Palestinian Judaism*, xii–xiii.

43. O'Brien, "Was Paul a Covenantal Nomist?," 264. For examples, see 4 Maccabees 6:28–29; *Apocalypse of Zephaniah* 3:5–9, 2 *Baruch* 85:1–2, 12–15; 1 *Enoch* 5:5–10; 47:1–4; 2 *Enoch* 41:1–2; 4 *Ezra* 7:88–99, 102–15; *Testament of Abraham* 7:8.

other strands? Does obedience in Sanders's view comprise what clearly appears to be a merit theology in 2 Enoch, 4 Ezra and 2 Baruch? And what are we to make of the apparently atoning deaths of the martyrs in 4 Maccabees? Are these part of the category of covenantal nomism "as an explanatory bulwark against all suggestions that some of this literature embraces works-righteousness and merit theology?" But it cannot achieve this end because covenantal nomism includes within its broad spectrum works-righteousness and merit theology.[44]

Therefore, although Sanders attempted to free Pauline scholarship from the presumption of the distorted readings of Augustine and the Reformation, in the end, he simply produced "an analysis that was as distortive of the sources as the ones he was overturning . . ."[45] Because of the overarching control which covenantal nomism has held over Paul's understanding of justification, the gospel, and final judgment, the credibility of these terms as used by proponents of the movement must be revisited in light of a more comprehensive view of Jewish thought.

PAUL'S USE OF THE ABRAHAM STORY IN ROM 4:1–25

The Function of Rom 4:1–25 in the Argument of Romans

From the outset of his epistle to the Romans, Paul claimed that the gospel of Jesus Christ, a gospel which he had received and of which he was a steward, was not a new gospel but, rather, a continuation of the same gospel of the seed which the Old Testament had anticipated (Rom 1:1–5; 3:21–22). It was to the stewardship of this gospel message—which God had promised beforehand through the prophets concerning Jesus the Davidic heir—that Paul had received his apostleship (1:1–3).[46] Although the righteousness of

---

44. O'Brien, "Was Paul a Covenantal Nomist?," 264. Allman notes that Sanders omitted Josephus from his model of covenantal nomism which demonstrates merit based righteousness in his discussion of Noah (*Legum Allegoriae* 3.77). See Allman, "Gaining Perspective on the New Perspective on Paul," 66. The Dead Sea Scrolls (1QS and 4QMMT) also provide evidence that such merit based theology existed with Judaism during the Second Temple period. For the text and translation of these texts, see García Martínez and Tigchelaar, *Dead Sea Scrolls Study Edition*, 68–98 and 790–803.

45. Carson, "Mystery and Fulfillment," 2:394.

46. "[T]he heart of the gospel is the Son of God as descended from David. Actually, there are two points in verse 3: his preexistence and his earthly existence. His preexistence is seen in that the Son 'came into being' (γενομένου–NIV, *was*) as a human. His earthly existence shows his royal messianic status . . . The idea goes back to 2 Sam 7:12–16, where David was promised an eternal throne. This led to the idea of a Davidic

God (δικαιοσύνη θεοῦ)[47] was, in the present dispensation, revealed in the gospel of this Jesus (1:17), the manifestation of this righteousness had already been made known in the Old Testament.[48] "But now apart from the Law the righteousness of God has been manifested, being witnessed by the Law and the prophets, even the righteousness of God through faith in Jesus Christ for all those who believe, for there is no distinction . . ." (3:21–22; NASB). If the righteousness required by the Law had always been achieved apart from the Law through faith in Jesus, then faith-obedience was how one fulfilled the requirements of the Law, not self-effort. This theological truth held profound implications for both Jews and gentiles alike. For the Jew, righteousness apart from the Law meant that the role of the Law in Judaism had to be reevaluated. Although the Law revealed God's standard of righteousness, it did not provide for such righteousness. Only faith in Jesus provided what the Law could not.[49] For the gentile, righteousness apart from the Law meant that such believers were under no obligation to become Jews to fulfill and to receive the righteousness the Law required. Like the

---

Messiah who would deliver the nation (Ps 89:3–4; Is 11:1; Jer 23:5–6; Ezek 34:23–24), an idea recognized both in Judaism (Psalms of Solomon 17–18; Qumran 1QM 11:1–8; 4QFlor 1:11–14) and in the early church (Mt 1:1–16; Mk 10:47; 12:35–37; Jn 7:42; 2 Tim 2:8)" (Osborne, *Romans*, 3).

47. The precise meaning of δικαιοσύνη θεοῦ has been the subject of some debate. For a good discussion surrounding the interpretive options of this phrase, see Moo, *Epistle to the Romans*, 81–86; O'Brien, "Justification in Paul and Some Crucial Issues of the Last Two Decades," 70–78; Williams, "The 'Righteousness of God' in Romans," 241–90. It is important to note that the phrase δικαιοσύνη θεοῦ is connected with εὐαγγέλιον and δύναμις θεοῦ (Rom 1:16), the message of salvation manifesting God's saving power, and πίστις (1:17), the means of salvation. Therefore, it is likely that δικαιοσύνη θεοῦ emphasizes both God's saving activity as well as the status given by God. See Käsemann, *Perspectives on Paul*, 76–77; Käsemann, *Commentary on Romans*, 23–30; Schrenk, "δικαιοσύνη," 202–10.

48. Regarding this revelation of God's righteousness, Everett Harrison writes, "The fact that in the gospel, a righteousness from God is revealed (1:17) could suggest that justification is a new thing, peculiar to the Christian era. To discover that it was already present in the OT serves to engender confidence in an ongoing purpose of God and in the basic unity of the Bible" (Harrison, "Romans," 47).

49. How did the Jews miss the clear Old Testament anticipation of Paul's gospel revealed in Jesus of Nazareth? In 2 Cor 3:14–16 Paul says that their eyes were veiled, prohibiting them from understanding what the Hebrew Scriptures foretold. As Leonhard Goppelt writes, "Diese Interpretation des Christus-geschehens vom Alten Testament her ist allerdings nicht rational zu erechnen; sie kann immer nur, wenn 'die Decke weggenommen wird' (2 Kor. iii. 14–16), von Christus her und auf Christus hin entwickelt werden." ["This interpretation of the Christ event from the Old Testament cannot be calculated rationally; it can only ever be developed from Christ and towards Christ when "the veil is removed" (2 Cor. iii. 14-16)."] See Goppelt, "Paulus und die Heilsgeschichte," 33.

Jews, such righteousness was available apart from the Law. By placing faith in Jesus Christ, a gentile could receive the righteousness required by the Law as a gentile.

If what Paul preached was true, then to pursue the righteousness of the Law through self-effort was to abandon God's gracious provision for such righteousness in the person of Christ and to pursue righteousness in a manner inconsistent with the Old Testament Scripture. Those who foolishly ignored Paul's gospel—Jew or gentile—would then, most certainly, never experience the righteousness of faith (1:17) as did the saints in the Old Testament but would find themselves as objects of God's wrath (1:18).

In light of the serious claims which Paul makes in the opening chapters of Romans, both Jewish and gentile believers must have wondered if Paul's claims were in fact true. Was it true that the Old Testament bore witness to the gospel of the seed which Paul preached and claimed had been fulfilled in Jesus? Was it true that righteousness has always been *received* apart from the Law through faith in Jesus rather than *achieved* through self-effort? To prove that his understanding of the gospel was not new, Paul looked to Abraham to provide an apologetic for his theological claims. In Abraham, Paul's theology found meaning for both Jew and gentile alike. Paul's use of the Abraham story in Rom 4, then, functioned as what Anthony Guerra refers to as "apologetic theology."[50] As apologetic theology, Rom 4 is not properly understood as *midrash* or diatribe, but theological exegesis intended to defend the theological position which Paul proposed. Because of the unique implications the Abraham story held for both Jews and gentiles alike, a proper understanding was critical to apprehend the nature of the gospel message as the acquisition of righteousness apart from the Law through faith in Jesus Christ. As Goppelt notes, "Sicher wurde der Hinweis auf Abraham . . . sind jedoch hier wie an anderen Stellen nicht lediglich situationsbedingtes Mittel der Apologetik, der Polemik oder traditioneller Schriftgelehrsamkeit, sondern ein von der Sache her gegebenes zentrales Mittel zur Interpretation des Evangeliums."[51]

---

50. Guerra, "Romans 4 as Apologetic Theology," 251.

51. Goppelt, "Paulus und die Heilsgeschichte: Schlussfolgerungen aus Röm 4 und 1 Kor 10:1–13," 32. The author's translation is as follows: "The reference to Abraham was intentional . . . However here and elsewhere they are not merely situational means of apologetics, polemics, or traditional writing, but a central means of interpreting the gospel."

The Abraham Story in Rom 4:1–8: Justification by Faith apart from Works[52]

In Rom 3:27–31, Paul argued that justification (δικαιόω) by faith established the Law and existed apart from works, the deeds of the Law, and circumcision.[53] Because justification was a gracious gift given apart from human merit or ritual (3:21–24; 4:3–8; cf. Eph 2:8–9), neither Jews nor gentiles had any grounds to boast. Additionally, as justification existed apart from Jewish ritual or Law, these elements were unnecessary for gentiles to experience God's gracious provision of justification. Through faith in Jesus, both Jew and gentile received and fulfilled the righteousness required by the Law. To both prove and illustrate his theology, Paul began his use of the Abraham story by explaining the means by which Abraham received a right standing before God (4:1–5). His theological exposition of the Abraham story in these opening verses corrected some of the faulty thinking surrounding this Jewish patriarch within elements of Jewish thought.

While it is hard to determine precisely how widespread the belief was, it is important to understand that elements within Judaism during Paul's day believed that Abraham was justified because of his works. In the pseudepigraphal work the Prayer of Manasseh, the author writes, "You, therefore, O Lord, God of the righteous ones, did not appoint grace for the righteous ones such as Abraham, and Isaac, and Jacob, those who did not sin against you . . ." (*Pr. Man.* 8).[54] Likewise, in The Book of Jubilees, the author states, "For Abraham was perfect in all his deeds with the Lord, and well-pleasing in righteousness all the days of his life . . ." (*Jub.* 23:10).[55] In light of this

52. While the nature of the current study eliminates the possibility to demonstrate that the proposed reading of Rom 4 is the only possible reading, it will be shown to be a legitimate reading of the text.

53. In Romans, "justification" (δικαιόω) is a forensic declaration of righteousness by God upon the believing sinner. That this is true can be seen from Paul's use of the term in the text of Romans itself. In Rom 4:3, Paul quotes from Ps 51:4 where David addresses God after his adulterous affair with Bathsheba. Here Paul notes that David claimed God was justified (δικαιωθῇς) in his adjudication of David's sin. David did not *make* God righteous but *declared* that he was righteous in his judgments. See Allman, *Accept One Another*, 62. "In Paul the legal usage is plain and indisputable . . . For Paul the word δικαιοῦν does not suggest the infusion of moral qualities, a *justum efficere* in the sense of the creation of right conduct. It implies the justification of the ungodly who believe, on the basis of the justifying action of God in the death and resurrection of Christ" (Schrenk, "δικαιόω," 2.215).

54. This translation was taken from Charlesworth, "Prayer of Manasseh," 636. For other examples, see Strack and Billerbeck, *Kommentar zum Neuen Testament aus Talmud und Midrasch*, 186–201.

55. This translation was taken from Charles, *Apocrypha and Pseudepigrapha of the*

belief, it is not surprising that Paul began his apologetic theology in Rom 4 by putting this erroneous theology on trial.

In his opening words of chapter 4, Paul began with a question to his Jewish audience. How did their biological forefather (προπάτορα ἡμῶν κατὰ σάρκα), Abraham, discover (εὑρηκέναι) his justification (4:1)?[56] Since the topic of the passage centered around justification by faith apart from works, the initial question implied two possible means. Was it by works? Or, was it by faith? The implications of the answer were developed by Paul in 4:2. If Abraham was justified (ἐδικαιώθη) by works, then he had every right to boast (ἔχει καύχημα), but as the story of Abraham in Genesis revealed, he did not have the right to boast before God (ἀλλ᾽ οὐ πρὸς θεόν).[57] The reason Abraham had no grounds to boast before God was to be found in the Scripture's own testimony concerning his justification. Quoting Gen 15:6, Paul provided scriptural proof that Abraham was justified by faith and not by works (Rom 4:3). "For what does the Scripture say? 'And Abraham believed [ἐπίστευσεν] God, and it was reckoned [ἐλογίσθη] to him as righteousness [δικαιοσύνη].'"[58] Justification was therefore a *grace-method* and not a

---

Old Testament in English, 48. It also appears that many within Judaism believed faith to be a meritorious work (2 Esd 9:7; 13:23).

56. There are two textual issues in 4:1 that affect its translation. The first involves the authenticity of the term "forefather" (προπάτορα). The word is a *hapax legomenon*. Although the word occurs only here, it has better manuscript support and is likely part of the original reading of the verse. See Metzger, *Textual Commentary on the Greek New Testament*, 450; Longenecker, *Epistle to the Romans*, 471. The second textual issue concerns the placement of the verb εὑρηκέναι. Should it be placed before Ἀβραάμ or after ἡμῶν? Regarding its placement, Metzger writes, "Of the two readings that include the word, the sequence ἡμῶν εὑρηκέναι was judged inferior both in sense and external support" (Metzger, *Textual Commentary on the Greek New Testament*, 450). A syntactical question concerns the phrase κατὰ σάρκα. Does it modify εὑρηκέναι in which Paul, for the sake of argument, is engaging with the notion of a works-based righteousness? Or, does κατὰ σάρκα modify προπάτορα ἡμῶν, in which case Paul is highlighting the Christian Jews' physical ancestry to their forefather Abraham; an ancestry in which they took great pride (cf. Matt 3:9; Luke 3:8). Paul has already used the phrase to connect Jesus' physical ancestry with David (Rom 1:3). Therefore, it seems likely that Paul's use of the term προπάτορα in 4:1 brings the physical ancestry of Paul and his imaginary Jewish interlocutors to the fore. Thus the latter syntactical option seems preferable. See Fitzmyer, *Romans*, 372.

57. The apodosis of the conditional sentence in 4:2, ἀλλ᾽ οὐ πρὸς θεόν, seems to be refuting the conclusion of the protasis, ἔχει καύχημα, namely that Abraham's justification by works gave him the basis to boast. For a good discussion of the syntax of 4:2, see Cranfield, *Critical and Exegetical Commentary on the Epistle to the Romans*, 228.

58. This translation was taken from the NASB. Paul's Greek translation of Gen 15:6 is nearly identical to the reading found in the LXX: καὶ ἐπίστευσεν Αβραμ τῷ θεῷ καὶ ἐλογίσθη αὐτῷ εἰς δικαιοσύνην. See Brenton, *Septuagint with Apocrypha*, 16–17. See also Fitzmyer, *Romans*, 373–74. As S. Lewis Johnson observes, he "varied the wording a

wage-method. One who worked (τῷ ἐργαζομένῳ) received a wage (μισθὸς) not grace (χάριν; 4:4), but one who did not work (τῷ δὲ μὴ ἐργαζομένῳ) but believed in God, the One who justified the ungodly (πιστεύοντι δὲ ἐπὶ τὸν δικαιοῦντα τὸν ἀσεβῆ)—that is, those who did not deserve justification— such faith was graciously accounted to them for righteousness (4:5). The *requirement* for justification was *faith* and the *object* of Abraham's faith was *God* who had promised him an heir.

To the Jewish interlocutor, Paul's opening remarks in Rom 4:1–5 demonstrated that the Jew who attempted to acquire a right standing before God on the basis of his works could only claim Abrahamic fatherhood in the physical sense alone. While he was a genuine physical offspring of Abraham, he had not acquired Abraham's spiritual heritage. If a Jew were to be Abraham's offspring in the fullest sense, the record of Scripture clearly demonstrated that physical decent was not enough. Like Abraham, he needed to acquire his right standing before God through faith in God apart from works. To the gentile reader, Paul's apologetic theology implied that justification could be attained apart from Judaism. If what Paul observed from Scripture were true, a gentile could possess a right standing before God as a gentile. Just as a believing Jew found in Abraham his biological and spiritual heritage, perhaps a gentile could also find sonship in Abraham as well, at least in a spiritual sense. Did the Scriptural account of Abraham really make him the father of two distinct peoples in the one family of God? What 4:1–5 implied, Paul would make explicit in the next two sections (4:9–12; 13–17).

To conclude this opening section of chapter 4, Paul briefly departed from the Abraham story (4:6–8) to validate his thesis of faith-based righteousness by citing David's words in Psalm 32:1–2. "Blessed [Μακάριος] are those whose lawless deeds have been forgiven, and whose sins have been covered. Blessed [Μακάριος] is the man whose sin the Lord will not take into account [λογίσηται]" (NASB). While a complete discussion of these verses is beyond the scope of the current discussion, the use of David's words in this

---

bit to emphasize that Abraham believed. In Paul's Greek letter, he threw forward the word 'believed' in order to underscore it" (Johnson Jr., *Discovering Romans*, 70). In his lexicon, William Danker defines ἐπίστευσεν in Rom 4:3 as belief in God's disclosures without doubt or contradiction. See Danker, ed., *Greek-English Lexicon of the New Testament and Other Early Christian Literature*, 816–17. He also notes that λογίζομαι in Rom 4:3, 4, and 5 means to "place to one's account" or "to credit." See Wright, "The Letter to the Romans," 597. See also Heidland, "λογίζομαι," 284–92. The word "righteousness" (δικαιοσύνη) denotes a right standing before God (Danker, *Greek-English Lexicon*, 247). See also Schrenk, "δικαιοσύνη," 2:206–7. See Longenecker for a good discussion of these words (Longenecker, *Epistle to the Romans*, 496–97).

penitential psalm show that, even during the dispensation of Law, a right standing before God was something *received* and not *achieved*.[59]

The Abraham Story in Rom 4:9–12: Justification by Faith apart from Circumcision

Having demonstrated that justification by faith in God apart from works was to be found in the Scripture's own account of Abraham (Gen 15:6), Paul began to unpack the implications of this profound theology for the believers in Rome. The logical link to the previous section (Rom 4:1–6) is achieved through the use of the inferential conjunction "therefore" or "then" (οὖν) which Paul employed to introduce another question. "Is this blessing [μακαρισμός] then [οὖν] upon the circumcised [τὴν περιτομήν], or upon the uncircumcised [τὴν ἀκροβυστίαν] also? For we say, 'Faith was reckoned to Abraham as righteousness'" (4:9; NASB).[60] Here, Paul asked his Jewish audience to ponder the Scriptural account of Abraham. If Scripture revealed that Abraham was justified by faith apart from works, then was justification available only to those who were circumcised or could those who were uncircumcised receive this blessing as well? In answer to his own question, Paul emphatically asserted that the blessing of justification was given to Abraham in an uncircumcised state (οὐκ ἐν περιτομῇ ἀλλ' ἐν ἀκροβυστίᾳ; 4:10). The chronological sequence in the Abrahamic narrative revealed the function of his circumcision. Since his circumcision happened after his justification, circumcision could not have been a *requirement* for his justification but, rather, functioned as a *sign* (σημεῖον) or *seal* (σφραγῖδα)[61] of the righteousness he had already received by faith while uncircumcised (4:11a).

---

59. See Moo, *Epistle to the Romans*, 265–67. Regarding Paul's use of Ps 32:1–2 Schreiner writes, "[P]aul brings Gen. 15:6 into the argument here to shed light on the meaning of Ps. 32. Genesis 15:6 is the hermeneutical key for unlocking the significance of Ps. 32. Paul suggests that if Abraham was righteous by faith, then circumcision is inconsequential. Covenantal grace does not depend on circumcision. Faith alone is the path to blessing" (Schreiner, *Romans*, 224).

60. The "blessing" (μακαρισμός) in Rom 4:9 connects Paul's question to his quotation of Ps 32:1–2 which used the same word to relate forgiveness to Abraham's justification in Gen 15:6. The subject of Rom 4:9–12 continues to develop the theology of justification by faith begun in 4:1–8. See Jewett, *Romans*, 317.

61. The terms "sign" (σημεῖον) and "seal" (σφραγῖδα) exist in apposition to each other and should both be taken to communicate the idea that circumcision was not essential to justification but functioned to provide an external marker signifying what had taken place spiritually. See Käsemann, *Commentary on Romans*, 114–15; Schreiner, *Romans*, 224–25. Gottfried Fitzer says that no distinction should be made between the meaning of "sign" and "seal" in Rom 4:11. See Fitzer, "σημεῖον," 7:258. Regarding the

Through the use of two εἰς clauses, Paul indicated that the manner of Abraham's justification was part of God's divine intent so that he might be the father of Jews and gentiles alike.[62] In the first of the two clauses, Paul revealed that Abraham's justification occurred in order (εἰς) to make Abraham the father of the gentiles—those who received justification by faith in an uncircumcised state as he had (4:11b; cf. Gal 3:28–29). The second εἰς clause revealed Abraham's justification occurred in order (εἰς) to make him the father of the Jews—those who, like him, were circumcised and had also received justified by faith (Rom 4:12; cf. Gal 4:1–5).

The implications of Paul's exposition of the Abrahamic story in Rom 4:9–12 held profound implications for both Jew and gentile believers. For the Jew, circumcision did not make one a spiritual offspring of Abraham. Only justification by faith could do that (cf. Gal 5:1–14). If circumcision were truly a sign of the righteousness received by faith, then the physical act of circumcision held no value if it did not accompany, or signify, a spiritual circumcision of the heart (cf., Deut 10:16; 30:6).[63] Jesus had taught this same theology during his ministry earth. Although the Jews who opposed him claimed to be Abraham's *true offspring*, Jesus told them that Abraham's true children were those who did what Abraham did. "If you are Abraham's children, do the deeds of Abraham" (John 8:39 NASB).[64]

For the gentile, Paul's theology enabled him to understand his own relationship to this father of the Jewish nation. Despite having no biological relationship to Abraham, a gentile could obtain a righteous standing before God as he responded to the gospel in faith and was justified according to the pattern set forth by Abraham. Because the act of circumcision was merely a sign (σημεῖον) for Abraham of what had taken place spiritually, the gentile was under no obligation to perform this Jewish ritual to obtain

---

term "seal" (σφραγῖδα), Moo writes, "[P]aul uses the word to denote something that 'confirms' the truth or reality of something else, as in 1 Cor. 9:2, where Paul describes the Corinthian believers themselves as the 'seal,' the confirmation and authentication of his apostleship" (Moo, *Epistle to the Romans*, 269).

62. For a good discussion of the grammar of these two prepositional phrases, see Cranfield, *Critical and Exegetical Commentary on the Epistle to the Romans*, 236–37.

63. Paul's theology here was foundational and prepared the reader for his defense of God's dealings with Israel later in the book (9–11) where he stated emphatically that "they are not all Israel who are descended from Israel" (9:6). Significantly, in Deut 10:16, Moses exhorts the second generation of Israel to circumcise their hearts. "Circumcise then your heart, and stiffen your neck no more." He would later reveal that a future time would come when God would circumcise their hearts (Deut 30:6). This exhortation to circumcise their hearts came before this generation experienced physical circumcision (Josh 5:2–8). Therefore, even during the dispensation of Law, physical circumcision was simply a sign of what should have taken place spiritually.

64. This translation was taken from the NASB.

a right standing before God. He had already experienced the circumcision necessary, a circumcision of the heart. While a believing Jew could claim both a *physical* and *spiritual* standing through Abraham, the gentile believer was not excluded for he, too, could share in this *spiritual* standing through Abraham, as Abraham became the father of all who believe (Rom 4:11; cf. 2:28–29; Gal 5:1–14; Col 2:11).

Paul's theological exposition of the Abraham story, likely, stood in contrast to the manner in which many Jews in Paul's day understood the rite of circumcision. Recognizing the importance of this particular rite within Judaism, Morris observes,

> The Jews put a good deal of emphasis on circumcision, that divinely ordained ceremony which formally admitted one to membership in the people of God. It was this that marked him off from other people and that was the seal of his place before God. No matter who a man's parents were, if he was not circumcised he was not a Jew . . . The Jews could say explicitly, "uncircumcised is but used as a name for the gentiles" (*Ned.* 3:11).[65]

But whereas the Jews in Paul's day took circumcision as a sign that signified their right standing before God through a distinctly Jewish heritage, Paul looked to Abraham and saw the true role of circumcision. If Abraham's justification preceded his circumcision, then circumcision functioned as a mnemonic sign that reminded Abraham of God's promise and provision—chief of which was the provision of a natural heir through whom God would bless the nations of the earth (Gen 15:3–4)—and a sign that signified the faith response through which he was justified (Gen 15:6; 17:1–14).[66] Cir-

---

65. Morris, *Epistle to the Romans*, 201. In Jubilees 15:26 the Jewish author writes, "And anyone who is born whose own flesh is not circumcised on the eight day is not from the sons of the covenant which the Lord made for Abraham since (he is) from the children of destruction. And there is therefore no sign upon him so that he might belong to the Lord because (he is destined) to be destroyed and annihilated from the earth and to be uprooted from the earth because he has broken the covenant of the Lord our God." This translation was taken from Wintermute, "Jubilees," 2:87. It is important to understand that circumcision was a common practice in the ancient Near East, particularly among the Canaanites and did not, as instituted in Gen 17, necessarily distinguish a Jew from a gentile in the ancient world. For a good discussion of the practice of circumcision in the ancient world, see Sasson, "Circumcision in the Ancient Near East," 473–76; De Vaux, *Bible and the Ancient Near East*, 46–48.

66. Helfmeyer observed that a mnemonic sign functioned in part to "give expression" to Israel's faith (Helfmeyer, "אות," in *Theological Dictionary of the Old Testament*, 179). Michael Fox observed that mnemonic signs "bring to consciousness something already known (which may or may not have been forgotten)" (Fox, "Sign of the Covenant," 563). While the current discussion cannot give attention to the different views regarding the nature of circumcision as a sign, the works cited in this note provide a

cumcision, in a sense, was both a preaching of the covenant promises and a call to respond in justifying faith. This pedagogical function of circumcision was revealed in the narrative account in Gen 17 where the covenant rite was first instituted.[67]

The precise relationship between Gen 15 and 17 has engendered some debate. Some have argued that Gen 17 is merely a reaffirmation of the covenant ratified in 15,[68] while others believe that Gen 17 exists as a covenant distinct from that revealed in chapter 15.[69] However, a credible case can be made that Gen 15 and 17 reveal two separate stages in the development of a single Abrahamic covenant.[70] While the covenant ratification in Gen 15 emphasized the *promissory aspects* and the *existence* of the covenant, Gen 17 revealed the *obligatory aspects* previously unstated related to the *function* of the covenant in history.[71] This new stage of covenant development was communicated by the author in a couple of different ways. In the opening of chapter 17, the author said that Yahweh "appeared" (וַיֵּרָא יְהוָה) to Abram at ninety-nine years of age (17:1). While this, at face value, may seem trivial, it becomes important once the reader realizes that this verb is used more broadly in Genesis to introduce both the Abrahamic promises (12:7) as well as covenant pericopes (17:1; 18:1; 26:2, 24; 35:9).

Moreover, the author used specific verbs to communicate the progress in covenant revelation in these two texts. In the ratification ceremony of Gen 15, the covenant was said to be "cut" (כרת; 15:18) at the time the covenant was ratified and brought into existence (15:7–21). In chapter 17, the covenant is not said to be "cut" but "given" by God (נתן; 17:2) and "established" by God (קום; 17:7). Although the covenant existed when it was "cut" (כרת) in Gen 15, chapter 17 reveals that the covenant would be "given" (נתן) or "established" (קום) as the obligatory aspects were upheld by Abram and his descendants after him (17:1, 10).[72] The introduction of a covenant

---

good overview of the current debate. The current discussion has attempted to provide an understanding of circumcision consistent with Paul's theology.

67. For a comprehensive study on circumcision in Gen 17, see Benton, "Genesis 17:9–1."

68. For an example of this, see Keil and Delitzsch, *Biblical Commentary on the Old Testament*, 222–23.

69. For an example of this view, see Gunkel, *Genesis*, 266.

70. For an excellent overview of the various views on this topic, see Williamson, *Abraham, Israel, and the Nations*, 26–77.

71. It is important to understand that the term "everlasting" (עֹלָם) is used four times in Gen 17. This observation is significant because it reveals that any obligatory elements added here are *placed alongside* the promissory aspects previously revealed in chapter 15. See Hamilton, *Book of Genesis*, 465.

72. See Johnson, *Dispensational Biblical Theology*, 98–99.

obligation did not affect one's justification. This Abraham had experienced prior to the existence of the covenant itself. Justification could only be received by faith (15:6). Rather, the obligations affected the experience of the covenant blessings in one's lifetime. When the covenant obligations in 17:1 are understood in connection with the promissory covenant in chapter 15 (cf. 12:3, 7; 13:14–16), it becomes clear that God necessarily obligated himself to provide a seed who would fulfill the covenant requirements and bring about the experience of the Abrahamic promises in history. If this were not the case, God could not ensure that the covenant promises—which he had given unconditionally in chapter 15—would ultimately be realized. In history, no descendant of Abraham but Jesus fulfilled the covenant requirements (cf. Matt 5:17; 1 Pet 2:22; 2 Cor 5:21), so it is only through him that the covenant blessings could fully be experienced in history. Thus, the righteous standing of Abraham's offspring before God and their experience of covenant blessings as those party to the covenant must be received by grace through faith.

It is important to observe that the Hebrew verbs used in the development of the Davidic covenant also follow the Genesis pattern when moving from the *promissory* to the *obligatory* functions of the covenant. In 2 Chron 7:18, God appeared to Solomon and said, "And as for you [Solomon], if you walk before Me as your father David walked even to do according to all that I have commanded you and will keep My statutes and My ordinances, then I will establish [קוּם] your royal throne as I covenanted [כרת] with your father David, saying, 'You shall not lack a man *to be* ruler in Israel'" (cf. 2 Kgs 2:1–4) While the promissory covenant was "cut" (כרת) with David (2 Sam 7) and ratified by oath (Ps 89:3), its function depended on Solomon's adherence to the Law. Only by meeting these obligations would the promissory covenant which existed be "established" (קוּם) with Solomon. To the degree that Solomon obeyed, he experienced the promised blessings in history, however only Jesus—David's perfect seed—could bring about the full realization of God's covenant promises. Once again the juxtaposition of the promissory and obligatory aspects of the Davidic covenant obligated God to provide a perfect King who would fulfill the covenant requirements so that he might be faithful to bring about his promises to David. The covenant obligations, then, affected a Davidic king's experience of the covenant blessings in his lifetime, but Jesus, God's perfect king, is the only one who can ensure the ultimate fulfillment of the covenant promises in history.

Although the current discussion cannot put forth this understanding as the only valid view regarding the relationship between Gen 15 and 17, the proposed view seems to be a credible understanding of the covenant. First, it recognizes the unity between 15 and 17 found in the promise of seed.

Second, the distinction of stages in the development of a single covenant explains the move from the promissory aspect of the covenant (15:1–7) to the introduction of covenant obligations (17:1–21). Third, it explains why the author of Genesis could bring together the covenant revelations of 15 and 17 (and the promises of 12:1–3) into a unified covenant description later in the book.[73] "Abraham will surely become a great and mighty nation, and in him all the nations of the earth will be blessed? For I have chosen him, in order that he may command his children and his household after him to keep the way of the LORD by doing righteousness and justice; in order that the LORD may bring upon Abraham what He has spoken about him" (Gen 18:18; cf. 22:16–18; NASB).

In Gen 17, the narrative pericope began as the Lord once again "appeared" (וַיֵּרָא יְהוָה) to Abram to reaffirm and develop the covenant promises of Gen 15 to multiply Abraham and to give his descendants the land which he had promised beforehand (12:1–3, 7; 15:1–21). This covenant was for Abraham and for his descendants after him (17:4, 7). In order to experience the blessings of the covenant, Abraham was told that he was to be blameless in his life before God (17:2)[74] and this condition of covenant blessing was applied to Abraham's lineage after him (17:9; cf. 18:18–19).[75]

In its development in Gen 17, both the promissory and obligatory aspects of the covenant were brought to the fore through God's use of the phrase "my covenant" (בְּרִיתִי). God's references to the Abrahamic covenant as "my covenant" referred both to his promissory obligations (17:2, 4, 7) as well as to the obligatory responsibilities of Abraham and his offspring (17:9, 10, 11, 13, 14).

While circumcision existed as a covenant obligation—"This is My covenant, which you shall keep, between Me and you and your descendants

---

73. See Williamson, *Abraham, Israel, and the Nations*, 75–77.

74. In Gen 17:1, God's command to Abraham that he "walk before him and be blameless," (הִתְהַלֵּךְ לְפָנַי וֶהְיֵה תָמִים) introduces a covenant obligation. The nature of this blameless walk is clarified in 18:18–19 when God says, "Abraham will surely become a great and mighty nation, and in him all the nations of the earth will be blessed? For I have chosen him, in order that he may command his children and his household after him *to keep the way of the LORD by doing righteousness and justice*; in order that the LORD may bring upon Abraham what He has spoken about him" (NASB). Emphasis mine. For a good overview of the word "blameless" (תָמִים) used in 17:1, see Kedar-Kopfstein, *tāmîm*, 699–711.

75. Once again it is important to emphasize that while Abraham and his descendants were responsible to fulfill the covenant obligations, no one in history but Jesus fulfills them perfectly. Therefore it is only through faith in him that the descendants of Abraham, who are party to the covenant, will experience the covenant promises in history (Gal 4:1–5), and it is only in him that gentiles will share in this inheritance through faith (Gal 3:28–29).

after you: every male among you shall be circumcised"[76] (17:10)—God revealed that its importance went far beyond a mere *pro forma* ritual. As a "sign" of the covenant arrangement, circumcision was to be a synecdoche for the Abrahamic covenant arrangement, which included both *promissory* and *obligatory* aspects. It represented God's promissory obligations (12:1–3, 7; 15:1–21; 17:1–9) as well as the covenant obligation of obedience imposed upon Abraham and his posterity for the covenant to function in history (17:2; 17:10; cf., 18:17–19). As a "sign" (אות), circumcision would remind Abraham and his posterity of God's commitments and their own responsibility before him.[77]

The imposition of the *karath* (כרת) penalty for the uncircumcised male (17:14), whether slave or free, ensured that the pedagogical function of the sign would continue throughout Israel's history so that every generation might receive the message of the covenant and respond in faith like their father, Abraham (15:6).[78] Circumcision was, in a sense, a speech-act in sign form. The *locutionary, illocutionary, and perlocutionary force* of the covenant promises were subsumed in the physical mark of circumcision (17:13) so that the *perlocutionary intention* of the covenant might be fulfilled in the life of the Israelite. For the one who, like Abraham, responded with the *intended perlocution*—faith—his circumcision assumed additional symbolism as it also signified what had occurred spiritually (cf. Deut 30:6).[79] The introduction of this covenant obligation did not make the Abrahamic covenant a gospel of works, for this would go against the Abrahamic narrative in Genesis and Paul's theology in Rom 4. Rather, it established a rite that would remind the Israelites of God's promise and his standard. As sin inevitably caused an individual in the community to fall short of God's standard (17:1), rather than pursue blessing in his own failed strength he would rest on God's promise of an heir who would meet the covenant obligations he could not so that, through him, he might be blessed as Abraham himself was blessed (15:6; cf. Gal 3:10–19). For the Jew whose response was an *unintended perlocution*—unbelief—his circumcision existed as an empty

76. This translation has been taken from the NASB.

77. As F. J. Helfmeyer notes, "[A] sign has different aspects: on the one hand, the God who provides it regards man, and on the other hand, man acknowledges the presence and activity of God" (Helfmeyer, "1:175, אות).

78. Most understand this penalty to refer to either the threat of expulsion from the community or as a reference to premature death. Choosing between these options is not necessary for the purposes of the study at hand. For a good discussion of the options, see Mathews, *Genesis 11:27—50:26*, 205.

79. These speech-act terms have been previously defined on pages 19–20 of the current work.

pro forma mutilation that held not value whatsoever. Since no descendant of Abraham could fully live up to God's standard revealed in the covenant obligations (17:1), such a circumcision could never attain one a right standing before God (15:6) or the assurance of a future covenant inheritance. Although such a one had received the physical mark of the covenant, he had not responded in faith like Abraham who rested on the promised of the heir. Elliott Johnson recognized this pedagogical function when he wrote,

> This brand [circumcision] placed the responsibility on fathers to communicate about the reality of a relationship with God and the existence of the covenant to the next generation. God had personally revealed the covenant to Isaac and Jacob. But fathers had to communicate what God no longer openly revealed to subsequent generations.[80]

Some, like Alice Laffey, have concluded that the practice of circumcision in Israel gave a soteriological priority to males in an ancient and patriarchal society. In her discussion on the role of circumcision in Israel, Laffey argues that, prior to Deut 10 and 30, circumcision was an exclusively male rite that excluded women from sharing in the same soteriological advantages as men in Israelite society.

> [M]aking circumcised hearts rather than circumcised bodies the appropriate sign of the covenant relationship with Yahweh makes that relationship more directly available to women; access to that relationship is no longer only through the penis of father and husband.[81]

However, Paul's apologetic theology demonstrated that circumcision was not a requirement for possessing a right standing before God. It was not, as Laffey suggests, necessary for a woman to go through her husband or father to receive a right standing before God. As the men in her community were circumcised in accordance with the divine command, or as a wife shared in the fullness of a sexual relationship with her circumcised husband, the mnemonic function of the sign preached to her as well calling her to faith in God's promises and in his provision through the promised seed. As Israelite women shared Abraham's faith in God's provision (Gen 15:6), they too experienced the circumcision that truly mattered, the circumcision of the heart.

80. Johnson, *Dispensational Biblical Theology*, 99–100.

81. Laffey, *Introduction to the Old Testament*, 66.

The Abraham Story in Rom 4:13–18:
Inheritance by Faith apart from Law

Having removed justification from any notion of human ritual merit, Paul continued to develop his argument by addressing the question of inheritance. If Abraham was not justified by works, on what basis did he receive the promise of inheritance? Was it, too, by faith? Or, did justification and inheritance operate by two different methods? Paul began his answer by stating that Abraham did not receive the promise of inheritance through the Mosaic Law (διὰ νόμου) but through the righteousness of faith (διὰ δικαιοσύνης πίστεως: Rom 4:13).[82] Since the Law could only bring wrath, it could never be the means by which a person inherited the promise of God for wrath and promise were opposites (4:14–15). Since no one but Jesus fulfilled God's righteous requirements, the promise had to operate on the gracious principle of faith so that both those of the Law—Jews—and the gentile who shared Abraham's faith in the promised seed (Gen 15:6) might participate in this inheritance (Rom 4:16). As S. Lewis Johnson observed,

> But what means, or instrumentality, is compatible with grace?
> For the human means of receiving the promise must be set out.
> Paul's answer is that faith is the only means that is harmonious
> with the principle of grace, for in faith humans do nothing but
> believe, or receive, the gifts of God.[83]

To understand more fully what Paul here argued, it is important to give some special consideration to the content of the promise to which Paul referred. In 4:13, Paul wrote that "the promise [ἡ ἐπαγγελία] to Abraham or to his descendants that he would be heir of the world [τὸ κληρονόμον αὐτὸν εἶναι τοῦ κόσμου] was not through the Law, but through the righteousness of faith." Cranfield was correct when he noted that "Nowhere in the Old Testament is the promise to Abraham expressed in terms at all close to 'that he should be heir of the world.'"[84] Although God had promised to give Abraham and his offspring a land in the Genesis account (Gen 12:7; 13:14–15; 15:7–21; 17:8), this promised inheritance had specific geographic boundaries (15:7–21). How, then, did Paul understand the Abraham account? In the Septuagint, the Hebrew word for land (אֶרֶץ) used in the Abraham narrative is translated with the Greek term, γῆ, and never κόσμος as Paul employed

---

82. "Just as Abraham's acceptance by faith was independent of circumcision, so it was independent of the Mosaic law" (Morris, *Epistle to the Romans*, 205).

83. Johnson, *Discovering Romans*, 74.

84. Cranfield, *Romans*, 90.

here in Rom 4:13.[85] In light of this, some scholars, such as Kenneth Bailey, believed that Paul found his understanding in the theological milieu of Second Temple Judaism where such expanded notions of the land promise could be found.[86] In the Book of Jubilees (*Jub.* 32:18–19; cf. 22:14), the author related the vision of God to Jacob at Bethel in the following manner,

> I am the Lord who created heaven and earth, and I shall increase you and multiply you very much. And there will be kings from you; they will rule everywhere that the tracks of mankind have been trod. And I shall give to your seed all of the land under heaven and they will rule in all nations as they have desired. And after this all of the earth will be gathered together and they will inherit it forever.[87]

Likewise, in *Ben Sirach* 44:21, the author described God's promise to Abraham in expansive terms when he wrote, "God promised him [Abraham] with an oath to bless the nations through his descendants, to make him numerous as the grains of dust, and exalt his posterity like the stars, giving them an inheritance from sea to sea, and from the River to the ends of the earth."[88] Although Second Temple parallels to Paul's theology in Rom 4 may certainly exist, the force of his argument depended on the truth of Old Testament revelation and, therefore, could not have been built upon intertestamental expansion in theology. If God had not actually promised Abraham that he would inherit the earth, then Paul's argument in Rom 4 becomes powerless, since Abraham never received what Paul claimed he received by faith. If Abraham did not receive it, then those who share Abraham's faith could never participate in it either, as the text in Romans claims they do (4:16).

The use of the term κόσμος to define the scope of Abraham's inheritance may provide a textual clue suggesting that Paul had interpreted the Abraham story in light of the theology of Genesis as a whole. God had created the world to be a realm over which he ruled through humans (Gen 1:28). The mediatorial rule established by God was interrupted by the serpent who led Adam and Eve into sin, and the serpent (i.e., Satan) became

---

85. Bailey, "St. Paul's Understanding of the Territorial Promise of God to Abraham," 60.

86. Bailey, "St. Paul's Understanding of the Territorial Promise of God to Abraham," 60.

87. Charles, *Apocrypha and Pseudepigrapha of the Old Testament*, 117–18.

88. This translation was taken from Skehan, *Wisdom of Ben Sira*, 503. For a good summary of the land promise during the Second Temple period, see Davies, *Territorial Dimension of Judaism*, 28–44.

the ruler of this world (Eph 2:2). In his pronouncement of judgment, God declared the end of the serpent's reign through the agency of the seed of the woman who would resolve the conflict initiated at the fall (Gen 3:15). In God's revelation to Abraham, the seed of Gen 3:15 was revealed to be Abraham's natural heir through whom all the nations of the earth would be blessed, that is, justified through faith in him (12:3; 15:4–6; Gal 3:6–9).[89] This heir would be Abraham's natural offspring and his provision from the Lord (Gen 15:1–4). As the promised heir both judged the serpent (3:15) and blessed humanity (12:3), Abraham's reward included a reclaimed κόσμος in which God's mediatorial rule was once again established over the earth.[90] Seen in this light, the promise of a land (12:7; 13:14–15; 15:7–21; 17:8) was merely a *token* of a greater inheritance to come.[91]

It is this inheritance that Paul could claim was promised to Abraham and received by faith so that believing Jews and gentiles—through faith apart from the Law—might participate in the promise (ἡ ἐπαγγελία) of inheritance with him (Rom 4:13–16; Matt 5:5; Gal 3:6–9).[92] Faith is the means by which a person receives what God has promised. Later in the chapter, Paul will connect the promise of 4:13 with the promise of Abraham's heir (4:20). As Paul has already looked to the Davidic rule of Christ and would later focus on the reconstitution of national Israel in the kingdom, the proposed view seems valid (Rom 1:2–4; 9–11).

In his development of the Abraham story, Paul argued that as believing Jews and gentiles shared in the promise of Abraham, he became the father of all who believe (4:16). While Paul completed this thought in 4:17b by noting that Abraham received this fatherhood "in the sight of Him whom he believed, *even* God, who gives life to the dead and calls into being that which

89. Although the ministry of the seed of Abraham is revealed in the early revelation of God to Abraham (12:1–3, 7), it is not understood and accepted until 15:6. See footnotes 110 and 145 in chapter 3.

90. This promise will be realized in the millennial kingdom under the reign of Messiah, the promised heir.

91. For a good discussion of the various views related to Rom 4:13, see Hsieh, "Abraham as 'Heir of the Word,'" 95–110. In this article, Hsieh argues that κόσμος is best understood as referring to Abraham's inheritance of spiritual nations rather than to the created world. While lexically possible, the view fails to observe that while the promise is made to Abraham, it is also *shared* by believing Jews and gentiles (Rom 4:16). While believing Jews and gentiles cannot share in the inheritance of spiritual nations, they can share in the inheritance of a reclaimed earth. See Hsieh, "Abraham as 'Heir of the Word,'" 106–8.

92. Some scholars adopt a universal kingdom inheritance based on the similarity between this passage and Matthew 5:5. See Moo, *Epistle to the Romans*, 274; Dunn, *Romans 1–8*, 213. However, it is interesting that few provide explanation regarding its consistency with an Old Testament theology.

does not exist" (NASB).[93] Then, he briefly interrupted the flow of thought with a parenthetical καθώς clause citing Gen 17:5 from the Septuagint:[94] "as [καθώς] it is written, 'A father of many nations have I made you'" (NASB).[95] In its original context, the verse explained why God changed Abram's name to Abraham. Bruce Waltke observed,

> His [Abraham's] former name spoke of his noble God, of his noble ancestry, or of his own eminence; his new name speaks of his many offspring. This is the name God will make great (12:2). Abram, composed of *'āb* ("father") and *rām* ("to be high"), means "Exalted Father," a reference either to God, Terah, or himself. His new name Abraham, by a word play of *'āb* ("father") plus *hām* (*hāmôn*, "crowd"), sounds like "father of a multitude."[96]

The name, then, as given by God existed as a token, a surety, of God's promise to make Abraham the father of a multitude of nations (Gen 17:5). Paul's use of this Old Testament quotation raises an important hermeneutical dilemma in his development of the Abraham story and its application to the believers in Rome. While the overall emphasis in Gen 17 is on Abraham's *natural offspring*, many commentators believe that Paul expanded the meaning to include a *spiritual progeny* in order to prove his assertion that Abraham is the father of all who believe (Rom 4:16).[97] Fitzmeyer represented this view well when he wrote, "While the promise was made to Abraham in the physical sense in Genesis, Paul now shows that the promise has found a *fuller fulfillment*: 'many nations' has come to include all those who become believers in Christ, who are reckoned upright through faith."[98]

93. Regarding the syntax of 4:16–17 Mounce understands it differently when he writes, "The NIV connects the phrase 'in the sight of God' (v.17b) to 'father of us all' (repeated as 'our father'). But what it means to be 'our father in the sight of God' is less than clear. It may be better to take vv.16–17a as a parenthesis and connect the phrase with 'guaranteed to all Abraham's offspring' (in v.16)" (Mounce, *Romans*, 128).

94. The KJV, NASB, NET, and NKJV understand 17b as a parenthetical clause. For a good discussion of this view in relation to alternatives, see Moo, *Epistle to the Romans*, 279–81.

95. The text of Gen 17:5 from the LXX reads as follows: ὅτι πατέρα πολλῶν ἐθνῶν τέθεικά σε. See Wevers, *Septuaginta*, 177.

96. Waltke and Fredricks, *Genesis*, 259–60.

97. See Cranfield, *Critical and Exegetical Commentary on the Epistle to the Romans*, 243. Waltke attempts to find both natural and spiritual progeny in the original context of 17:5, but this interpretation imports two disparate interpretations to the same sequence of words. God's promise in 17:5 cannot promise both biological and non-biological nations at the same time. See Waltke and Fredricks, *Genesis*, 260. Something cannot mean "A" and "not A" at the same time and in the same way. For a similar view, see Moo, *Epistle to the Romans*, 280–81.

98. Fitzmyer, *Romans*, 386. Emphasis mine. Brendan Byrne argues for the same

According to this view, the καθώς clause introduced a fulfillment of Paul's assertion in 4:16. However, if Gen 17:5 promised Abraham natural nations, then spiritual nations cannot fulfill the terms of the promise since they did not form part of God's promissory obligations to Abraham in the original context.

In Gen 12:2, God promised that he would make Abraham—who was Abram at the time—into a great nation (גוֹי). Although Abraham doubted that his heir and promised nation would form part of a biological provision from the Lord, God clarified that both his heir and the nation he would receive would be from his own body (15:1–6). When God appeared to Abraham in Gen 17, God promised him "nations" (17:4, 5, 6; גּוֹיִם) from which kings (מְלָכִים) would come forth (17:6). What was the relationship between the "nation" promised by God (12:2; 15:1–21) and the "nations" (17:4, 5, 6) that now formed part of God's covenant obligations to Abraham? Are the "nations" *in addition to* the "nation," or do the "nations" in some sense *define* the "nation" already promised? Many commentators, understand the "nations" of Gen 17:4–6 to refer to the biological nations that come from Abraham through his sexual relationships with Sarah, Hagar, and Keturah (cf. 17:20; 25:1–4, 12–18; 36:1–43).[99] While the genealogical lists included in the book do provide some textual support for this view, it seems to minimize an important aspect found in the text of Gen 17. The promise given to Abraham—that of nations and kings—was also given to Sarah who was to bear Abraham's heir (17:15–16). According to the divine plan, the promise made to both Abraham and Sarah would meet and be fulfilled through Isaac (17:16), their natural son who would be heir to these covenant promises (17:19). If Abraham and Sarah *shared this promise*, it is reasonable to assume that one should seek to understand their terms in a sense that can be true of both.

Desmond Alexander recognized this important fact when he wrote, "Since this promise is later associated with Sarah—'She will be the mother of nations' (17:6)—it is unlikely that it includes the nations descended from Abraham through his relationships with Hagar (cf. 17:20) and Keturah (25:1–4)."[100] It is possible, however, that God's giving of the promise to Sarah clarified the sense in which the promise was intended for Abraham as well.

---

position when he writes, "Since the same term *ethne* does service for both 'nations' and 'gentiles' in biblical Greek, Paul can cite this text as confirmation of what he has been arguing all through" (Byrne, *Romans*, 153).

99. See Waltke and Fredricks, *Genesis*, 260; Westermann, *Genesis 12–36*, 260–61; Kidner, *Genesis*, 129. Waltke also extends the concept of "nations" to include Abraham's spiritual progeny.

100. Alexander, *From Paradise to the Promised Land*, 101.

"And I will bless her, and indeed I will give you a son by her. Then I will bless her, and she shall be a mother of nations [גּוֹיִם]; kings of peoples [עַמִּים] shall come from her" (17:16; NASB) In the promise as given to Sarah, the term "peoples" (עַמִּים) seems to clarify the sense in which "nations" (גּוֹיִם) is to be understood. While the term "nations" (גּוֹיִם) could carry the sense of distinct ethnic groups,[101] the term "peoples" (עַמִּים) is most naturally understood to refer to those with a close biological kinship as would be the case with tribes or clans.[102] Therefore, the nations promised to both Abraham and Sarah could be understood as a reference to the twelve tribes of Israel.

This interpretation finds additional support when one observes the terms used when the covenant was given to Jacob. When God initially gave the covenant, he promised Jacob that he would become a "company of peoples" (28:3; לִקְהַל עַמִּים). However, when the covenant was reaffirmed to him later in the narrative, God clarified that Jacob would be a "nation [גּוֹי] and a company of nations [35:11) "[גּוֹיִם וּקְהַל]).[103] As with Sarah, this would likely have been a reference to the twelve tribes of Israel for no other nation but Israel would come from Jacob. Because of this use of the terms "nation" (גּוֹי) and "people" (עַמִּים) in the development of the Abrahamic covenant, Franz Delitzsch did not believe that one should draw too great a distinction between these terms in such covenant contexts in Genesis.[104] As the focus of God's covenant with Abraham was on the greatness of his blessings to the patriarchs, the use of the term "nations" to describe the tribes of Israel would certainly reveal the magnanimous nature of God's promised posterity.

Others believe that "nations" denote Abraham's spiritual fatherhood.[105] While canonically, this is certainly a development which could be associated with Abraham, the overwhelming tenor of Gen 17 in both its near and broad context is on God's promise of biological children as seen in his divine direction of Abraham's lineage through Sarah. While certainly a difficult issue, it seems valid to understand God's promise of "nations" to both Abraham and Sarah as clarifying the sense in which the one nation

101. See Koehler and Baumgartner, *Hebrew and Aramaic Lexicon of the Old Testament*, 182–83.

102. See Koehler and Baumgartner, *Hebrew and Aramaic Lexicon of the Old Testament*, 837–38.

103. It is very possible that the *waw* in Gen 35:11 functions in an epexegetical way to clarify and intensify the sense of the nation initially promised. See Waltke and O'Connor, *Introduction to Biblical Hebrew Syntax*, 652.

104. Delitzsch, *New Commentary on Genesis*, 33. Interestingly, Delitzsch made a single exception to his general rule in Gen 17:5. See Delitzsch, *New Commentary on Genesis*, 33.

105. See Sarna, *Genesis*, 124; Hamilton, *Book of Genesis*, 464–65; Alexander, *From Paradise to the Promised Land*, 101–2.

promised (12:2; 15:1–21) will take shape. Although the nation promised through Abraham and Sarah would be a single nation, Gen 17 predicted its future tribal configuration according to the divine plan.

If this is the case, how then is one to understand Paul's use of Gen 17:5 in Rom 4:17a? Rather than take the καθώς clause to introduce a fulfillment through Abraham's spiritual fatherhood of Jews and gentiles, the clause must introduce a type of comparison. Just as God had made Abraham the father of a physical family (Israel) consisting of a multitude of nations (i.e. tribes) through their biological relationship with him—a unity in diversity—God had also made Abraham the father of a spiritual family consisting of Jews and gentiles—a unity in diversity—whose members attained their relationship to Abraham of a right standing before God as they shared his faith (cf., 9:25–26).[106]

Having established that Abraham's justification was *by faith in God* apart from works (Rom 4:1–8; cf. Gen 15:6) and circumcision (Rom 4:9–12; cf. Gen 15:6; 17), and that this faith was the same means by which he and those who shared his faith inherited the promise of life in the kingdom, Paul now returned to his key passage in the Abraham story (Gen 15:6) to begin his shift to the *content* of Abraham's faith. Because Abraham had believed in the God who gives life to the dead and calls into being what did not yet exist (Rom 4:17b), he believed God's promise despite the seeming impossibility of its realization. Humanly speaking, the impossibility of the promise was so great that Paul described Abraham's faith as "hope against hope" (παρ' ἐλπίδα ἐπ' ἐλπίδι; 4:18).[107] Yet, despite its seeming impossibility, Abraham believed with the result that he became the father of many nations (εἰς τὸ γενέσθαι αὐτὸν πατέρα πολλῶν ἐθνῶν), that is, of the federated tribes of Israel (Gen 17:5). This statement referred back to Paul's previous point (Rom 4:16–17) and explained how it was possible for Abraham to be the father of Jews and gentiles alike. If Abraham's fatherhood of the federated tribes of Israel was inherited by faith in God, then faith not physical descent was the necessary requirement to join the family of Abraham. Because of faith, Abraham's lineage was able to comprise two peoples with a right standing— Jew and gentile—in the one family of God.

106. Regarding Paul's use of Gen 17:5 in Rom 4:17a, James Stifler writes, "The quotation is cited hardly in confirmation of what Paul has said, but to show the harmony between him and the Scripture" (Stifler, *Epistle to the Romans*, 64).

107. As Schreiner rightly observes, the difference between "faith" and "hope" in 4:18 is nearly indistinguishable in Paul's use of the words with reference to Abraham. See Schreiner, *Romans*, 237.

Some commentators understand the εἰς clause in Rom 4:18 as the only content of Abraham's faith.[108] However, as Wallace observes, the use of the construction, εἰς τὸ + the infinitive, as is the case in the present text, is a structural clue that the author intends to convey a purpose or result.[109] This clause introduced a quotation from the Septuagint's translation of Gen 15:5 in which God promised Abraham that his descendants would be as numerous as the stars in the heavens (κατὰ τὸ εἰρημένον, Οὕτως ἔσται τὸ σπέρμα σου).[110]

Unfortunately, some commentators have overemphasized *creatio ex nihilo* in their interpretation of Rom 4:17–18 and thereby missed the important means by which Paul transitioned to the final section where he discussed the content of Abraham's faith.[111] While it is certainly true that the passage emphasized God's ability to create what does not yet exist, it neglects the important means by which he accomplished this creation. It was by his word. As the text said, Abraham believed in the God who "calls into being that which does not exist" (4:17).[112] Just as the performative force of God's word created the cosmos (Gen 1:1–25), God created a future reality for Abraham in promise by his word (Rom 4:17). The faith by which Abraham was justified, the faith by which he received the promise that he would inherit the world, and the faith by which he became the father of Israel was not a blind faith or some generic trust in God but faith in God's word of promise (cf. Gen 15:6). This promise had a specific content which Paul would go on to discuss.

---

108. See Byrne, *Romans*, 154.

109. Wallace, *Greek Grammar Beyond the Basics*, 590–93. See also Cranfield, *Critical and Exegetical Commentary on the Epistle to the Romans*, 246. See also Schreiner, *Romans*, 237; Moo, *Epistle to the Romans*, 283; Longenecker, *Epistle to the Romans*, 519.

110. See Morris, *Epistle to the Romans*, 210–11. In the context of Gen 15:5, the descendants which God promised Abram referred to the nation of Israel, for immediately following this promise, God explains that these are the offspring of Abram to whom he will give the land (Gen 15:7–21). Paul's juxtaposition of Gen 15.5 with the promise of "nations" in 17:5 supports the idea that the "nations" spoken of are the federated tribes of Israel. The text of Gen 15:5 in the Septuagint reads as follows: ἐξήγαγεν δὲ αὐτὸν ἔξω καὶ εἶπεν αὐτῷ ἀνάβλεψον δὴ εἰς τὸν οὐρανὸν καὶ ἀρίθμησον τοὺς ἀστέρας εἰ δυνήσῃ ἐξαριθμῆσαι αὐτούς καὶ εἶπεν οὕτως ἔσται τὸ σπέρμα σου. Wevers, *Septuaginta*, 168.

111. For an example of this, see Cranfield, *Critical and Exegetical Commentary on the Epistle to the Romans*, 244.

112. Paul used two participial phrases to describe the creative activity of God in 4:17. God is the one who "gives life to the dead" (τοῦ ζῳοποιοῦντος τοὺς νεκρούς) and the one who "calls into being that which does not exist" (καλοῦντος τὰ μὴ ὄντα ὡς ὄντα). Translation is from the NASB.

The Abraham Story in Rom 4:19–25:
Justification by Faith in Messiah[113]

To this point in his discussion of the Abraham story, Paul focused his attention exclusively on the multiplicity of Abraham's descendants—both Israel
and gentiles who shared his faith and right standing before God. God had
chosen Abraham to be the conduit through which all the nations of the
earth would be blessed, his *principal promise*. In the progress of revelation,
Paul recognized that the justification which Abraham received by faith in
God had clarified the sense in which God intended to bless both Israel and
the nations of the earth. The blessing which Abraham himself received from
God (Gen 12:2; 15:6) was the blessing which the nations of the earth were to
receive as they shared his faith (12:3; Gal 3:8–9). In the development of the
Abraham narrative, God had revealed the means by which he would accomplish this *principal promise*. The promise would not become reality through
one such as Eliezer but through a natural-born heir who would be Abraham's
own offspring (15:1–4). It was only after Abraham believed in this promised
heir that he was justified before God (15:6). However, God had not revealed
the identity of the heir to Abraham at the time of the promise. As promise,
the illocutionary commitment of God obligated him to provide Abraham
with an immediate heir to whom the covenant promises might pass. In the
case of a delayed, the promise of an heir obligated God to provide a lineage
of heirs through whom the promise might stay alive until the ultimate heir
was revealed in history. The promise governed a history of "fulfilling" and
ensured the final "fulfillment." It is worth remembering the contribution
that Willis Beecher made to the hermeneutics of promise when he wrote,

> From some points of view there is no difference between per-
> forming something that has been promised or threatened and
> the coming to pass of something that has been foretold; but from
> other points of view there is a great difference. For example,
> when we think of a promise and its fulfillment, we think of the
> means employed for that purpose. *The promise and the means
> and the result are all in mind at once*, and our conception of each
> is modified by our conception of the others . . .Every fulfilled
> promise is fulfilled prediction; but it is exceedingly important to
> look at it as a promise, and not as mere prediction.[114]

113. Not all commentators see the beginning of a new section in 4:19. See Fitzmyer,
Romans, 382; Moo, *Epistle to the Romans*, 271; Schreiner, *Romans*, 234. However, as
4:19 begins to focus attention on the content of Abraham's faith, it is legitimate to distinguish the verse as beginning a new phase in Paul's thought.

114. Beecher, *Prophets and the Promise*, 376. Emphasis mine.

Since belief in this heir was the means by which the promised blessing would come to both Abraham and the nations, it was important for Paul to return to this important element in God's program of salvation in his climactic ending to Rom 4.

Paul had already revealed that Abraham had believed in a God "who gives life to the dead [τοὺς νεκρούς] and calls into being that which does not exist" (Rom 4:17b NASB) and that at the time God had promised Abraham an heir and nation, the circumstances of his life made their fulfillment impossible from a human point of view (4:18). He now revealed the two most significant obstacles standing against the promise of God. Abraham, nearly one hundred years old (Gen 17:1; cf. Heb 11:12), was well beyond the normal age for procreation ("as good as dead"), and the age of his wife, Sarah, made her womb dead (νέκρωσιν) since she was well past her childbearing years (4:19).[115] However, since Abraham believed in a God who gave life to the dead and called into being what did not exists (4:17b), "he did not become weak in faith" (μὴ ἀσθενήσας τῇ πίστει) when he considered these obstacles (4:19; NASB).[116] Rather, "with respect to the promise [εἰς τὴν ἐπαγγελίαν] of God, he did not waver in unbelief, but grew strong in faith, giving glory to God, and being fully assured that what He had promised, He was able also to perform" (4:20–21 NASB).[117] The promise, here, formed the content of Abraham's faith

115. As Moo observes, "Since the word 'deadness' is not the normal word for a woman's barrenness, Paul has deliberately chosen his language to make clear that Abraham's faith with respect to this promise was specifically faith in the 'God who gives life to the dead' (v. 17b)." Moo, *Epistle to the Romans*, 284. The phrase "as good as dead" (τὸ ἑαυτοῦ σῶμα [ἤδη] νενεκρωμένον) with reference to Abraham's body (σῶμα) should be interpreted within the present context of sexual reproduction. For this reason, Byrne writes that "'body'(*sōma*) here, as in 1:24, has an evident sexual tone." See Byrne, *Romans*, 160. The aspect of deadness, then relates to the fact that Abraham was well past the age when a man was likely to produce offspring. There are two textual issues in 4:19. The first relates to the presence of οὐ before the verb κατενόησεν and the second relates to the legitimacy of ἤδη in the verse. These textual issues, however, are unimportant to the current study and therefore will not be discussed. For a good discussion of these issues, see Metzger, *Textual Commentary on the Greek New Testament*, 451.

116. Many scholars take the participle "weakening" (ἀσθενήσας) to be subordinate to the finite verb "observed" (κατενόησεν). For an example, see Longenecker, *Epistle to the Romans*, 519. While this is certainly a legitimate reading of the text, it is also grammatically possible for the finite verb to be subordinate to "weakening," rendering the translation "he did not become weak in faith when he observed . . ." This latter grammatical construction fits the context better as it draws a sharper connection between Abraham's stalwart faith in the face of the physical obstacles standing in the way of the promise. See Moo, *Epistle to the Romans*, 283.

117. The phrase "Abraham grew strong in faith" (ἀλλ' ἐνεδυναμώθη τῇ πίστει), should retain the passive force of the aorist passive form of the verb, ἐνεδυναμώθη, ("he was made strong in faith"). For a good discussion on this phrase, see Cranfield, *Critical and Exegetical Commentary on the Epistle to the Romans*, 248–49. The

and centered around belief in God's provision of an heir through whom the nations would be blessed, as will be demonstrated in a moment.[118]

To the keen observer of Scripture, Paul's statement that Abraham "did not waver in unbelief but grew strong in faith" (οὐ διεκρίθη τῇ ἀπιστίᾳ ἀλλ᾽ ἐνεδυναμώθη τῇ πίστει) seems to go against the testimony of Scripture, which recounts Abraham's use of Hagar to ensure a physical offspring for himself (Gen 16:1–4) as well as his seeming doubt in Sarah's ability to produce offspring in her old age (17:17).[119] This doubt even manifested itself in Abraham's request that Ishmael might be his heir (17:18). To understand Paul's interpretation of this element in the Abraham story a couple of observation are in order. First, the word translated as "unbelief" (ἀπιστίᾳ) means to actively reject the truth of something.[120] Although it is clear from the Abrahamic narrative in Genesis that Abraham did have moments of doubt, these moments were never active rejections of the truth of God's promise and, therefore, were never moments of ἀπιστία. As Moo notes,

> When Paul says that Abraham did not "doubt . . .because of unbelief," he means not that Abraham never had momentary hesitations, but that he avoided a deep-seated and permanent attitude of distrust and inconsistency in relationship to God and his promises. Unlike the "double-souled" person who displays a deeply rooted division in his attitude towards God (Jas 1:6–8), Abraham maintained a single-minded trust in the fulfillment of God's promise.[121]

Second, it is important to remember that the opposite of faith is not doubt but unbelief. Since doubt and faith are not opposites, they may at times coexist in a person's relationship with God throughout his life.

---

two participial phrases in 4:20–21 explain how it was that Abraham grew strong in his faith (ἐνεδυναμώθη τῇ πίστει). It was by "giving glory to God" (δοὺς δόξαν τῷ θεῷ) and by "being fully convinced that what God had promised he was able to perform" (πληροφορηθεὶς ὅτι ὃ ἐπήγγελται, δυνατός ἐστιν καὶ ποιῆσαι). Schreiner, *Romans*, 238.

118. Some translators understand the εἰς in a causal sense and believe that it was *because of* the promise that Abraham did not weaken in the faith. However as numerous commentators have noted, it is more natural here to understand the preposition εἰς as introducing the object of his stalwart faith and should be translated as "with respect to" the promise. See Fitzmyer, *Romans*, 387–88; Morris, *Epistle to the Romans*, 212; Cranfield, *Critical and Exegetical Commentary on the Epistle to the Romans*, 248. This latter translation of the preposition fits the context better which as a whole is focusing on Abraham's faith in God's promissory revelation.

119. Later in the narrative, Abraham admits to a habit of lying (Gen 20:10–13).

120. Danker, *Greek-English Lexicon*, 103–4.

121. Moo, *Epistle to the Romans*, 284–85.

Therefore, Paul's understanding of this element in the Abraham story need not be at odds with the testimony of Scripture.

An important question arises concerning Paul's use of the phrase "the promise of God" (τὴν ἐπαγγελίαν τοῦ θεοῦ) in Rom 4:20 when referencing the content of Abraham's unwavering faith. Since this content will be connected to his justification in 4:22, it is essential to examine its reference. To what did this promise refer and how did it relate to Paul's previous use of the term to refer to Abraham's future inheritance of the world (4:13)? It is quite remarkable to note that this issue is almost wholly ignored in the current literature available on the topic.[122] However, those who do make brief reference to the phrase believe it either refers to the promise of a descendant/descendants[123] or refers back to the promise of 4:13.[124]

In order to understand the likely content of the promise of 4:20 an important observation must be made. The reference to Abraham's reproductive age and the deadness of Sarah's womb in 4:20 indicates that Paul had the promise of Abraham's heir in mind. While the historical reference seems to be to Gen 17, where God promised Abraham that Isaac would be his offspring through Sarah, it is important to observe that Paul's testimony of Abraham's faith at this point is sandwiched between two references—the first to Gen 15:5 and the second to 15:6 (Rom 4:18, 22). How could Abraham's faith in chapter 17 be credited to him as righteousness in chapter 15 as Rom 4:19–22 seems to suggest? Unless one wishes to accuse Paul of historical error, it seems that the faith of Abraham in the heir (Gen 15:6) had not wavered despite the obstacles to its fulfillment detailed in chapter 17 (cf. Rom 4:19–20). This is why Paul could say that his faith at this point was counted to him as righteousness (4:22).

Although this heir was first promised in Gen 15:4 as the conduit through which God would bless the nations of the earth, God later clarified that this heir would be the offspring of both Abraham and Sarah (17:16, 19). Paul's focus on the promise of this ultimate heir may explain why he did not mention Isaac when he referenced Abraham's faith "in the promise of God" (4:20) since the identity of the heir in Abraham's day was still a mystery. Although Abraham's immediate heir was Isaac (17:19; 21:1–3), Isaac never

---

122. See Cranfield, *Critical and Exegetical Commentary on the Epistle to the Romans*, 248–49; Longenecker, *Epistle to the Romans*, 520–21; Schreiner, *Romans*, 238.

123. Byrne, *Romans*, 154; Moo, *Epistle to the Romans*, 285, note 81; Lopez, *Romans Unlocked*, 96–97; Johnson, *Discovering Romans*, 76. James Boice believes that the promise includes everything God promised to Abraham. "God made a multi-faceted promise to Abraham, involving personal blessing, a land to be given to him and his posterity, blessing on his descendants, and a Redeemer to come" (Boice, *Romans*, 478).

124. Morris, *Epistle to the Romans*, 212.

accomplished what God promised the heir would do. Though Isaac was an heir, and therefore fulfilled God's promise *in part*, he was ultimately not the heir God committed to provide for Abraham or, ultimately, the heir in which Abraham believed (15:6). Isaac was part of God's "fulfilling" of his promise, but he was not the "fulfillment" of the promise. It is Paul's focus on the heir that connected the promise of Rom 4:20 with his previous use of the term (4:13–16) and, perhaps, clarified the sense in which Paul understood this previous promise to have been made. It would be through the promised heir that the inheritance of the world would be received.

Abraham's unwavering faith in the promised heir despite the physical obstacles which he and Sarah faced was the *promissory content* that led to his justification before God. This connection between Abraham's faith in God's promised heir and his justification is made by Paul's use of the inferential conjunction, διό, to begin 4:22.[125] As Paul wrote, "Therefore [διὸ] also it was reckoned to him as righteousness" (διὸ [καὶ] ἐλογίσθη αὐτῷ εἰς δικαιοσύνην; 4:22).[126] Because of Abraham's belief in God's promised heir, he was justified before God. Justifying faith for Abraham, then, involved faith (requirement) in God (object) to provide an heir (content) through whom the promises would be realized. This faith was exercised in a God who gave life to the dead and called into being things that did not exist (4:17b).

It is at this point in the chapter that Paul applied Abraham's belief in God's promise of an heir to the believers in Rome. In 4:23–25 Paul wrote, "But the words 'it was counted to him' were not written for his sake alone, but for ours also. It will be counted to us who believe [requirement] in him [object] who raised from the dead Jesus our Lord [content], who was delivered up for our trespasses and raised for our justification" (ESV). The method of Abraham's justification was recorded for the benefit of the readers so that they, too, might experience justification as they modeled their faith after that of Abraham. Just as Abraham was justified when he expressed faith in God's promise of an heir through whom all nations would be blessed, believers were justified as they believed in God's provision of Jesus, the promised heir, whose death burial and resurrection purchased justification for those who shared Abraham's faith.[127] In his comments on

125. See Wallace, *Greek Grammar Beyond the Basics*, 673.

126. Concerning the inclusion of καὶ in the text of 4:22, Metzger writes, "In order to represent the balance of external evidence for and against the presence of καὶ, the Committee decided to print it within square brackets" (Metzger, *Textual Commentary on the Greek New Testament*, 452).

127. Whether or not this additional content—the death, burial, and resurrection of Messiah—was necessary for salvation in the Old Testament, is beyond the scope of the current study, which is merely attempting to show continuity found in Messiah as part of the content of faith.

Rom 4:1–25, Walter Kaiser acknowledged the continuity in God's plan of salvation when he wrote,

> Now all of this [salvation] was not new, for in Romans 4:1–25 Paul showed that Abraham was similarly "justified," but not by his works. Rather it happened just as "the Scriptures say" (4:3): "Abraham believed God and it was credited to him as righteousness" (Gen 15:6). This did not mean that Abraham became a theist, one who now believed in God for the first time—and that was all that happened! No, it meant that he put his faith in the coming Man of promise, his own "seed," which God had just disclosed to him in Genesis 15:1–5. The object of his faith was in principle the same as it ever was or ever will be: the Messiah himself. On that basis, God declared Abraham righteous.[128]

As Abraham believed in this heir, he received the promise of inheriting the world—life in the kingdom—when this heir arrived and completed his work (4:13). As Christians believed in Jesus, the heir in whom Abraham hoped, they shared in this promise and could also look forward to life in the kingdom (4:14–16) under Messiah. Justification by faith in God's promised heir, Jesus, was the means by which this inheritance could be experienced.

Paul's treatment of the Abraham story revealed the nature of the discontinuity in God's one method of salvation. While continuity was to be found in Messiah, *what could be known about Messiah and his work* differed from dispensation to dispensation. The heir who was unknown in Abraham's day was revealed to be Jesus of Nazareth. Yet, despite this aspect of discontinuity in content, salvation included faith Messiah. In this way, the gospel message, trans-dispensationally, had always been distinct in content. In the Old Testament, then, as illustrated by Abraham, God's promissory revelation of Messiah set up a "Situation Vacant" type of meaning.[129] The revelation was clear enough in its original context to be understood and, therefore, sufficient to provide the basis for genuine faith, however the details were revealed in generic terms. In Abraham's day, he believed in God's promised heir through whom the nations of the earth would be blessed. This was true and correct at the level at which it was expressed. However, the generic nature of these promises left much unstated. Who was this promised heir? Would it be Isaac or someone else? How, precisely, would this seed bless all the nations of the earth in response to sin? In the progress of history, the promised heir would reveal himself as he fulfilled the terms of the vacancy expressed in the original context. Therefore, while Abraham

---

128. Kaiser Jr., *Promise-Plan of God*, 282.

129. Caird, *Language and Imagery of the Bible*, 157.

believed in the same Messiah as New Testament believers, his faith was in what could be understood in the generic terms of the promise as God revealed it in his day. The faith of New Testament believers recognized the arrival of this heir in Jesus of Nazareth.

CONCLUSION

The apostle Paul wrote the book of Romans to address a problem that had arisen in the church in Rome concerning his gospel and ministry. Paul's failure to visit the believers in Rome had caused some in that community to accuse him of avoiding the church out of shame in the gospel he preached (Rom 1:10–16; 15:22–25). Paul had preached that justification by grace through faith in the person and work of Christ was equally available to both Jew and gentile apart from works of the Law (3:24). In the gospel, then, Jews and gentiles were co-heirs of salvation and should experience unity in the church. Neither the Law nor circumcision provided the Jew with any superior standing in the sight of God. For the Jew, Paul's gospel required a proper understanding of the role that the Law and circumcision played in Israel's history (2:17–29). Since neither were salvific acts, the gentile believer was under no obligation to pursue righteousness by the Law to attain a right standing before God. The avoidance of God's wrath (1:18) and unity in the body (15:7) could only come by grace through faith in Jesus.

However, to the Jewish believer, Paul's gospel sounded like a new teaching—a gospel different from what the Old Testament anticipated. In order to convince them that the gospel he preached was the same gospel the Old Testament foresaw, Paul needed to show that the method of salvation by which Old Testament saints were justified was no different than the gospel he now proclaimed had been fulfilled in Jesus Christ. Because it was Paul's gospel that accurately represented the Scriptures, it was his gospel in which the believers in Rome needed to persevere.

In Rom 3:21–22, Paul announced that the gospel he preached, justification by grace through faith in Jesus was the same gospel that the Law and the prophets had anticipated (cf. 1:1–3). "But now apart from the Law the righteousness of God has been manifested, being witnessed by the Law and the prophets, *even the righteousness of God through faith in Jesus Christ for all who believe*, for there is no distinction."[130] However, this announcement itself raised a series of important questions. How could the Law and prophets bear witness to a gospel including Christ before the revelation of Christ in his advent? Did the Old Testament really preach a gospel through faith apart from

---

130. Translation is from the NASB. Emphasis mine.

circumcision and the Law? To answer these questions, Paul turned to the life of Abraham in Rom 4:1–25 to show that justification in God's one plan of salvation had always been by grace through faith in the Messiah. Because of the method of Abraham's justification, believing Jews and believing gentiles in the Church could and should experience unity through their shared faith.

The truthfulness of Paul's gospel is dependent on a real, not imagined or fabricated, continuity with the Old Testament's witness. Paul's argument, therefore, could not transform the meaning of Old Testament revelation, for to do so would be to undermine the credibility of the very thing he attempted to prove. To convince his readers that the Law and prophets bore witness to his gospel, he turned to the life of Abraham to demonstrate the continuity of the gospel in its relationship to the one he now preached.

In his development of the Abraham story, Paul revealed that the faith by which Abraham was justified existed apart from works and therefore was a gracious gift rather than a wage that could be earned (4:1–8; cf. Gen 15:6). Abraham's justification was not only received by faith apart from works but was received apart from circumcision (4:9–12) and the works of the Law (4:13–18). However, so that his audience did not conclude that Abraham's faith was a general belief in God, Paul revealed that the content of the faith through which Abraham was justified came when he believed in God's promise of an heir. Although the identity of this heir was unknown in Abraham's day, in the present dispensation the heir had been revealed to be Jesus Christ whose death and resurrection purchased justification for those who believed (4:19–25).

Romans 3:21—4:25, then, provides a complete picture of God's one method of salvation both past and present. According to Paul, the *basis for salvation* is the death of Jesus Christ (Rom 3:25), the *requirement* is faith apart from works, rituals, or the Law (Rom 4:1–18), the *object of faith* is God who declares the sinner righteous (Rom 4:3), and the *content of faith* includes Messiah, Abraham's promised heir revealed to be Jesus of Nazareth (4:19–25). In Paul's treatment of the Abraham story, the element of discontinuity pertained to *what could be known of Messiah*. Yet, despite this aspect of discontinuity in content, salvation always included faith in him.

In the Old Testament, then, as illustrated in the Abraham story, God's promissory revelation of Messiah set up a "Situation Vacant" type of meaning.[131] The revelation was clear enough in its original context to be understood and, therefore, sufficient to provide the basis for genuine faith, however the details were revealed in generic terms. In Abraham's day, he believed in God's promised heir through whom the nations of the earth would

---

131. Caird, *Language and Imagery of the Bible*, 157.

be blessed. This was true and correct at the level at which it was expressed. However, the generic nature of these promises left much unstated. Who was this promised heir? Would it be Isaac or someone else? How would he bless all the nations of the earth in response to sin? In the progress of history, the promised heir would reveal himself as he fulfilled the terms of the vacancy expressed in the original context. Therefore, while Abraham believed in the same Messiah as New Testament believers, his faith was in what could be understood in the generic terms of the promise as God revealed it in his day. In the progress of revelation, the New Testament believer's faith recognized the arrival of this heir in Jesus of Nazareth.

5

Summary and Future Direction

SUMMARY

Purpose of the Study

When considering God's one method of salvation in dispensational theology, Rom 4:1–25 becomes a sort of *crux interpretum* for it is here that Paul used the Abraham story from Genesis to speak to the role that faith played in God's singular program for salvation both past and present. The purpose of this study was to show that Paul's use of the Abraham story in Rom 4:1–25 demonstrated that faith in the promised seed, Messiah, was a *sine qua non* of God's one method of salvation as Paul interpreted this theology in light of the argument of Genesis as a whole and its progress in history.[1] In order to accomplish this purpose, it was shown that Abraham's faith in Genesis, by which he was justified, was in God's promised seed of blessing, Abraham's heir. Although Isaac was an immediate seed and heir, he was not the seed or heir which God had promised or ultimately the heir in which Abraham believed. In Rom 4:1–25, Paul announced that the heir whose full identity was unknown in Abraham's day was revealed to be Jesus of Nazareth. The change, then, between Abraham's faith and the faith of New Testament believers was found in *what could be known of this heir* in the progress of revelation. When understood in conjunction with preceding literary unit, Rom 3:21—4:25 existed as a thought unity that described

---

1. This is the thesis statement of this study.

God's one method of salvation as having a common *basis* (Christ's death), a common *requirement* (faith), a common *object* (God), and a common *content* (faith in the promised Messiah). The purpose of this study was merely to demonstrate that the content of saving faith included belief in Messiah. It was not meant to determine what must be believed about Messiah in each dispensation.

The Issue within Dispensational Theology

The interpretation of the Abraham story in Rom 4:1–25 within the dispensational tradition evidenced a diversity in the movement. Although widespread agreement existed with respect to the continuity found in the basis of salvation, requirement for salvation, and the object of faith, there was never a consensus on whether any continuity was to be found in the content of faith. Since its beginning, there were those, like Darby, who maintained that the efficacious nature of saving faith only required that a person believe in God. However, there were also dispensationalists, like William Kelly, who believed that God's method of salvation involved more than a common object—it included belief in Messiah. Therefore, within the dispensational tradition, disagreement surrounded the nature of discontinuity in God's program for salvation.

The debate, as it pertained to Rom 4, hinged on what the interpreter believed was capable of being shared through the language of the original text. To use literal interpretation consistently, one could not go further than to assign meanings capable of being expressed in the historical context in which the passage was written. To read New Testament meanings back into an Old Testament context was to depart from the literal method of interpretation demanded by the dispensational tradition.[2]

Dispensationalists who believed that the content of Abraham's faith in Gen 15:6 looked no further than a belief in God's provision of Isaac or a multiplicity of offspring saw the content of Abraham's faith to be different than the faith of the New Testament believer, for the Christian did not place his faith in Isaac or a multiplicity of offspring for salvation but in the person and work of Jesus Christ. However, those dispensationalists who saw the faith of Abraham to look beyond God's immediate provision of Isaac, or numerous descendants, to an ultimate fulfillment of covenant promise through his seed and heir, opened the door to a greater continuity in the

2. Ryrie observed that the consistent use of a literal hermeneutic is an essential component of dispensationalism (Ryrie, *Dispensationalism*, 93).

content of faith throughout the dispensations. Therefore, it was essential to establish what Abraham could have believed in Gen 15:6

The Faith of Abraham in Gen 15:6

Using the genre of narrative history, the author of Genesis developed the expectation of a coming male descendant of Eve who would be God's agent of judgment on the serpent (Gen 3:15; cf. Num 24:17). The performative nature of God's speech act in Gen 3:15 obligated God to provide Eve with this coming seed. Historically, God's illocutionary commitment provided Adam and Eve the lens through which to exegete history. Literarily, these divine commitments provided the lens through which the reader must interpret the narrative to follow. The lineage of this individual was traced from Adam through Seth (5:1–32), Shem (11:10–26), Abraham (11:31; 15:4) to a coming ruler out of Judah (49:10) through Perez (38:29; 46:12; cf. Ruth 4:18–22; Ps 72:17). Although none of the individuals in Genesis accomplished God's word of judgment on the serpent, the continued provision of offspring to Eve existed as a testimony to God's commitment to bring about the seed as he had promised.

While God had revealed that this coming seed would be his agent of judgment, God revealed that this the coming seed would also be an agent of blessing through a partnership with Abram. In a series of performative speech acts (12:1–3, 7), God obligated himself to accomplish a *principal promise* in his governance of history. Through Abram, God committed himself to bless all the nations of the earth (12:3c). Abram's early response to the illocutionary commitments of God evidenced an immature faith as he exhibited both *intended* (12:5–6; 7) and *unintended perlocutions* (11:31; 12:10–20; 13:1–12) in his early response to the revelation of God. However, in his dialogue with God in Gen 15:1–3, Abram revealed that despite God's promises that he would make him into a great nation (12:2) and give the land to his offspring (12:7; 13:14–15)—promises that implied an heir and natural posterity—Abram had not yet trusted that God would indeed provide him with an heir and therefore had not yet accepted the means by which God intended to bless the nations of the earth. It was not God's intention to bless humanity through Abram's servant but through a natural heir of Abram (12:4). This future heir would be a *male descendant* that God would provide (15:3–4).

To highlight Abram's response to this assurance from God as the climactic event in the dialogue (15:1–6), the author shifted from the use of the *wayyiqtol* form to the *weqatal* form. In response to God's assurance, Abram

believed in the Lord's word and he reckoned his faith to him as righteousness (15:6). While the *object* of Abram's faith was the God—and had been
all along—the *content* of his faith now included the belief that his future heir
would be *a natural male descendant* through whom God would bless the nations of the earth. Although at the time of their conversation, the provision
of this heir remained unfulfilled, Abram experienced a part of his blessing
from the Lord. In response to his faith, God gifted Abram a declaration of
righteousness. The blessing which Abram through his heir was to mediate
was the very blessing which he himself received from the Lord.

Paul's Use of the Abraham Story in Rom 4:1–25

The apostle Paul, built upon this Abraham narrative in his letter to the Romans. Paul wrote the book of Romans to address a problem that had arisen
in the church in Rome concerning his gospel and ministry. Paul's failure to
visit the believers in Rome had caused some in that community to accuse
him of avoiding the church out of shame in the gospel he preached (Rom
1:10–16; 15:22–25). Paul had preached that justification by grace through
faith in the person and work of Christ was equally available to both Jew
and gentile apart from works of the Law (3:24). In the gospel, then, Jews
and gentiles were co-heirs of salvation and could experience unity in the
church. Neither the Law nor circumcision provided the Jew with any superior standing in the sight of God. For the Jew, Paul's gospel required a proper
understanding of the role that the Law and circumcision played in Israel's
history (2:17–29). Since neither were salvific acts, the gentile believer was
under no obligation to pursue righteousness by the Law to attain a right
standing before God. The avoidance of God's wrath (1:18) and unity in the
body (15:7) could only come by grace through faith in Jesus Christ.

However, to the Jewish believers, Paul's gospel sounded like a new
teaching—a gospel different from what the Old Testament anticipated. In
order to convince them that the gospel he preached was the same gospel
the Old Testament foresaw, Paul needed to demonstrate that the method of
salvation by which Old Testament saints were justified was no different than
the gospel he now proclaimed had been fulfilled in Jesus. Because it was
Paul's gospel that accurately represented the Scriptures, it was his gospel in
which the believers in Rome needed to persevere.

In Rom 3:21–22, Paul announced that the gospel he preached, justification by grace through faith in Jesus, was the same gospel that the Law and
the prophets had anticipated (cf. 1:1–3). "But now apart from the Law the
righteousness of God has been manifested, being witnessed by the Law and

the prophets, *even the righteousness of God through faith in Jesus Christ for all who believe,* for there is no distinction."[3] However, this announcement itself raised a series of important questions. How could the Law and prophets bear witness to a gospel including Christ before the revelation of Christ in his advent? Did the Old Testament really preach a gospel through faith apart from circumcision and the Law? To answer these questions, Paul turned to the life of Abraham in Rom 4:1–25 to show that justification in God's one plan of salvation had been by grace through faith in the Messiah. Because of the method of Abraham's justification, believing Jews and gentiles in the Church could and should experience unity through their shared faith, a unity that would extend to their acceptance of Paul as well.

The truthfulness of Paul's gospel depended on a real, as opposed to an imagined or fabricated, continuity with the Old Testament's witness. Paul's argument, therefore, could not transform the meaning of Old Testament revelation, for to do so would be to undermine the credibility of the very thing he attempted to prove. Rather, to convince his readers that the Law and prophets did in fact bear witness to his gospel, he turned to the life of Abraham to demonstrate the continuity of the gospel in its relationship to the one he now preached.

In his development of the Abraham story, Paul revealed that the faith by which Abraham was justified had existed apart from works and therefore was a gracious gift rather than a wage that could be earned (4:1–8; cf. Gen 15:6). Abraham's justification was not only received by faith apart from works, but it was received apart from both circumcision (4:9–12) and the works of the Law (4:13–18). However, so that his audience did not conclude that Abraham's faith was a general belief in God, Paul revealed that the content of the faith through which Abraham was justified came when he believed in God's promise of an heir. Although the identity of this heir had been a mystery in Abraham's day, in the present dispensation the heir had been revealed to be Jesus Christ whose death and resurrection purchased justification for those who believed (4:19–25).

Romans 3:21—4:25, then, provided a complete picture of God's one method of salvation both past and present. According to Paul, the *basis for salvation* was the death of Jesus Christ (Rom 3:25), the *requirement* was faith apart from works, rituals, or the Law (Rom 4:1–18), the *object of faith* was God who declares the sinner righteous (Rom 4:3), and the *content of faith* included Messiah, Abraham's promised seed and heir revealed to be Jesus of Nazareth (4:19–25).

---

3. Emphasis mine.

Paul's treatment of the Abraham story revealed the nature of the discontinuity in God's one method of salvation. While continuity was to be found in Messiah, *what could be known about Messiah* differed from dispensation to dispensation. Yet, despite this aspect of discontinuity in content, salvation had included faith in him. In this way, the gospel message, transdispensationally, had always been distinct in content. In the Old Testament, then, as illustrated by Abraham, God's promissory revelation of Messiah set up a "Situation Vacant" type of meaning.[4] The revelation was clear enough in its original context to be understood and, therefore, sufficient to provide the basis for genuine faith, however the details were revealed in generic terms. In Abraham's day, he believed in God's promised seed and heir through whom the nations of the earth would be blessed. This was true and correct at the level at which it was expressed. However, the generic nature of these promises left much unstated. Who was this promised heir? Would it be Isaac or someone else? How would this heir bless all the nations of the earth in response to sin? In the progress of history, the promised heir would reveal himself as he fulfilled the terms of the vacancy expressed in the original context. Therefore, while Abraham believed in the same Messiah as New Testament believers, his faith was in what could be understood in his day. The New Testament believer's faith recognized the arrival of this heir in Jesus of Nazareth.

In summary, this study has attempted to provide validity to the historic dispensational position articulated by dispensationalists like William Kelly with reference to Rom 4:1–25.

> But the apostle [Paul] takes care to point out the difference as well as the analogy. The faith not of Abraham only but of all Old Testament saints was exercised on promise. They all in a large sense waited for the accomplishment of what God held out, sure that He could not lie, and was able also to perform. But in the great ulterior object of their hope they were expecting One who was only promised and not yet come.
>
> It is not so with the Christian; for though he, like the elders, obtains a good report by faith, and has his faith reckoned for righteousness, yet the personal object of hope is come, and has wrought the infinite work of redemption.[5]

4. Caird, *Language and Imagery of the Bible,* 157.

5. Kelly, *Notes on the Epistle of Paul,* 54.

FUTURE DIRECTION

The Gospel throughout the Dispensations

While this study has focused on Paul's use of the Abraham story in Rom 4:1–25 to argue for a trans-dispensational gospel message that includes Messiah as part of the essential content of a saving faith, this analysis has only looked at continuity with regard to two dispensations, the dispensation of promise and that of grace. More work needs to be done to expand this study. How did this single gospel function in the other dispensations in light of their added revelation? Can further continuity be found in the content of faith from such an analysis? Are there particular things one must believe about Messiah in order to be justified? Such future study is needed to provide greater clarity within dispensational theology.

Israel as a Steward of the Message of Messiah

If it is true that the Genesis account of the Abraham story elicits a critical soteriology in God's one program of salvation, then the function of Genesis in the Pentateuch must be reevaluated. As a single book composition, the Pentateuch held a special place for the nation of Israel for it provided them with their identity and ministry in the redemptive program of God. Recognizing the important role that the Pentateuch played in Israel's identity, Gary Knoppers and Bernard Levinson describe these five books of the Bible as the "constitution" of Israel.

> There is no doubt that the reception of the Pentateuch as authoritative *tôrâ* ("instruction") led to this *tôrâ*'s becoming one of the defining pillars of the religious practices of Jews and Samaritans. Since antiquity, the five books of Moses have served as a sacred constitution, foundational for both belief and practice.[6]

In an attempt to define the theme of this constitution, M. H. Segal writes, "[T]he real theme of the Pentateuch is the selection of Israel from the nations and its consecration to the service of God and His laws in a divinely-appointed land."[7] Within this foundational corpus the book of Genesis functions to provide Israel with her ancestry in the redemptive program of God centering around the hope of a future "king from the house of Judah

---

6. Knoppers and Levinson, "How, When, Where, and Why Did the Pentateuch Become the Torah?," 2.

7. Segal, *Pentateuch.*

who will reign over Israel and the nations."[8] If the Abraham narrative reveals critical content to the gospel message, then the function of Genesis must extend beyond these suggestions to include the soteriological stewardship of Israel. Among other things, the book of Genesis would identify Israel as God's steward of the gospel message and would provide clarity to the way Israel was to function as God's kingdom of priests (Exod 19:5–6). Further attention needs to be given to this stewardship found in the Pentateuch and its function in Israel's history.

CONCLUSION

It is the hope of this writer that future generations of dispensationalists will rediscover the important soteriological heritage found throughout dispensational history that has emphasized a continuity in the content of the gospel found in Messiah. While such a view has always been present within dispensationalism's heritage, it has not garnered enough attention in recent years. Like other orthodox Christian theologies, dispensationalism as a system has always been home to those who have affirmed that God's method of salvation in past and present includes a common *basis* (the substitutionary death of Jesus Christ), a common *requirement* (faith), a common *object* (faith in God), and a common *content* in every age (belief in Messiah).

8. Sailhamer, *Meaning of the Pentateuch*, 603. In a previous work, Sailhamer expanded this discussion when he observed two theological interests of the author of Genesis. "Nearly every section of the work displays the author's theological interest, which can be summarized in two points. First, he intends to draw a line connecting the God of the fathers and the God of the Sinai covenant with the God who created the world. Second, he intends to show that the call of the patriarchs and the Sinai covenant have as their ultimate goal the reestablishment of God's original purpose in Creation." See Sailhamer, *Pentateuch as Narrative*, 81.

Bibliography

Alexander, T. Desmond. "From Adam to Judah: The Significance of the Family Tree in Genesis." *Evangelical Quarterly* 61 (1989) 5–19.

———. *From Paradise to the Promised Land: An Introduction to the Pentateuch.* 3rd ed. Grand Rapids: Baker, 2012.

———"Further Observations on the Term 'Seed' in Genesis." *Tyndale Bulletin* 48 (1997) 363–67.

———. "Genealogies, Seed and the Compositional Unity of Genesis." *Tyndale Bulletin* 44 (1993) 255–70.

Allis, Oswald T. "Modern Dispensationalism and the Doctrine of Unity of Scripture." *Evangelical Quarterly* 8 (1936) 22–35.

———. "Modern Dispensationalism and the Law of God." *Evangelical Quarterly* 8 (1936) 272–89.

Allman, James E. *Accept One Another: A Practical and Expository Commentary on the Book of Romans.* Lebanon, TN: Seven Interactive, 2017.

———. "Gaining Perspective on the New Perspective on Paul." *Bibliotheca Sacra* 170 (2013) 51–68.

Alston, William P. *Illocutionary Acts and Sentence Meaning.* Ithaca, NY: Cornell University Press, 2000.

Alter, Robert. *The Art of Biblical Poetry.* New York: Basic Books, 2011.

Altman, Amnon. *The Historical Prologue of the Hittite Vassal Treaties: An Inquiry into the Concepts of Hittite Interstate Law.* Bar–Ilan Studies in Near Eastern Languages and Culture. Ramat-Gan, Israel: Bar Ilan University Press, 2004.

Arnold, Bill T. *Genesis.* New Cambridge Bible Commentary. Edited by Ben Witherington III. Cambridge, UK: Cambridge University Press, 2009.

Arnold, Bill T., and John H. Choi. *A Guide to Biblical Hebrew Syntax.* Cambridge, UK: Cambridge University Press, 2003.

Austin, John L. *How to Do Things with Words.* Edited by J. O. Urmson and Marina Sbisá. 2nd ed. Cambridge, MA: Harvard University Press, 1975.

Bahnsen, Greg L. "Response to Wayne G. Strickland." In *Five Views on Law and Gospel.* Edited by Stanley N. Gundry, 290–301. Grand Rapids: Zondervan, 1996.

Bailey, Kenneth E. "St. Paul's Understanding of the Territorial Promise of God to Abraham: Romans 4:13 in Its Historical and Theological Context." *Theological Review* 15 (1994) 59–69.

Baker, Charles F. *A Dispensational Theology*. Grand Rapids: Grace Bible College Publications, 1971.

Balmer, Randall. "Arno C. Gaebelein." In *Encyclopedia of Evangelicalism*, 235–35. London: Westminster John Knox, 2002.

———. "H. A. Ironside." In *Encyclopedia of Evangelicalism*, 298. London: Westminster John Knox, 2002.

———. "John Nelson Darby." In *Encyclopedia of Evangelicalism*, 170–71. London: Westminster John Knox, 2002.

———. "Lewis Sperry Chafer." In *Encyclopedia of Evangelicalism*, 120–21. London: Westminster John Knox, 2002.

Baltzer, Klaus. *Das Bundesformular*. Wissenschaftliche Monographien zum alten und neuen Testament 4. Edited by Günther Bornkamm and Gerhard von Rad. Freudenstadt, Germany: Neukirchener, 1964.

Bar-Efrat, Shimon. *Narrative Art in the Bible*. New York: T. & T. Clark, 2004.

Barker, Kenneth L. "False Dichotomies Between the Testaments." *Journal of the Evangelical Theological Society* 25 (1982) 3–16.

Baron, David. *Rays of Messiah's Glory: Christ in the Old Testament*. Winona Lake, IN: BHM Books, 1979.

Barr, James. "The Meaning of 'Mythology' in Relation to the Old Testament." *Vetus Testamentum* 9 (1959) 1–10.

Batto, Bernard F. *In the Beginning: Essays on Creation Motifs in the Ancient Near East and the Bible*. Winona Lake, IN: Eisenbrauns, 2013.

Baylis, Charles P. "Creation of the Nation Israel (Jacob) to Represent God (27–50)." 2013. http://thebiblicalstory.org/baylis/wp-content/uploads/2015/02/11SettingCreationNationJacob110713.pdf.

Beckman, Gary. *Hittite Diplomatic Texts*. Edited by Harry A. Hoffner. 2nd ed. Society of Biblical Literature: Writings from the Ancient World 7. Edited by Simon B. Parker. Atlanta: Scholars Press, 1999.

Beecher, Willis J. *The Prophets and the Promise*. New York: n.p., 1905. Reprint, Grand Rapids: Baker, 1963.

Ben-Barak, Zafrira. "Meribaal and the System of Land Grants in Ancient Israel." *Biblica* 62 (1981) 73–91.

Benton, Steven S. "Genesis 17:9–14: An Exegetical and Theological Study of the Relation of Circumcision to the Covenant." ThM thesis, Dallas Theological Seminary, 1988.

Bergen, Robert D. "Text as a Guide to Authorial Intention: An Introduction to Discourse Criticism." *Journal of the Evangelical Theological Society* 30 (1987) 327–36.

Berlin, Adele. *Poetics and Interpretation of Biblical Narrative*. Winona Lake, IN: Eisenbrauns, 1994.

Beyerlin, Walter, ed. *Near Eastern Religious Texts Relating to the Old Testament*. Translated by John Bowden. Old Testament Library. Edited by Peter Ackroyd et al. Philadelphia: Westminster, 1978.

Blaising, Craig A., and Darrell L. Bock. *Progressive Dispensationalism*. Grand Rapids: Baker, 1993.

Boice, James M. *Romans: Justification by Faith Romans 1–4*. Vol. 1. 2 vols. Grand Rapids: Baker, 1991.

Bornkamm, Günther. "μυστήριον." In *Theological Dictionary of the Old Testament*. Vol. 4. 15 vols. Edited by Gerhard Kittel, 802–28. Translated by Geoffrey W. Bromiley. Grand Rapids: Eerdmans, 1967.

Botterweck, G. Johannes, and Helmer Ringgren, eds. *Theological Dictionary of the Old Testament*. Vol. 9. 15 vols. Translated by David E. Green. Grand Rapids: Eerdmans, 1977.

Brenton, Lancelot C. L. *The Septuagint with Apocrypha: Greek and English*. London: Samuel Bagster & Sons, 1851. Reprint, Grand Rapids: Zondervan, 1982.

Brooks, Peter. *Reading for the Plot: Design and Intention in Narrative*. Cambridge, MA: Harvard University Press, 1992.

Brown, Francis, S. R. Driver, and Charles A. Briggs. *A Hebrew and English Lexicon of the Old Testament: With an Appendix Containing the Biblical Aramaic*. Oxford: Clarendon, 1907.

Brown, Jeannine K. *Scripture as Communication: Introducing Biblical Hermeneutics*. Grand Rapids: Baker, 2007.

Brueggemann, Walter. *Genesis: A Bible Commentary for Teaching and Preaching*. Interpretation. Edited by James Luther Mays, et al. Louisville: Westminster John Knox, 1982.

Buss, Martin J. "The Contribution of Speech Act Theory to Biblical Studies." In *Speech Act Theory and Biblical Criticism*, 125–34. Semeia 41. Edited by Hugh C. White. Decatur, GA: Scholars Press, 1988.

Byrne, Brendan. *Romans*. Sacra Pagina Series 6. Edited by Daniel J. Harrington. Collegeville, MN: Liturgical Press, 1996.

Caird, G. B. *The Language and Imagery of the Bible*. London: Duckworth, 2009.

Carson, D. A. "Mystery and Fulfillment: Toward a More Comprehensive Paradigm of Paul's Understanding of the Old and the New." In *Justification and Variegated Nomism*. Vol. 2. 2 vols. Edited by D. A. Carson, Peter O'Brien, and Mark A. Seifrid, 393–436. Grand Rapids: Baker, 2004.

Carson, D. A., Peter T. O'Brien, and Mark A. Seifrid, eds. *Justification and Variegated Nomism*. Vol. 2. 2 vols. Grand Rapids: Baker, 2001.

Chafer, Lewis S. *Dispensationalism*. Dallas: Dallas Seminary Press, 1936.

———. "Dispensational Distinctions Denounced." *Bibliotheca Sacra* 101 (1944) 257–60.

———. "Editorials: Justification." *Bibliotheca Sacra* 103 (1946) 129–34.

———. "Inventing Heretics through Misunderstanding." *Bibliotheca Sacra* 102 (1945) 1–5.

———. *Systematic Theology: Ecclesiology*. Vol. 4. 8 vols. 1948. Reprint, Grand Rapids: Kregel, 1976.

———. *Systematic Theology: Soteriology*. Vol. 3. 8 vols. 1948. Reprint, Grand Rapids: Kregel, 1976.

———. *Systematic Theology: Christology*. Vol. 5. 8 vols. 1948. Reprint, Grand Rapids: Kregel, 1976.

Charles, R. H., ed. *The Apocrypha and Pseudepigrapha of the Old Testament in English: With Introduction and Critical Explanatory Notes to the Several Books*. Vol. 2. 2 vols. Oxford: Clarenden, 1913.

Charlesworth, James H. "Prayer of Manasseh." In *The Old Testament Pseudepigrapha: Expansions of the 'Old Testament' and Legends, Wisdom and Philosophical Literature, Prayers, Psalms, and Odes, Fragments of Lost Judeo-Hellenistic Works*. Vol. 2. 2 vols. Edited by James H. Charlesworth, 625–37. Peabody, MA: Hendrickson, 2009.

Chisholm, Robert B., Jr. *From Exegesis to Exposition: A Practical Guide to Biblical Hebrew*. Grand Rapids: Baker, 1998.

Christian Reformed Church. *Psalter Hymnal: Including the Psalms, Bible Songs, Hymns, Ecumenical Creeds, Doctrinal Standards, and Liturgical Forms of the Christian Reformed Church in North America*. Grand Rapids: CRC, 1988.

Clark, David H. "The Genealogies of Genesis Five and Eleven." PhD diss., Dallas Theological Seminary, 1967.

Coats, George W. *Genesis: With an Introduction to Narrative Literature*. Grand Rapids: Eerdmans, 1983.

Cohen, L. Jonathan. *The Diversity of Meaning*. London: Methuen, 1966.

Collins, John C. "A Syntactical Note (Genesis 3:15): Is the Woman's Seed Singular or Plural." *Tyndale Bulletin* 48 (1997) 139–48.

Cranfield, Charles E. B. *A Critical and Exegetical Commentary on the Epistle to the Romans*. Vol. 1. 2 vols. International Critical Commentary. Edited by J. A. Emerton, et al. Edinburgh: T. & T. Clark, 1975.

———. *Romans: A Shorter Commentary*. Grand Rapids: Eerdmans, 1985.

Crutchfield, Larry V. *The Origins of Dispensationalism: The Darby Factor*. New York: University Press of America, 1992.

Dallas Theological Seminary. "David K. Lowery." https://voice.dts.edu/contributor/david-k-lowery/.

———. "DTS Doctrinal Statement." https://www.dts.edu/about/doctrinal-statement.

Danker, Frederick W., ed. *A Greek-English Lexicon of the New Testament and Other Early Christian Literature*. Chicago: University of Chicago Press, 2000.

Darby, John N. *The Collected Writings of John Nelson Darby: Doctrinal No. 2*. Vol. 7. 34 vols. Edited by William Kelly. Sunbury, PA: Believer's Bookshelf, 1971.

———. *The Collected Writings of John Nelson Darby: Doctrinal No. 7*. Vol. 23. 34 vols. Edited by William Kelly. Sunbury, PA: Believer's Bookshelf, 1971.

———. *The Collected Writings of John Nelson Darby: Doctrinal No. 8*. Vol. 29. 34 vols. Edited by William Kelly. Sunbury, PA: Believer's Bookshelf, 1971.

———. *The Collected Writings of J. N. Darby: Expository No. 1*. Vol. 19. 34 vols. Edited by William Kelly. Sunbury, PA: Believer's Bookshelf, 1971.

———. *The Collected Writings of J. N. Darby: Expository No. 5*. Vol. 26. 34 vols. Edited by William Kelly. Sunbury, PA: Believer's Bookshelf, 1971.

———. *The Collected Writings of John Nelson Darby: Miscellaneous No. 2*. Vol. 33. 34 vols. Edited by William Kelly. Sunbury, PA: Believer's Bookshelf, 1971.

Davies, W. D. *The Territorial Dimension of Judaism*. Berkeley: University of California Press, 1982.

Davis, John J. *Paradise to Prison: Studies in Genesis*. Grand Rapids: Baker, 1975.

De Catanzaro, Carmino J. "Man in Revolt: A Study in the Primeval History of the Book of Genesis." *Canadian Journal of Theology* 4 (1958) 285–92.

De Vaux, Roland. *The Bible and the Ancient Near East*. Translated by Damian McHugh. New York: Doubleday, 1971.

De Wette, W. M. L. *A Critical and Historical Introduction to the Canonical Scriptures of the Old Testament*. Boston: Charles C. Little and James Brown, 1850.

Delitzsch, Franz. *A New Commentary on Genesis*. Vol. 1. 2 vols. Translated by Sophia Taylor. Clark's Foreign Theological Library 36. Edinburgh: T. & T. Clark, 1899.

———. *A New Commentary on Genesis*. Vol. 2. 2 vols. Translated by Sophia Taylor. Edinburgh: T. & T. Clark, 1888. Reprint, Minneapolis: Klock & Klock, 1978.

DeRouchie, Jason S. "The Blessing-Commission, the Promised Offspring, and the *Toledot* Structure of Genesis." *Journal of the Evangelical Theological Society* 56 (2013) 219–47.

DeRouchie, Jason S., and Jason C. Meyer. "Christ or Family as the 'Seed' of Promise? An Evaluation of N. T. Wright on Galatians 3:16." *Southern Baptist Journal of Theology* 14 (2010) 36–48.

Detweiler, Robert. "Speaking of Believing in Gen. 2–3." In *Speech Act Theory and Biblical Criticism*, 135–42. Semeia 41. Edited by Hugh C. White. Decatur, GA: Scholars Press, 1988.

Dumbrell, William J. *Covenant and Creation: An Old Testament Covenant Theology.* Revised and enlarged edition. Milton Keynes, UK: Paternoster, 2013.

———. *Covenant and Creation: A Theology of the Old Testament Covenants.* Carlisle, UK: Paternoster, 1993.

Dunn, James D. G. "The New Perspective on Paul." *Bulletin of the John Rylands Library* 65 (1983) 95–122.

———. "The Justice of God: A Renewed Perspective on Justification by Faith." *Journal of Theological Studies* 43 (1992) 1–22.

———. *The New Perspective on Paul.* Rev. ed. Grand Rapids: Eerdmans, 2008.

———. *Romans 1–8.* Word Biblical Commentary 38a. Edited by David A. Hubbard and Glenn W. Barker. Waco, TX: Word, 1988.

———. "A New Perspective on the New Perspective on Paul." *Early Christianity* 4 (2013) 157–82.

———. *Romans 9–16.* Word Biblical Commentary 38b. Edited by Bruce M. Metzger et al. Dallas: Word, 1988.

———. *The Theology of Paul the Apostle.* Grand Rapids: Eerdmans, 1998.

Eissfeldt, Otto. *Die Genesis der Genesis: Vom Werdegang des ersten Buches der Bibel.* Tübingen, Germany: J. C. B. Mohr-Siebeck, 1958.

Ellis, E. Earle. *Prophecy and Hermeneutic in Early Christianity: New Testament Essays by E. Earle Ellis.* Grand Rapids: Eerdmans, 1978.

Enns, Paul P. "Charles C. Ryrie." In *Handbook of Evangelical Theologians*, edited by Walter A. Elwell, 366–78. Grand Rapids: Baker, 1993.

Erickson, Michael E. "'Faith Credited as Righteousness': An Evaluation of N. T. Wright's Perspectives on Justification through Paul's Use of Psalm 32 in Romans 4." ThM thesis, Capital Bible Seminary, 2009.

Fabry, H. J., and H. Simian-Yofre. "נחם." In *Theological Dictionary of the Old Testament.* Vol. 9. 15 vols. Edited by G. Johannes Botterweck et al., 340–55. Translated by David E. Green. Grand Rapids: Eerdmans, 1977.

Feinberg, John S., ed. *Continuity and Discontinuity: Perspectives on the Relationship between the Old and New Testaments.* Westchester, IL: Crossway, 1988.

———. "Salvation in the Old Testament." In *Tradition and Testament: Essays in Honor of Charles Lee Feinberg.* Edited by John S. Feinberg and Paul D. Feinberg, 39–77. Chicago: Moody, 1981.

Fishbane, Michael. *Text and Texture: Close Readings of Selected Biblical Texts.* New York: Schocken, 1979.

Fitzer, G. "σημεῖον." In *Theological Dictionary of the New Testament.* Vol. 7. 10 vols. Edited by Gerhard Friedrich and Geoffrey W. Bromiley, 200–261. Translated by Geoffrey W. Bromiley. Grand Rapids: Eerdmans, 1975.

Fitzmyer, Joseph A. *Romans*. Anchor Bible 33. Edited by William Foxwell Albright and David Noel Freedman. New York: Doubleday, 1993.

Fox, Michael V. "The Sign of the Covenant: Circumcision in the Light of the Priestly *'ôt* Etiologies." *Revue Biblique* 81 (1974) 557–96.

Frye, Northrop. *Anatomy of Criticism*. Oxford: Oxford University Press, 2000.

Fuller, Daniel P. *Gospel and Law: Contrast or Continuum?* Grand Rapids: Eerdmans, 1980.

———. "The Hermeneutics of Dispensationalism." PhD diss., Northern Baptist Theological Seminary, 1957.

Gaebelein, A. C. *The Annotated Bible: The Holy Scriptures Analysed and Annotated*. Vol. 1. 9 vols. Wheaton, IL: Van Kampen, 1913.

———. *The Epistle to the Romans*. New York: Francis Emory Fitch, 1916.

———. *Gaebelein's Concise Commentary on the Whole Bible*. Rev. ed. Neptune, NJ: Loizeaux Brothers, 1985.

García Martínez, Florentíno, and Eibert J. C. Tigchelaar, eds. *The Dead Sea Scrolls Study Edition*. Leiden, Netherlands: Brill, 1999.

Gaster, Theodore H. *Myth, Legend, and Custom in the Old Testament: A Comparative Study with Chapters from Sir James G. Frazer's Folklore in the Old Testament*. Gloucester, MA: Peter Smith, 1981.

George, Andrew. *The Epic of Gilgamesh: The Babylonian Epic Poem and Other Texts in Akkadian and Sumerian*. New York: Barnes & Noble, 1999.

Gertner, John H. *Wrongly Dividing the Word of Truth: A Critique of Dispensationalism*. Edited by Don Kistler. 2nd ed. Morgan, PA: Soli Deo Gloria, 2000.

Gestenberger, Erhard. "Book Review: Treaty and Covenant." *Journal of Biblical Literature* 83 (1964) 198–99.

Goppelt, Leonhard. "Paulus und die Heilsgeschichte: Schlussfolgerungen aus Röm 4 und 1 Kor 10:1–13." *New Testament Studies* 13 (1966) 31–42.

Green, William H. "Primeval Chronology." *Bibliotheca Sacra* 47 (1890) 285–303.

Guerra, Anthony J. "Romans 4 as Apologetic Theology." *Harvard Theological Review* 81 (1988) 251–70.

Gunkel, Hermann. *Genesis: Translated and Interpreted by Hermann Gunkel*. Translated by Mark E. Biddle. Mercer Library of Biblical Studies. Edited by Joseph Blenkinsopp et al. Macon, GA: Mercer University Press, 1997.

———. *Schöpfung und Chaos in Urzeit und Endzeit: Eine religionsgeschichtliche Untersuchung über Gen 1 und Ap Joh 12*. Göttingen, Germany: Vandenhoeck und Ruprecht, 1921.

Hamilton, Victor P. *The Book of Genesis: Chapters 1–17*. New International Commentary on the Old Testament. Edited by R. K. Harrison and Robert L. Hubbard Jr. Grand Rapids: Eerdmans, 1990.

Harrison, Everett F. "Romans." In *The Expositor's Bible Commentary: Romans–Galatians*, 2–171. Expositor's Bible Commentary 10. Edited by Frank E Gaebelein. Grand Rapids: Zondervan, 1976.

Harrison, R. K. *Introduction to the Old Testament*. Grand Rapids: Eerdmans, 1969.

Healey, Joseph P. "Faith." In *The Anchor Bible Dictionary*. Vol. 2. 6 vols. Edited by David Noel Freedman et al., 744–49. New York: Doubleday, 1992.

Heidland, H. W. "λογίζομαι." In *Theological Dictionary of the New Testament*. Vol. 4. 10 vols. Edited by Gerhard Kittel, 284–92. Translated by Geoffrey W. Bromiley. Grand Rapids: Eerdmans, 1967.

Helfmeyer, F. J. "חאו." In *Theological Dictionary of the Old Testament*. Vol. 1. 10 vols. Edited by G. Johannes Botterweck and Helmer Ringgren, 167–88. Translated by John T. Willis. Grand Rapids: Eerdmans, 1977.

Hess, Richard S. "The Genealogies of Genesis 1–11 and Comparative Literature." *Biblica* 70 (1989) 241–54.

Hirsch, E. D., Jr. *The Aims of Interpretation*. Chicago: University of Chicago Press, 1976.

———. "Transhistorical Intentions and the Persistence of Allegory: Part 1." *New Literary History* 25 (1994) 549–67.

———. *Validity in Interpretation*. New Haven: Yale University Press, 1967.

Hodge, Charles. *Systematic Theology*. Vol. 2. 4 vols. London: James and Clarke, 1960.

Hoffmeier, James K. "Genesis 1–11 as History and Theology." In *Genesis: History, Fiction, or Neither?* Edited by Charles Halton. CounterPoints. Edited by Stanley N. Gundry. Grand Rapids: Zondervan, 2015.

———. "Historiography: King Lists." In *The Context of Scripture*. Vol. 1. 3 vols. Edited by William W. Hallo, 68–73. Leiden, Netherlands: Brill, 2003.

Holsteen, Nathan D. "The Hermeneutic of Dispensationalism." In *Dispensationalism and the History of Redemption: A Developing and Diverse Tradition*. Edited by D. Jeffrey Bingham and Glenn R. Kreider, 101–21. Chicago: Moody, 2015.

Hsieh, Nelson S. "Abraham as 'Heir of the Word': Does Romans 4:13 Expand the Old Testament Abrahamic Land Promises?" *The Masters Seminary Journal* 26 (2015) 95–110.

Irenaeus. *Against the Heresies*. Translated by Dominic J. Unger. Ancient Christian Writers 64. Edited by Boniface Ramsey et al. New York: Newman, 2012.

Ironside, H. A. *Lectures on the Epistle to the Romans*. New York: Loizeaux Brothers, 1927.

Jepsen, Alfred. "āman." In *Theological Dictionary of the Old Testament*. Vol. 1. 15 vols. Edited by G. Johannes Botterweck and Helmer Ringgren, 292–323. Translated by John T. Willis. Grand Rapids: Eerdmans, 1977.

Jewett, Robert. *Romans: A Commentary*. Hermeneia. Edited by Helmut Koester et al. Minneapolis: Fortress, 2007.

Johnson, Elliott E. *A Dispensational Biblical Theology*. Allen, TX: Bold Grace Ministries, 2016.

———. *Expository Hermeneutics: An Introduction*. Grand Rapids: Zondervan, 1990.

Johnson, S. Lewis, Jr. *Discovering Romans: Spiritual Revival for the Soul*. Edited by Mike Abendroth. Grand Rapids: Zondervan, 2014.

Johnston, Gordon H., "Revisiting Moshe Weinfeld's Comparative and Traditio-Historical Analysis of the Promissory and Obligatory Passages Related to the Abrahamic Covenant." A paper presented at the National Meeting of the Society of Biblical Literature (Atlanta, 2010).

Kaiser, Walter C., Jr. *The Messiah in the Old Testament*. Grand Rapids: Zondervan, 1995.

———. *The Promise-Plan of God: A Biblical Theology of the Old and New Testaments*. Grand Rapids: Zondervan, 2008.

———. "Is It the Case That Christ is the Same Object of Faith in the Old Testament? (Genesis 15:1–6)." *Journal of the Evangelical Theological Society* 55 (2012) 291–98.

———. "The Single Intent of Scripture." In *Evangelical Roots: A Tribute to Wilbur Smith*. Edited by Kenneth S. Kantzer, 123–41. Nashville: Nelson, 1978.

Karlberg, Mark W. "Legitimate Discontinuities between the Testaments." *Journal of the Evangelical Theological Society* 28 (1985) 9–20.

Käsemann, Ernst. *Commentary on Romans*. Translated by Geoffrey W. Bromiley. Eerdmans: Grand Rapids, 1980.

———. *Perspectives on Paul*. Translated by Margaret Kohl. Philadelphia: Fortress, 1971.

Kass, Leon R. *The Beginning of Wisdom: Readings Genesis*. New York: Free Press, 2003.

Kautzsch, E. *Gesenius' Hebrew Grammar: As Edited and Enlarged by the Late E. Kautzsch*. Translated by A. E. Cowley. 2nd English ed. Oxford: Clarendon, 1910.

Kedar-Kopfstein, B. "tāmîm." In *Theological Dictionary of the Old Testament*. Vol. 15. 15 vols., 699–711. Edited by G. Johannes Botterweck et al. Translated by David E. Green. Grand Rapids: Eerdmans, 1977.

Keil, C. F., and F. Delitzsch. *Biblical Commentary on the Old Testament: The Pentateuch*. Translated by James Martin. Edinburgh: T. & T. Clark, 1866. Reprint, Grand Rapids: Eerdmans, 1949.

Kelly, William. *Lectures Introductory to the Study of the Epistles of Paul the Apostle*. London: W. H. Broom, 1869.

———. *Notes on The Epistle of Paul, the Apostle to the Romans with a New Translation*. London: G. Morrish, 1873.

Kidner, Derek. *Genesis: An Introduction and Commentary*. Tyndale Old Testament Commentaries 1. Edited by D. J. Wiseman. Downers Grove: InterVarsity, 1967.

Kitchen, Kenneth A. *On the Reliability of the Old Testament*. Grand Rapids: Eerdmans, 2003.

Kline, Meredith. *Kingdom Prologue: Genesis Foundations for a Covenantal Worldview*. Eugene, OR: Wipf & Stock, 2006.

———. *Treaty of the Great King: The Covenant Structure of Deuteronomy*. Grand Rapids: Eerdmans, 1963.

Klooster, Fred H. "The Biblical Method of Salvation: A Case for Continuity." In *Continuity and Discontinuity: Perspectives on the Relationship between the Old and New Testaments, Essays in Honor of S. Lewis Johnson*. Edited by John S. Feinberg, 131–60. Westchester, IL: Crossway, 1988.

Knoppers, Gary N. "Ancient Near Eastern Royal Grants and the Davidic Covenant: A Parallel?" *Journal of the American Oriental Society* 116 (1996): 670–97.

Knoppers, Gary N., and Bernard M. Levinson. "How, When, Where, and Why Did the Pentateuch Become the Torah?" In *The Pentateuch as Torah: New Models for Understanding Its Promulgation and Acceptance*. Edited by Gary N. Knoppers and Bernard M. Levinson, 1–19. Winona Lake, IN: Eisenbrauns, 2007.

Köhler, Lidwig. *Old Testament Theology*. Translated by A. S. Todd. Philadelphia: Westminster, 1957.

Koehler, Ludwig, and Walter Baumgartner, eds. *The Hebrew and Aramaic Lexicon of the Old Testament*. Vol. 1. 5 vols. New York: E. J. Brill, 1994.

———. *The Hebrew and Aramaic Lexicon of the Old Testament*. Vol. 2. 5 vols. New York: E. J. Brill, 1995.

Kreider, Glenn R. "What is Dispensationalism?" In *Dispensationalism and the History of Redemption*. Edited by D. Jeffrey Bingham and Glenn R. Kreider, 15–46. Chicago: Moody, 2015.

Kuruvilla, Abraham. *Genesis: A Theological Commentary for Preachers*. Eugene, OR: Resource Publications, 2014.

Laffey, Alice L. *An Introduction to the Old Testament: A Feminist Perspective*. Philadelphia: Fortress, 1988.

Lambrecht, Jan. "Romans 4: A Critique of N. T. Wright." *Journal for the Study of the New Testament* 36 (2013) 189–94.

Levenson, Jon D. "The Davidic Covenant and Its Modern Interpreters." *Catholic Biblical Quarterly* 41 (1979) 205–19.

———. "On the Promise to the Rechabites." *Catholic Biblical Quarterly* 38 (1976) 508–14.

Loewenstmm, S. E. "The Divine Grants of Land to the Patriarchs." *Journal of the American Oriental Society* 91 (1971) 509–10.

Long, V. Philips. *The Art of Biblical History*. Foundations of Contemporary Interpretation 5. Edited by Moisés Silva. Grand Rapids: Zondervan, 1994.

———. *The Reign and Rejection of King Saul: A Case for Literary and Theological Coherence*. Society of Biblical Literature: Dissertation Series 118. Edited by David L. Petersen and Charles Talbert. Atlanta: Scholars Press, 1989.

Longacre, Robert E. "*Weqatal* Forms in Biblical Hebrew Prose: A Discourse-modular Approach." In *Biblical Hebrew and Discourse Linguistics*. Edited by Robert D. Bergen, 50–98. Winona Lake, IN: Summer Institute of Linguistics, 1994.

Longacre, Robert E., and Andrew C. Bowling. *Understanding Biblical Hebrew Verb Forms: Distribution and Function across Genres*. Dallas: SIL International, 2015.

Longenecker, Richard N. *The Epistle to the Romans*. New International Greek Testament Commentary. Edited by I. Howard Marshall and Donald A. Hagner. Grand Rapids: Eerdmans, 2015.

Longman, Tremper, III. "Biblical Narrative." In *A Complete Literary Guide to the Bible*. Edited by Leland Ryken and Tremper Longman III, 69–79. Grand Rapids: Zondervan, 1993.

———. *Literary Approaches to Biblical Interpretation*. Foundations of Contemporary Interpretation 3. Edited by Silva Moisés. Grand Rapids: Academie, 1987.

Lopez, René A. "Christ, the End of the Law in Romans 10:4." In *Dispensationalism, Israel and the Church: The Search for Definition*. Edited by Craig A. Blaising and Darrell L. Bock, 230–47. Grand Rapids: Zondervan, 1992.

———. *Romans Unlocked: Power to Deliver*. Springfield, MO: 21st Century, 2005.

Lowery, David K. "A Theology of Paul's Missionary Epistles." In *A Biblical Theology of the New Testament*. Edited by Roy B. Zuck, 243–97. Chicago: Moody, 1994.

Macpherson, John. *The Westminster Confession of Faith: With Introduction and Notes by the Rev. John Macpherson*. 2nd ed. Handbook for Bible Classes. Edited by Marcus Dods and Alexander Whyte. Edinburgh: T. & T. Clark, 1882.

Marshall, I. Howard. "Romans 16:25–27—An Apt Conclusion." In *Romans and the People of God: Essays in Honor of Gordon Fee on the Occasion of His 65th Birthday*. Edited by Sven K. Soderlund and N. T. Wright, 170–84. Grand Rapids: Eerdmans, 1999.

Martin, R. A. "The Earliest Messianic Interpretation of Genesis 3:15." *Journal of Biblical Literature* 84 (1965) 425–27.

Mathews, Kenneth A. *Genesis 1–11:26: An Exegetical and Theological Exposition of the Holy Scripture*. New American Commentary 1A. Edited by E. Ray Clendenen. Nashville: Broadman & Holman, 1996.

———. *Genesis 11:27—50:26: An Exegetical and Theological Exposition of the Holy Scripture*. New American Commentary 1B. Edited by E. Ray Clendenen. Nashville: Broadman & Holman, 2005.

McCarthy, Dennis J. "Covenant in the Old Testament: The Present State of Inquiry." *Catholic Biblical Quarterly* 27 (1965) 217–40.

———. *Old Testament Covenant: A Survey of Current Opinions*. Richmond, VA: John Knox, 1972.

———. *Treaty and Covenant: A Study in Form in the Ancient Oriental Documents and in the Old Testament*. Analecta Biblica 21. Rome: Biblical Institute, 1963.

McClain, Alva J. *The Greatness of the Kingdom: An Inductive Study of the Kingdom of God*. Winona Lake, IN: BMH Books, 1974.

McKeown, James. *Genesis*. Two Horizons Old Testament Commentary. Edited by J. Gordon McConville and Craig Bartholomew. Grand Rapids: Eerdmans, 2008.

Mendenhall, George E. *Law and Covenant in Israel and the Ancient Near East*. Pittsburgh, PA: Presbyterian Board of Colportage, 1955.

Mendenhall, George E., and Gary A. Herion. "Covenant." In *The Anchor Bible Dictionary: A–C*. Vol. 1. 6 vols. Edited by David Noel Freedman, 1179–1202. New York: Doubleday, 1992.

Metzger, Bruce M. *A Textual Commentary on the Greek New Testament*. 2nd ed. New York: American Bible Society, 2002.

Miller, Patrick D., Jr. "Syntax and Theology in Genesis XII 3a." *Vetus Testamentum* 34 (1984) 472–75.

Moberly, R. W. L. "*āmēn*." In *New International Dictionary of Old Testament Theology & Exegesis*. Vol. 1. 5 vols. Edited by Willem A. VanGemeren, 427–33. Grand Rapids: Zondervan, 1997.

Moo, Douglas J. *The Epistle to the Romans*. New International Commentary on the New Testament. Edited by Ned B. Stonehouse et al. Grand Rapids: Eerdmans, 1996.

———. "Foreword." In *New Covenant Theology: Description, Definition, Defense*. Edited by Tom Wells and Fred G. Zaspel, xiii–xiv. Frederick, MD: New Covenant Media, 2002.

Moran, W. L. "Gen 49,10 and Its Use in Ez 21, 32." *Biblica* 39 (1958) 405–25.

Morris, Leon. *The Epistle to the Romans*. Grand Rapids: Eerdmans, 1988.

Mounce, Robert H. *Romans*. New American Commentary 27. Edited by E. Ray Clendenen. Nashville: Broadman & Holman, 1995.

Mowinckel, Sigmund. *Tetrateuch-Pentateuch-Hexateuch: Die Berichte über Landnahme in den drei altisraelitischen Geschichtswerken*. Berlin: Alfred Töpelmann, 1964.

Mullen, E. Theodore, Jr. "The Divine Witness and the Davidic Royal Grant: Ps 89:37–38." *Journal of Biblical Literature* 102 (1983) 207–18.

———. "The Royal Dynastic Grant to Jehu and the Structure of the Book of Kings." *Journal of Biblical Literature* 107 (1988) 193–206.

Nevin, Paul D. "Some Major Problems in Dispensational Interpretation." PhD diss., Dallas Theological Seminary, 1965.

O'Brien, Peter T. "Justification in Paul and Some Crucial Issues of the Last Two Decades." In *Right with God: Justification in the Bible and the World*. Edited by D. A. Carson, 69–95. Grand Rapids: Baker, 1992.

———. "Was Paul a Covenantal Nomist?" In *Justification and Variegated Nomism: The Paradoxes of Paul*. Vol. 2. 2 vols. Edited by D. A. Carson et al., 249–96. Grand Rapids: Baker, 2001.

Ojewole, Afolarin Olutunde. "The Seed in Genesis 3:15: An Exegetical and Intertextual Study." PhD diss., Andrews University, 2002.

Osborne, Grant R. *Romans*. IVP New Testament Commentary Series. Edited by D. Stuart Briscoe and Haddon Robinson. Downers Grove: InterVarsity, 2004.

Patte, Daniel. "Speech Act Theory and Biblical Exegesis." In *Speech Act Theory and Biblical Criticism*, 85–102. Semeia 41. Edited by Hugh C. White. Decatur, GA: Scholars Press, 1988.

Pehlke, Helmuth. "An Exegetical and Theological Study of Genesis 49:1–28." PhD diss., Dallas Theological Seminary, 1985.

Pentecost, J. Dwight. *A Faith That Endures: The Book of Hebrews Applied to the Real Issues of Life*. Grand Rapids: Discovery House, 1992.

Petrey, Sandy. *Speech Acts and Literary Theory*. London: Routledge, 1990.

Pettingill, William L. *Bible Questions Answered*. 6th ed. Findlay, OH: Fundamental Truth, 1935.

———. *Bible Questions Answered*. Wheaton, IL: Van Kampen, n.d.

Porter, J. R. "Old Testament Historiography." In *Tradition and Interpretation: Essays by the Members of the Society for Old Testament Study*. Edited by G. W. Anderson, 125–62. Oxford: Clarendon, 1979.

Poythress, Vern S. *Understanding Dispensationalists*. 2nd ed. Phillipsburg, NJ: P & R Publishing, 1994.

Pratt, Mary L. *Towards a Speech Act Theory of Literary Discourse*. Bloomington, IN: Indiana University Press, 1977.

Pritchard, James B., ed. *Ancient Near Eastern Texts Relating to the Old Testament*. Princeton: Princeton University Press, 1969.

Pröbstle, Martin. "'Lion of Judah': The Blessing on Judah in Genesis 49:8–12." In *"For You Have Made Me Glad": Biblical and Theological Studies in Honor of Gerhard Pfandl in Celebration of His 65th Birthday*. Edited by Martin Pröbstle et al., 23–49. St. Peter am Hart: Seminar Schloss Bogenhofen, 2007.

Rad, Gerhard von. *Genesis: A Commentary*. Translated by John H. Marks. Rev. ed. Old Testament Library 1. Edited by G. Ernest Wright. Philadelphia: Westminster, 1961.

Richelle, Matthieu. "La structure littéraire de l'histoire primitive (Genese 1,1–11,26) en son état final." *Biblische Notizen* 151 (2011) 3–22.

Ritner, Robert K. "Denderite Temple Hierarchy and the Family of Theban High Priest Nebwenenef: Block Statue OIM 10729." In *For His Ka: Essays Offered in Memory of Klaus Baer*. Edited by David P. Silverman, 205–26. Studies in Ancient Oriental Civilization 55. Edited by Thomas A. Holland and Thomas G. Urban. Chicago: University of Chicago Press, 1994.

Rogers, Cleon L., Jr. "The Covenant with Abraham and Its Historical Setting." *Bibliotheca Sacra* 127 (1970) 241–56.

Ross, Allen P. "The Biblical Method of Salvation: A Case for Discontinuity." In *Continuity and Discontinuity: Perspectives on the Relationship between the Old and New Testaments, Essays in Honor of S. Lewis Johnson*. Edited by John S. Feinberg, 161–78. Westchester, IL: Crossway, 1988.

———. *Creation and Blessing: A Guide to the Study and Exposition of Genesis*. Grand Rapids: Baker, 1998.

———. *Introducing Biblical Hebrew*. Grand Rapids: Baker, 2001.

Ryken, Leland. *How to Read the Bible as Literature and Get More Out of It*. Grand Rapids: Zondervan, 1984.

Ryrie, Charles C. *Biblical Theology of the New Testament*. Chicago: Moody, 1959.

———. *Dispensationalism*. Rev. ed. Chicago: Moody, 2007.

———. *Dispensationalism Today*. Chicago: Moody, 1965.

———. *The Ryrie Study Bible*. Chicago: Moody, 1986.

———. *So Great a Salvation: What It Means to Believe in Jesus Christ*. Wheaton: Victor, 1989.

Sailhamer, John H. "Genesis." In *The Expositor's Bible Commentary: With the New International Version of the Holy Bible*, 3–284. Expositor's Bible Commentary 2. Edited by Frank E. Gaebelein and Richard P. Polcyn. Grand Rapids: Regency, 1990.

———. "Johann August Ernesti: The Role of History in Biblical Interpretation." *Journal of the Evangelical Theological Society* 44 (2002) 193–206.

———. *The Meaning of the Pentateuch: Revelation, Composition, and Interpretation.* Downers Grove, IL: IVP Academic, 2009.

———. *The Pentateuch as Narrative: A Biblical-Theological Commentary.* Grand Rapids: Zondervan, 1992.

Sanders, E. P. *Paul, the Law, and the Jewish People.* Minneapolis: Fortress, 1983.

———. *Paul.* Oxford: Oxford University Press, 1991.

———. *Paul and Palestinian Judaism: A Comparison of Patterns of Religion.* Philadelphia: Fortress, 1977.

Sarna, Nahum M. *Genesis.* JPS Torah Commentary. Edited by Nahum M. Sarna and Chaim Potok. New York: Jewish Publication Society, 1989.

Sasson, Jack M. "Circumcision in the Ancient Near East." *Journal of Biblical Literature* 85 (1966): 473–76.

Schreiner, Thomas R. *Romans.* Baker Exegetical Commentary on the New Testament 6. Edited by Moisés Silva. Grand Rapids: Baker, 1998.

Schrenk, G. "δικαιοσύνη." In *Theological Dictionary of the New Testament.* Vol. 2. 10 vols. Edited by Gerhard Kittel, 192–210. Translated by Geoffrey W. Bromiley. Grand Rapids: Eerdmans, 1964.

———. "δικαιόω." In *Theological Dictionary of the New Testament.* Vol. 2. 10 vols. Edited by Gerhard Kittel, 211–19. Translated by Geoffrey W. Bromiley. Eerdmans: Grand Rapids, 1964.

Scofield, C. I. *The Scofield Reference Bible.* New York: Oxford University Press, 1909.

Searle, John R. *Speech Acts: An Essay in the Philosophy of Language.* Cambridge: Cambridge University Press, 1969.

Segal, M. H. *The Pentateuch: Its Composition and Its Authorship and Other Biblical Studies.* Jerusalem: Magnes, 1967.

Seifrid, Mark A. "Paulus und seine neue Perspektive." *Kerygma und Dogma: Zeitschrift für theologische Forschung und kirchliche Lehre* 58 (2012) 268–83.

Selman, M. J. "Comparative Customs and the Patriarchal Age." In *Essays on the Patriarchal Narratives.* Edited by A. R. Millard and D. J. Wiseman, 93–138. Leicester, UK: InterVarsity, 1980.

Skehan, Patrick W. *The Wisdom of Ben Sira.* Anchor Bible 39. Edited by William Foxwell Albright and David Noel Freedman. New York: Doubleday, 1987.

Soderlund, Sven K., and N. T. Wright, eds. *Romans and the People of God: Essays in Honor of Gordon D. Fee on the Occasion of His 65th Birthday.* Grand Rapids: Eerdmans, 1999.

Soula, Don E. "The Meaning of 'I Will Give You Rest' in Matthew 11:28." ThM thesis, Dallas Theological Seminary, 2004.

Stallard, Michael D. *The Early Twentieth-Century Dispensationalism of Arno C. Gaebelein.* Studies in American Religion 77. Lewiston: Edwin Mellen, 2002.

———. "The Interpretation of the New Covenant in the History of Dispensationalism." In *Dispensational Understanding of the New Covenant.* Edited by Mike Stallard, 73–106. Schaumburg, IL: Regular Baptist Press, 2012.

Stendahl, Krister. "The Apostle Paul and the Introspective Conscience of the West." *Harvard Theological Review* 56 (1963) 199–215.

———. *Paul Among Jews and Gentiles and Other Essays*. Philadelphia: Fortress, 1976.

Sternberg, Meir. *The Poetics of Biblical Narrative: Ideological Literature and the Drama of Reading*. Bloomington, IN: Indiana University Press, 1985.

Stifler, James M. *The Epistle to the Romans*. Chicago: Moody, 1983.

Strack, H. L., and Paul Billerbeck. *Kommentar zum Neuen Testament aus Talmud und Midrasch*. Vol. 3. 4 vols. Munich: Beck, 1974.

Svigel, Michael J. "The History of Dispensationalism in Seven Eras." In *Dispensationalism and the History of Redemption*. Edited by D. Jeffrey Bingham and Glenn R. Kreider, 69–100. Chicago: Moody, 2015.

Thomas, Matthew A. *These Are the Generations: Identity, Covenant, and the 'Toledot' Formula*. Library of Hebrew Bible: Old Testament 551. Edited by Claudia V. Camp and Andrew Mein. New York: T. & T. Clark, 2011.

Thordarson, Thorir Kr. "The Mythic Dimension." *Vetus Testamentum* 24 (1974) 212–20.

Van Til, Cornelius. "Covenant Theology." In *Twentieth Century Encyclopedia of Religious Knowledge*. Vol. 1. 2 vols. Edited by Lefferts A. Loetscher, 306. Grand Rapids: Baker, 1955.

Vanhoozer, Kevin J. *Is There a Meaning in This Text? The Bible, the Reader, and the Morality of Literary Knowledge*. Grand Rapids: Zondervan, 2009.

———. "The Semantics of Biblical Literature." In *Hermeneutics, Authority, and Canon*. Edited by D. A. Carson and John D. Woodbridge, 49–104. Grand Rapids: Academie, 1986.

Venema, Cornelis P. *The Gospel of Free Acceptance in Christ: An Assessment of the Reformation and New Perspectives on Paul*. Carlisle, PA: Banner of Truth Trust, 2006.

Visscher, Gerhard H. *Romans 4 and the New Perspective on Paul*. Studies in Biblical Literature 122. Edited by Hemchand Gossai. New York: Peter Lang, 2009.

Wallace, Daniel B. *Greek Grammar Beyond the Basics: An Exegetical Syntax of the New Testament*. Grand Rapids: Zondervan, 1996.

Waltke, Bruce K., and Cathi J. Fredricks. *Genesis: A Commentary*. Grand Rapids: Zondervan, 2001.

Waltke, Bruce K., and M. O'Connor. *An Introduction to Biblical Hebrew Syntax*. Winona Lake, IN: Eisenbrauns, 1990.

Waltke, Bruce K., and Charles Yu. *An Old Testament Theology: An Exegetical, Canonical, and Thematic Approach*. Grand Rapids: Zondervan, 2007.

Walton, John H. *Genesis*. NIV Application Commentary 1. Edited by Terry Muck. Grand Rapids: Zondervan, 2001.

Waters, Guy Prentiss. *Justification and the New Perspective on Paul: A Review and Response*. Phillipsburg, NJ: P & R Publishing, 2004.

Watts, James W. *Psalm and Story: Inset Hymns in Hebrew Narrative*. Journal for the Study of the Old Testament Supplement Series 139. Edited by David J. A. Clines and Philip R. Davies. Sheffield, UK: JSOT, 1992.

Weinfeld, Moshe. "B[e]rîth." In *Theological Dictionary of the Old Testament*. Vol. 2. 15 vols. Edited by G. Johannes Botterweck and Helmer Ringgren, 253–79. Translated by John T. Willis. Grand Rapids: Eerdmans, 1977.

———. "The Covenant of Grant in the Old Testament and in the Ancient Near East." *Journal of the American Oriental Society* 90 (1970) 184–203.

———. *Deuteronomy and the Deuteronomic School*. Winona Lake, IN: Eisenbrauns, 1992.

Wellhausen, J. *Die Composition des Hexateuches und der historischen Bücher des Alten Testaments.* 3rd ed. Berlin: Walter de Gruyter, 1963.

Wenham, Gordon J. *Genesis 1–15.* Word Biblical Commentary 1. Edited by David A. Hubbard and Glenn W. Barker. Waco, TX: Word, 1987.

———. *Genesis 16–50.* Word Biblical Commentary 2. Edited by David A. Hubbard et al. Waco, TX: Word, 1994.

Westerholm, Stephen. *Perspectives Old and New on Paul: The 'Lutheran' Paul and His Critics.* Grand Rapids: Eerdmans, 2004.

Westermann, Claus. *Genesis 12–36.* Vol. 2. 2 vols. Translated by John J. Scullion. Minneapolis: Augsburg Publishing, 1985.

Wevers, John W., ed. *Septuaginta: Vetus Testamentum Graecum Auctoritate Academiae Scientiarum Gottingensis editum; Genesis.* Vol. 1. Göttingen, Germany: Vandenhoeck & Ruprecht, 1974.

White, Hayden. "The Question of Narrative in Contemporary Historical Theory." *History and Theory* 23 (1984) 1–33.

White, Hugh C. "Speech Act Theory and Literary Criticism." In *Speech Act Theory and Biblical Criticism*, 1–24. Semeia 41. Edited by Hugh C. White. Decatur, GA: Scholars Press, 1988.

———. "The Value of Speech Act Theory for Old Testament Hermeneutics." In *Speech Act Theory and Biblical Criticism*, 41–64. Semeia 41. Edited by Hugh C. White. Decatur, GA: Scholars Press, 1988.

Williams, Sam K. "The 'Righteousness of God' in Romans.'" *Journal of Biblical Literature* 99 (1980) 241–90.

Williamson, Paul R. *Abraham, Israel, and the Nations: The Patriarchal Promise and Its Covenantal Development in Genesis.* Journal for the Study of the Old Testament Supplement Series 315. Edited by David J. A. Clines and Philip R. Davies. Sheffield, UK: Sheffield Academic Press, 2000.

Wilson, Robert R. *Genealogy and History in the Biblical World.* Yale Near Eastern Researches 7. Edited by William W. Hallo. London: Yale University Press, 1977.

Wintermute, O. S. "Jubilees." In *The Old Testament Pseudepigrapha: Expansions of the "Old Testament" and Legends, Wisdom and Philosophical Literature, Prayers, Psalms, and Odes, Fragments of Lost Judeo-Hellenistic Works.* Vol. 2. 2 vols. Edited by James H. Charlesworth, 35–142. Peabody, MA: Hendrickson, 2009.

Wiseman, P. J. *Clues to Creation in Genesis.* London: Marshall, Morgan, & Scott, 1977.

Wolff, Hans Walter. "The Kerygma of the Yahwist." *Interpretation* 20 (1966) 131–58.

Wolterstorff, Nicholas. *Divine Discourse: Philosophical Reflections on the Claim That God Speaks.* Cambridge, UK: Cambridge University Press, 1995.

Woodring, H. Chester. "Grace under the Mosaic Covenant." PhD diss., Dallas Theological Seminary, 1956.

Woolsey, Andrew A. *Unity and Continuity in Covenantal Thought: A Study in the Reformed Tradition to the Westminster Assembly.* Grand Rapids: Reformation Heritage Books, 2012.

Woudstra, M. H. "The *Toledot* of the Book of Genesis and Their Redemptive-Historical Significance." *Calvin Theological Journal* 6 (1971) 184–89.

Wright, N. T. *Justification: God's Plan and Paul's Vision.* Downers Grove: IVP Academic, 2009.

———. *Justification: God's Plan and Paul's Vision.* Downers Grove: IVP Academic, 2016.

———. "The Letter to the Romans." In *The New Interpreter's Bible: General Articles & Introduction, Commentary, & Reflections for Each Book of the Bible* 394–770. New Interpreter's Bible 10. Edited by Leander E. Keck. Nashville: Abingdon, 1994.

———. "New Perspective on Paul." In *Justification in Perspective: Historical Developments and Contemporary Challenges.* Edited by Bruce L. McCormack, 243–64. Grand Rapids: Baker, 2006.

———. "The Paul of History and the Apostle of Faith." *Tyndale Bulletin* 29 (1978) 61–88.

———. "Paul the Patriarch: The Role of Abraham in Romans 4." *Journal for the Study of the New Testament* 35 (2013) 207–41.